Down by the River

The Thames & Kennet in Reading

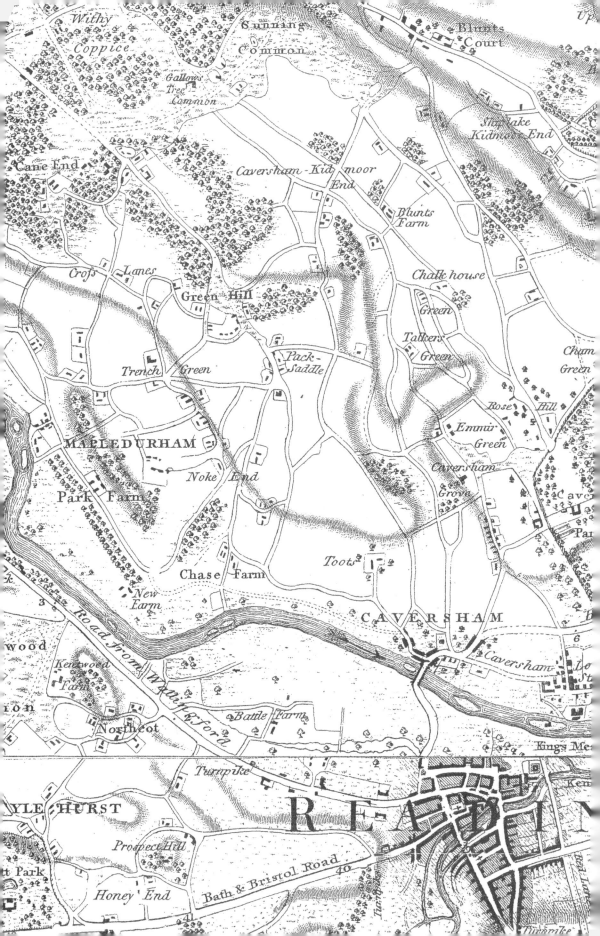

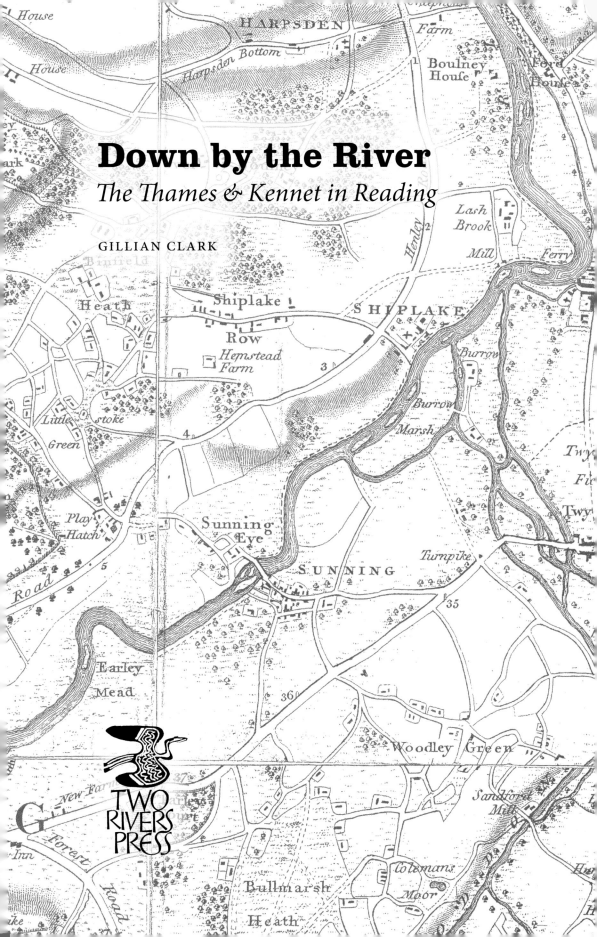

Down by the River

The Thames & Kennet in Reading

GILLIAN CLARK

TWO RIVERS PRESS

First published in the UK in 2009 by

Two Rivers Press

35–39 London Street

Reading

RG1 4PS

www.tworiverspress.com

Two Rivers Press is represented in the UK by
Inpress Limited www.inpressbooks.co.uk
and distributed by Central Books: www.centralbooks.com

DESIGN: www.designforprint.org
PRINTING: Quadgraphics, Newbury

ISBN 978-1-901677-58-4

FRONT COVER: Berkshire Record Office, D/EX 326 2b,
part of map, 1863

TITLE PAGE: Reading Local Studies Library, OS map,
Berkshire sheet XXXVII, 1878

Contents

Acknowledgements   *vii*

Introduction   *ix*

1   The early years at Caversham: 1100–1600   *1*

2   Commerce, civil war and settlement: 1600–1750   *14*

3   Navigating the Thames and Kennet: 1700–1750   *25*

4   Barges and bargemen in Reading: 1750–1820   *31*

5   Steam power on river and rail: 1800–1850   *41*

6   Caversham people and places: 1840–1870   *51*

7   Changes, real and perceived: 1860–1880   *64*

8   Rowing, fishing and baby farming: 1880–1900   *78*

9   Expansion of the pleasure boat businesses: 1880–1890   *88*

10   Rowing and regattas: 1870–1890   *101*

11   Leisure time along the riverside: 1870–1890   *107*

12   The peak years for pleasure boating: 1890–1896   *116*

13   The old riverside pattern begins to break up: 1896–1910   *128*

14   Two difficult decades: 1900–1920   *144*

15   Building and rebuilding: 1918–1939   *154*

16   World War II and after: 1937–1947   *167*

17   Post-war changes along the river: 1947–1960   *174*

18   Conclusion   *190*

Reading waterways workers: 1423–1930   *196*

Index,   *201*

TO MY GRANDCHILDREN

Eleanor, Thea and Jonathan Marsh

Acknowledgements

The author wishes to thank Mrs Jenny Freebody and Mr Roy Gyngell for sharing their family histories and photographs so generously and for supplying information about the two family businesses. Photographs provided by them, and for which they have copyright, are acknowledged in appropriate end notes.

She also thanks her family and friends who have read and discussed the text and provided photographs: Timothy Clark, Stephen Clark; Vanessa Clark; Nigel Marsh; Geoffrey Pearce; Susan Wheeler, Michael Wheeler, (who shared his expertise and knowledge of fishing), Margaret Dade, Janet King and Michael Vince.

Professional help was provided by staff of libraries, museums and record offices, and thanks are given in particular to David Cliffe of Reading Borough Libraries and Ken Wells of the Police Museum at Sulhamstead. Richard Wise provided information about 'The Fishery' in Caversham. Martin Andrews of the University of Reading generously lent a photograph of the launch of Robert Gibbings' boat *Willow*.

The author owes much to Barbara Morris and Adam Sowan of Two Rivers Press and to David Woodward of Design for Print. They have given encouragement, advice and professional help and this is warmly acknowledged with appreciation and thanks. Mrs Doris Woodward shared her memories of living and working 'down by the river'.

Thanks are due to the Richmond Local Studies Library for making copies of the *Lock to Lock Times* freely available and of course to the original editors, advertisers, authors, illustrators and photographers whose work has been so valuable in this volume.

Picture credits

Acknowledgement is made to the following organisations for permission to use illustrations for which they hold copyright:

BRITISH LIBRARY (COLINDALE): illustrations from *Lock to Lock Times*: Antonio Bona p 88; Browne and Lilly p 123; Pratt's Motor Spirit p 130; lock-keeper p 147; Naval recruitment p 149; outboard engine p 150; gramophone p 159.

MUSEUM OF ENGLISH RURAL LIFE: houses in Thames Side p 122; angling club group and prize distribution p 180.

ORTNER BOAT CLUB & READING UNIVERSITY BOAT CLUB (Mr Will Ortner): RUBC VIII at the boat house (1928) p 155; women's crew with boatman p 183.

OXFORDSHIRE COUNTY COUNCIL PHOTOGRAPHIC ARCHIVE: The Clappers and the Adams & Gyngell boathouse on View Island p 95; Caversham Bridge from Bona's boathouse p 97; Telegraph poles along Thames Side p 118.

READING BOROUGH COUNCIL: illustrations from *Reading Waterways: a plan for the river landscape* (RBC, 1978): map adapted to show Reading's two rivers p 1; Lorco sign p 191.

READING BOROUGH COUNCIL (BERKSHIRE RECORD OFFICE): Map of Fry's Island p 5; mouldings and newel post from the Old Rectory p 11; plan of proposed canal network p 35; map showing the Clappers p 57; basket made by one of the Knight family p 71; Bill Moss's boathouse p 76.

READING BOROUGH COUNCIL (READING BOROUGH LIBRARIES): W Havell, engraved by John Pye, *View on the Thames from Caversham Bridge near Reading* p 28; Southampton Street looking towards Seven Bridges Wharf; p 38; W Fletcher, engraved by W Newman, *View of Reading from the Great*

Western Railway embankment at Kennet Mouth p 47; part of OS map of Reading (1932) p 58; Caversham House on View Island p 125; Caversham Mill p 125; two steamers moored above Caversham Bridge p 129; launch of the *Queen of the Thames* p 161; celebrating the launch of the *Queen of the Thames* p 161.

READING BOROUGH COUNCIL (READING MUSEUM SERVICE): copyright, all rights reserved: H Morley *Trial by Combat* (1918) p 2; William Havell *Old Caversham Bridge from the Warren* p 22; the Talbot wharf looking towards Caversham Bridge p 60; Piper's ferry crossing to the Caversham bank p 62; Moss and Freebody premises at Caversham Bridge p 76; two boatmen who found babies murdered by Mrs Dyer p 80; looking from Moss's site towards Caversham Bridge p 112; the brig *King Alfred* at Knighton's meadow p 146; preparation for the new Caversham Bridge p 158; Elliotts launch a landing craft p 169.

SALTER BROTHERS RIVER THAMES PASSENGER BOATS website: the steamer *Majestic* p 135.

THAMES VALLEY POLICE ARCHIVE (Curator Ken Wells): Mrs Amelia Dyer p 80; Chief constable presents prizes after the police swim p 184.

THE NATIONAL ARCHIVES: will of Richard Alexander of Caversham p 9; plan of Crown lands held by John Blagrave and Henry Vansittart (1770) p 21; map by R Billing showing town centre wharfs p 37; plan of Crown Estate at Reading for sale (1832) p 44; plan of Crown lands at King's Meadow (1865) with boundaries and acreage p 45; plan of house at View Island p 126 and of the Old Rectory p 134, both from Inland Revenue survey (1910).

Place names in brackets are present day locations to help identify the sites of former buildings or land.

Abbreviations

BRO Berkshire Record Office; RLSL Reading Borough Council Local Studies Library; RM Reading Borough Council Museum; MERL Museum of English Rural Life; TNA The National Archives.

Introduction

The story of Reading's rivers, the Thames and the Kennet, and of their importance to the town and to Caversham for business and pleasure has not been fully told before. This book now tells that story through records of the barge businesses on the Kennet and the boatbuilding and boat-hire businesses between Caversham Bridge and Caversham Lock on the Thames. It also tells how the people working on the river, including some of the author's own family, earned their living and how trades and businesses flourished, declined,

adapted to new technology, and flourished again. It follows the changes of land ownership on the riverbanks over the centuries and looks at the many leisure activities, particularly rowing, fishing and swimming, that took place there. Above all, this account puts people into the riverside landscape.

The bridge at Caversham was for centuries the main river crossing point for road traffic going south to Southampton or to pick up the main London to Bristol route, and going north through the Chilterns to Oxford and beyond. Caversham Bridge is still one of only two road crossings for the town. It has played a role in the town's history and its presence has attracted commercial activity alongside it. Caversham Lock in its present position was built in 1778 about a mile downstream from the bridge. The position of the railway when it came in 1840 and the nearness of the station to the Thames were critical in the development of businesses and leisure activities. There is a footbridge across the weir between Lower Caversham and Reading and, before Reading Bridge was built in 1923, this was an important pedestrian link between the two places.

The Kennet carried the town's barge traffic for 700 years and was its commercial centre until the nineteenth century. The river collects up Foundry Brook near Rose Kiln Lane, and the Holy Brook near Chestnut Walk, and flows into the Thames downstream from Caversham Lock. It has four locks of its own within the town boundary: Blake's, County, Fobney and Southcote.

The county boundary between Berkshire and Oxfordshire followed the Thames backwater behind Fry's Island on the Caversham side until Reading extended its boundary in 1911, taking Caversham into Berkshire, and other administrative boundaries still follow that line. Much of the land alongside the river was, and is, in public ownership and this has been a significant influence in keeping it accessible.

In the late 1800s there were two names that were in every local trade directory: Moss and Freebody. A significant part of the book is the story of their boatbuilding and boat-letting businesses. The Freebody family had been in Caversham for centuries and for much of that time were connected with the river. Bill Moss

arrived on the scene from Greenham in the 1870s. Between them they carry the story of the river from commercial horse-drawn barges to pleasure boating and each offered opportunities for the increasing leisure time that local people had to spend on, in and by the river. Family and business records of these two companies and the memories of present-day family members, with information from local and specialist primary sources, have been used to show how and when those changes on the river took place. Fry's Island, midway between the bridge and the lock, has been fully researched for the first time: its ownership has been established, and a good case made to identify the original Mr Fry.

The story would not be complete without some account of the various regulating bodies to show how their presence and their actions affected life and work on the river. There was no central control over the Upper Thames until the formation of a Commission in 1694. It was replaced in the next century by two further Commissions with extended powers to regulate and improve the navigation. The Thames Navigation Commission, in severe financial difficulties because of competition for trade from the railways, was replaced in 1866 by the Thames Conservancy. This continued as the regulating body for the Upper Thames, being increasingly involved in maintaining water purity, public water supplies and drainage, until 1974 when the Thames Water Authorities took over from it. The main themes of the story are brought to an end at this point, the Moss and Freebody businesses having closed between 1950 and 1965. A look, from a present day perspective, at the Thames and Kennet in Reading and Caversham, now under the management of the Environment Agency, forms a conclusion.

1 The early years at Caversham: 1100–1600

Landowners

People have lived in the waterside areas between Reading and Caversham since Neolithic times. There are signs that the Romans were there in the fourth century at a farmstead site near the weir, and the early Christians too, near Dean's Farm.[1] The crossing point eventually became a bridge, the weir began to support fishing and a mill, and boats were big enough to need a lock to let them manage the changing river levels as they travelled up or down stream.

When the area reached this stage of its development, it was a surprisingly important place because of the status of the owners of the surrounding land. William the Conqueror gave Caversham Manor to William Gifford, the founder of Notley Abbey in Buckinghamshire. In 1162 Gifford gave St Peter's Church, just above the bridge on the Caversham side, to Notley Abbey. Battle Abbey in Sussex held land on the Reading side of the river, both upstream and downstream from the bridge. Reading Abbey stood on rising ground on the town side, within sight of the Thames, its position generating commercial activity around it and at mills and wharfs along the Holy Brook and the Kennet.

Henry I, son of William the Conqueror, had founded the Abbey in 1121. It was the site of Great Councils, Parliaments, royal marriages, and royal visits, all of which contributed to the importance of the area and kept the river crossings and wharfs busy.

The first significant dated happening in the riverside area took place in the presence of King Henry II, on 8 April 1163. This was a trial by combat between Robert de Montfort and Henry, Earl of Essex, on an island in the area. It is popularly believed, from the way the event is shown in a painting by Harry Morley in 1918, now held at Reading Museum, that the island where the trial took place was the big central island on the Thames, sometimes called De Montfort Island, but marked on nineteenth-century maps as Fry's Island. The painting (see overleaf) shows

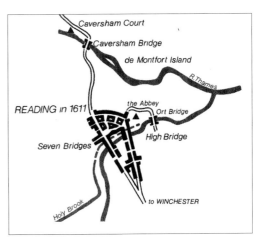

Reading and its two rivers, Thames and Kennet: adapted with permission from *Reading Waterways* published by Reading Borough Council, 1978.

the combat taking place, with the Abbey in the background, as if it was on the downstream tip of this island. The original source for the story simply says that the combat took place on an island not far from the Abbey and so the site could have been View Island or even one of the islands on the Kennet. De Montfort had accused his opponent of treachery and cowardice in battle and of casting away the Royal Standard and causing panic among the soldiers by falsely announcing the death of the King. Essex denied the charges and took up the challenge of trial by combat and so fought a duel in the presence of the King. During the fight it seems that Essex experienced a vision of two men he had wronged and he collapsed, leaving de Montfort as the victor, but although Essex was carried away for dead, he recovered and became a monk at the Abbey.[2]

By the next century there was a bridge across the river at Caversham. In 1233 Franciscan monks from the order of Friars Minor were given permission by Pope Gregory IX to settle in Reading. The Benedictines at the Abbey, who controlled most of the town, saw this as a challenge to themselves and

so the site near the bridge, which the newcomers were offered for their Friary, was outside the town centre, swampy and liable to flooding (present day Caversham Road). The Friars had oak from Windsor Forest for their building and this timber was likely to have been brought by river from Windsor. That in itself suggests that there was a wharf at the bridge and that there was commercial traffic on the river. By 1244 the friars had a substantial set of buildings on this damp and swampy site: a chapel, chapter house, dormitory, refectory and a two-storey privy chamber, at least some of which had good windows and a shingled roof. Eventually the Archbishop of Canterbury persuaded the Abbot of Reading to give the Franciscans a better site and in 1285 they moved closer to the town (where Greyfriars Church now stands). The site then presumably reverted to the Abbey.[3]

The mill, the flash lock and weir and the ferries, a mile downstream from the bridge, were part of the holdings of the manor or estate of Caversham, on the opposite side of the river to the Franciscans. This estate had passed by descent to William, Earl Marshall. He ruled as Regent

Trial by Combat, painting by H Morley of the fight between Robert de Montfort and Henry, Earl of Essex, in 1163.

The effigy of William, Earl Marshal, in the Temple Church, London. He was the first Earl of Pembroke.

during the minority of Henry III until his own death at Caversham in 1219. When his end was near, he was brought from London by boat and after his death his body was taken by river down to Reading Abbey to lie in state and then back to London for burial.[4]

On the north side of Caversham Bridge there was a Chapel of St Anne which had been founded by the Earl Marshall and by the Abbot of Reading. The chapel was a stopping place on the way to St Anne's Well (Priest Hill) and to the Chapel or Shrine of Our Lady in Caversham, said to have been in Lower Caversham near the river. The Shrine was a place of pilgrimage, because it housed a jewel-encrusted crowned statue of the Virgin and an important collection of relics: there was the spearhead that pierced Christ's side on the Cross, described as the principal relic of the Realm; a piece of the rope with which Judas hanged himself; and the knives that killed Saint-King Edward the Martyr and King Henry VI. Whether the pilgrims came by road or river, they made it a busy, thriving place.

The second Earl of Pembroke died in 1231 and the King commanded the Sheriff of Oxfordshire to go to the Chapel of St Anne to confirm that the joint arrangements between the Abbot and the next Earl for the chapel and the bridge were still properly in place. Later in the year the Keeper of Windsor Forest sent an oak to Andrew, Sergeant

of Caversham, to build a ferry for the use of the poor and more oaks were given to the canons of Notley Abbey for a ferry at Caversham for the use of pilgrims. The third Earl of Pembroke died in 1241 and there are life-sized effigies of all three of them, each dressed in chain mail and carrying a sword, in the circular Norman section of the Temple Church just behind the Strand in London.

The Caversham estate, with the weir and ferries, stayed in the hands of high-ranking people who were close to the monarch, coming eventually to Constance, widow of Thomas Despenser, daughter of Edmund, Duke of York, and granddaughter of Edward III. She died in Reading on 28 November 1416 and was buried before the high altar of the Abbey. Her daughter Isabel married Richard Beauchamp, and her granddaughter Anne Beauchamp, born in Caversham in 1426, married Richard Neville, Earl of Warwick, also known as Warwick the Kingmaker. He was first a supporter of Edward IV and later of Henry VI and both his daughters married members of the royal family. After Richard was killed in battle in 1471 the estate became a royal holding, but leased to Notley Abbey.[5] It was held by Edward IV's brother, Duke of Clarence, until his possessions were seized for treason in 1477 and he was executed in 1478, and then the manor, now known as Caversham Lodge, went back into the hands of the king. After this, the fulling (cloth) and the grain mill, let to Thomas Pynnock, were out of service for almost a year and the reeve and bailiff in 1481 had to employ contractors to cut and carry timber to get them repaired. The records of the four barge-loads of burnt lime delivered for the repair work are evidence of commercial river traffic on the Caversham reach. The bridge was still held by Reading Abbey, and the townspeople had to complain to Edward IV in 1480 that the Abbot had neglected to keep the bridge in good repair.

The names of some of those who kept the ferry in these early years are recorded: James Hyde in 1479 until at least 1502 when the manor of Caversham was on lease to Notley Abbey; and R[ichar]d Justice in 1510. The phrase 'kept the ferry' does not imply that Hyde and the others acted as ferrymen. They held the right to operate the ferry and to have the income from it. The ferry was just one of the waterside parts of the estate that could produce an income and which could be rented or leased from their owners: the wharf for goods and for passengers coming in and going out of the property; income and food from the fisheries; income from lock and mill and from osier growing on the islands around the fisheries; control over the level and flow of water which could have been used or directed to the benefit of the water mills or for the passage of commercial or passenger traffic through Caversham. All along the river this power to control the water flow, and to impose charges for navigation, set up conflicts between mill owners and bargemen which continued for centuries.

The value of these riverside assets was made clear when Caversham Manor was transferred in 1493 from Henry VII to the Abbot of Notley. The agreement covered not just the manor with all its gardens, orchards and meadows but was very specific about the profitable part of the estate: the two water mills, the mill barge, the lock called Caversham lock, the weirs and waters, banks and dams from the lock to the mills and beneath, fishing, Hergyn Eiate (eyot or island) and all the other eyots in Caversham and the waters to them, the ferry passage and the ferry barge in Caversham. There were references to the profits and revenues from the assets and requirements for repair and upkeep.[6]

The right to keep swans was another river-related asset. It was a status symbol amongst the wealthy and a privilege much sought after because the birds were a source of food and eggs and cygnets could be sold to landowners wanting ornamental birds for their lakes. The beaks of the birds were distinctively marked to denote individual ownership and the marking system was managed by the Master of the Thames. The Borough of Reading had marked swans on the Thames and the Kennet. The Guildhall and the Convent and Abbot of Reading were also sixteenth-century owners with their own sets of markings, as were William Gifford and William Knollys of Caversham Park and Thomas Vachel of Coley. Nicholas Niclas, alderman of Reading in 1546, was censured for exploiting the commercial aspect of swan-keeping and so exceeding his privileges.[7]

Change of ownership between 1535 and 1539

Henry VIII closed the monasteries, including of course the local riverside landowners, Battle, Notley and Reading Abbeys and the Franciscan Friary, and took their wealth and land for his own use. After this initial change to royal ownership, some of the rights and landholdings along the riverside were sold, rented or leased by the king to suitable owners or tenants. The right to present a clergyman to the living at St Peter's Church was granted to Christ Church, Oxford. One of the chapels on the bridge, and the island that supported it, was sold to Anthony Brigham, cofferer to the king. When the Abbey was demolished in 1549 all the contents and materials from which it was made, particularly the lead from the roofs, were sorted into lots and records were kept of the sale of even the smallest items. Much of the stonework from the Abbey was taken away by boat, some to Windsor and to Henley for building. Brigham was one of many people who bought materials, in his case a load of gravestones, both broken and whole.[8] Wills are very useful sources about landholdings and when the will of 'Anthony Bryghm, Gentleman of Caversham' was proved in the Prerogative Court of Canterbury in 1553 it showed that he had more riverside land than just the chapel site at Caversham. He held the leases of two pieces of land called Westmead and Frogmarshe, with their appurtenances, lying beside Caversham Bridge in the County of Berkshire and he left these leases to his wife, Margaret. Frogmarshe was originally part of Battle Abbey's lands and the holdings later became known as Brigham's Meads (present day Brigham Road). The Brigham family had a privately-owned chapel in St Peter's Church and

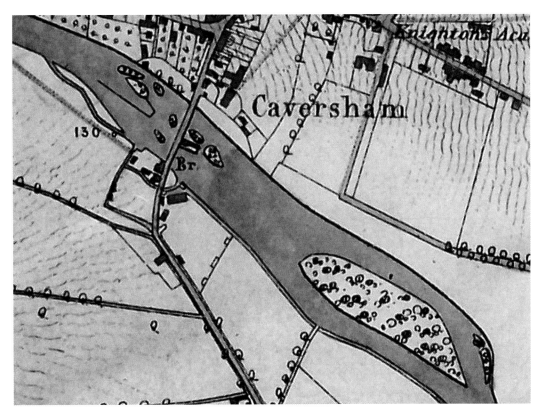

A marker point for the Borough boundary was on Caversham Bridge but the charter which defined the boundary did not say on which side of the large island the line should run.[11]

family burials continued to be made there.

Caversham Manor was leased in 1542 to Francis Knollys, a man with royal connections, and then granted to him in 1552. The grant specifically included the 'ferry and ferry barge of Caversham, all the watermills within the manor, the mill barge, Caversham lock and the weirs and waters from the said lock down to the mills.' There were at this time two corn mills and two fulling mills.[9] Knollys' son, Earl of Banbury, was a Privy Councillor and Treasurer of the Household to Queen Elizabeth. His wife, as a daughter of Mary Boleyn, was her first cousin. The Queen visited Knollys in Caversham in 1602. It was during his ownership of the estate that the house in Lower Caversham down near the water was replaced by one on the site where the BBC Monitoring Station now stands. When Anne, Queen of Denmark, visited the Knollys family in the new house in 1613, she arrived by river and because the house

was now some distance from the wharf, she was taken across the fields and up the hill towards Henley Road by a specially created road. During Knollys' ownership of the estate in 1585 the flash lock was kept by R[ichar]d Barton and the weir by 'one Salter'.[10] A flash lock was created by removing a panel in a palisade across the weir and water which had been allowed to build up behind the barrier would carry a boat through the gap and across the weir. Boats coming upstream had to be hauled through the gap. The Knollys land holdings extended over the river to Reading and up towards the town centre.

The Borough boundary

The centre of the bridge between Reading and Caversham was used as a marker point to define the boundaries of the Borough of Reading in a royal charter in 1559/60, the second year of the

LEFT: a gatepost at the top of steps in Caversham Court, whose stones may have come from the Abbey. RIGHT: a beast's head corbel set into the gatepost. The second head is a similar size and the face is slightly cat-like. Both are limestone and have therefore become eroded.

reign of Queen Elizabeth. Clause 7 of the Charter described the boundary as running

> … from a certain place upon the bridge where the Counties of Berk and Oxon are allotted and divided, and so from there eastward through the midstream of the River Thames in the County of Berk to its meeting the River Kennette called Kennettes Mouth …'

What this description misses, and it seems an extraordinary omission, is that the Thames at this point divides around the island now known as Fry's Island and that there are therefore two water-ways which the boundary might follow. Current town and earlier county and other administrative boundaries, where marked on maps, pass along the backwater on the Caversham side. Fry's Island therefore was, and is, in the parish of Reading St Laurence although the charter does not use it as a marker.

The charter transferred responsibility for the repair of the bridge within the boundary from the Crown to the Borough although this was sweetened by the right to timber and stone from various local sources and by revenues from various Berkshire lands around the bridge: the Chapel and the site of the Chapel at the bridge and a rood (a quarter of an acre) of meadow adjoining; a plot called the Hermitage and half an acre of meadow on the west part and all the site of former Holy Ghost Chapel and one little eyot (island) and parcels of land, all now in the tenure of John Salter.[12] A further charter in 1638/39 gave permission to the Borough to raise money from those crossing the bridge (the right of pontage), and the right to charge a toll on barges passing under the Reading half of the bridge, the charge to go towards repairing its foundations. Laden carts or wagons had to pay two pence, laden horses a halfpenny and barges four pence.[13] The bridge was the crossing point at one time for a packhorse route used by the wool trade that followed the line of the present Warren towards Wallingford.[14] The origin of this road lies in a land deal negotiated by Sir Richard Blount of Mapledurham, who wanted to improve access to his home from Caversham. He bought a parcel of land below Chazey Wood from the estate of Caversham Rectory, part of the former Notley Abbey lands, and in about 1600 created a level road to his house from what had been a bridleway.

The Old Rectory

A piece of riverside land below St Peter's Church, well above water level, was a perfect site for a house. A building was put on it by Notley Abbey for the rector of Caversham but it was later leased to a lay rector who had the duty to provide a priest for the church. At the Reformation, like other abbey and priory properties, it changed ownership. The site and the patronage, with much other land along the Caversham side of the river, passed from Notley Abbey to the Dean and Chapter of Christ Church, Oxford. By 1586 there was a large house on the site below the church and it was occupied by William Alexander (also known as Milward or Mylwarde), under lease from Christ Church. It was called the Old Rectory and known, from its timber and stucco construction, as the Striped House.[15]

The house was built round inner and outer courts and inside it was partly balustraded, with a long gallery running its whole length. The immediate estate consisted in 1584 of several barns, a stable, brew house, malt house, the Mount [sic], glebelands, a bounded and enclosed rabbit warren, an orchard, dove house and gardens which sloped down from a terrace to the river. There was a hedge along the river bank. The site was at some stage separated from the churchyard of St Peter's Church above it by the rippled curves of a 20ft-high crinkle-crankle brick wall. A set of steps going down from the terrace in present-day Caversham Court, the site of the Striped House, has a carved beast's head corbel set into each stone gatepost and these may have been part of the old garden and have come, before that, from Reading Abbey.[16]

William Alexander

William Alexander was born in Bushey in Hertfordshire in about 1540. His father's extensive estates at this time comprised the manor and church of Bushey, the demesne lands, fisheries, mill, coney warren and other royalties granted to him by the crown in 1543, with other profitable assets leased to him for 21 years. In 1543 he was also granted Bushey Hall Park, Hounslow Grove, Bushey Grove, and Bushey Heath. William succeeded to all these at his father's death in 1546 and in 1579 sold Bushey Hall and conveyed the advowson of the church, the watermill, free fishery, and coney warren to Anthony Brigham. William married Katherine Warde, daughter of Coleberry Lambert and Richard Warde of Hurst.[17]

William's income came principally from lending money and dealing in property and the records of the court cases concerning his business arrangements form a very rich source of information about him, his family, his household and events that took place at his riverside home. They provide a clearer picture of William and his lifestyle than exists for almost any other man in Caversham at the time. In 1577–78, before he left Bushey, he had brought proceedings against Anthony Brigham about a debt. In 1588, soon after his arrival in Caversham, Alexander was leasing out parts of the estate. The church, rectory and parsonage of Caversham were leased to William Skidmore of London who transferred the arrangement to Thomas Brigham. Once again the Alexanders and the Brighams met in court to sort out issues that arose from the transfer. The proceedings mention Alexander's son Richard and his wife's brother, Richard Warde.[18] Another case, on a much smaller scale, was about the failure of John Lane, woollen draper of Reading, to repay £40 that he had borrowed in about 1593 from William, and £80 that he had borrowed from William's son Richard, having agreed to the terms of repayment. The Alexanders said that he had wilfully intended to forfeit the bond.[19] Sarah Markham said 'a tenant to whom he had granted a lease complained that so much of the property had been conveyed away that what remained was not worth the 'consideration money' that he had paid.'[20] These are just examples of the many cases brought before the courts and for which the papers still remain.

Richard Alexander

The Alexander family name has become a much-quoted one in legal textbooks right down to the present day as a warning to students about the need to prepare court papers in clear and concise language. William and his eldest son Richard are the principal characters in the story. In 1594 and 1596 William met members of the Weldon family in court in two cases that were related in substance.[21] The earlier one was a bill of complaint brought by William Weldon against Alexander in connection with a debt. Weldon had borrowed money from Alexander, with an agreement about its repayment. At the time the situation between the two was one of great friendship, and it was likely that they would become closer through the proposed marriage of a kinswoman, Isabel Weldon, daughter of Edward and Katherine Weldon, to Richard Alexander, an arrangement which Weldon had initiated and encouraged. Alexander had been most willing and ready to lend the money, since the 'principall stait of [his] livinge [was] by letting out mony to use' and Weldon was of sufficient substance to repay the debt. However the relationship between them had cooled when the arrangement for the marriage was broken off because of a dislike that had arisen between the couple. Weldon was willing to give a new obligation to pay the debt and asked for a subpoena against Alexander to appear in the Court of Chancery to sort the issue out.

The second case was brought by Alexander (in the first case described as of Caversham but here as of New Windsor) against the Weldons in connection with the failure to agree about money to be settled on Richard and his future wife Isabel. Richard Alexander prepared the paperwork for the case.[22] When the Lord Keeper looked at the 120 sheets of paper on which it was set out, he said that the relevant material in it could just as well have been contained in 16 pages, that such abuse of the court was not to be tolerated, and that Richard, as the author, should be imprisoned, punished and fined as an example to others. Richard then had to prepare the case again, making sure that his presentation was short and to the point. This was the punishment that still serves as a reminder to students of the risk of wasting the time of the courts:

> It is therefore ordered, that the warden of the Fleet shall take the said Richard Mylward, alias Alexander, into his custody, and shall bring him into Westminster Hall on Saturday next, about 10 of the clock in the forenoon, and then and there shall cut a hole in the midst of the same engrossed Replication which is delivered unto him for that purpose, and put the said Richard's head through the same hole, and so let the same Replication hang about his shoulders with the written side outward, and then, the same so hanging, shall lead the said Richard bareheaded and barefaced round about Westminster Hall, whilst the Courts are sitting, and shall shew him at the Bar of every of the three Courts within the Hall, and then shall take him back again to the Fleet, and keep him prisoner until he shall have paid £10 to her Majesty for a fine, and 20 nobles to the defendant for his costs in respect of the aforesaid abuse, which fine and costs are now adjudged and imposed upon him by this court for the abuse aforesaid.

The lease of the Old Rectory at Caversham ran for three score years and at some point William conveyed the remainder of the years still to run on it to Richard. Unfortunately Richard died before his father and his death in 1601 was probably sudden and unexpected because the will that he made was a nuncupative or spoken one:

> In the name of God Amen. Memorandum that one daye happening in the moneth of March, a thousand six hundred and one or therabouts, Richard Alexander als Millward whilst he lyved of Caveysham in the Countie of Oxon gentleman deceased being of perfect mynde and memorie, and having an intent to make his last will and testament, did nuncupativley declare the same in

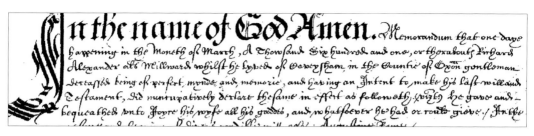

The will of Richard Alexander.

effect as followeth vizt: he gave and bequeathed unto Joyce his wyfe all his gooddes and whatsoever he had or could give. In the presence and hearing of divers credible wittnesses.[23]

After Richard's death, his widow Joyce married Hubert Earle of Chelsea. The family of her new husband claimed that the lease of the Parsonage at Caversham was hers for life and so the couple moved, or attempted to move, into the riverside house. William's claim was that the lease had reverted to him but he did not wait for legal proceedings. He got together a group, including his sons William the younger and Thomas, together with Thomas Piggot and Thomas Allaway, who were members of the household staff, Henry Salter or Campion, Nicholas Coles of Caversham and Leonard Welbeck of Reading, gent, to repel the Earles. The Alexanders were described as behaving towards the Earles in a threatening and warlike manner with swords, daggers and rapiers.

After this incident the Earles brought charges against them. The court papers include a list of the questions prepared for the witnesses, one of whom was William Smith of Caversham, who prepared deeds and conveyances for the Alexanders. The questioning covered Smith's knowledge of the affairs of the two men and of the conveyance, in particular about whether Richard had transferred the lease back to his father before he died and if so, if there were any deeds supporting it, and whether his death rendered the agreement void. The outcome of the case was that William Alexander, William Smythe, Roger Salter and Thomas Pyrkitt were issued with a writ of subpoena to appear before the Court of the Star Chamber.[24] However the Earles' case did not succeed and the Alexander family stayed in the riverside house.

Alexander's Catholic connections

William Alexander's name, because he was a Catholic and because he had living with him another Catholic, Robert Newport, was indirectly linked with one of the major political events of his time. The Gunpowder Plot of 1605 grew out of dislike of James I by people of the Catholic faith who had suffered persecution since he succeeded Elizabeth I as monarch. The plan was of course to blow up the King as he opened a new session of Parliament. After the discovery of the plan and the arrest of Robert Catesby, Thomas Wintour, John Wright, Guy Fawkes and Thomas Percy there were investigations into many Catholic families to seek out any knowledge of, or involvement in, the plot. Thomas Percy was an employee of the Earl of Northumberland and had visited him at his London home the night before the plot was discovered and so the Earl and his household and contacts were suspects. Robert Newport was another of the Earl's servants. A witness at the enquiry in November 1605, immediately after the plot was discovered, described him as an arrant papist who lived with William Mylwarde of Caversham.[25] There were suggestions that Newport had been aware of the conspiracy and he certainly knew Thomas Percy through their mutual connections with the Earl of Northumberland. Although the Earl spent 15 years in the Tower after the plot and Percy was shot while trying to avoid capture, there is no evidence that either Newport or Alexander suffered any punishments. However there was one further consequence. Newport had not attended the parish church of St Peter when he was living at the Rectory but the rector had been afraid to

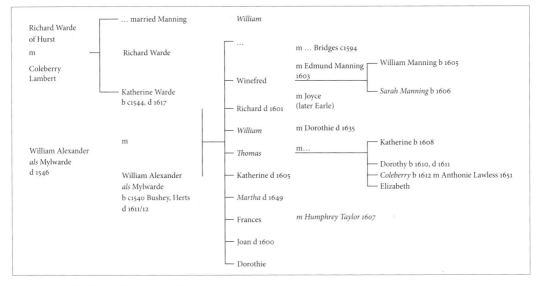

Family tree of William Alexander or Mylward, 1540–1611/12.

report this evidence of Catholicism to the authorities because William Alexander controlled his tenancy. It was to prevent such situations that legislation was introduced to prevent Catholics having the control of Anglican benefices.

The Alexander family tree

William died in March 1611/12, leaving half his plate (tableware of precious metal) and household goods to his wife Katherine, making bequests to his son Thomas, with conditions of good behaviour, his daughter Martha and to the children, William and Sarah, of his son [in-law] Manning. The rest of his estate went to his son William, with his brother-in-law Sir Alexander Hampden and his kinsman Paule Alexander as executors. William's widow Katherine died in 1617, appointing her sons William (his father's heir) and Thomas as executors, with bequests to her servants Goodwives Michell, Tristrame, Piggott and Alloway and to her maids Isabel Wydmoor and Margarett Palmer. Her clothing was to be shared between her daughter Martha, Sarah Manning and Coleberry Milward. She wished to be buried in the chancel of St Peter's Church, with money to be distributed on the day for the poor and for the bellringers.[26]

The diagrammatic family tree has been built up mainly from names and dates in parish registers, wills and court cases. Names in italic are those mentioned in Katherine's will in 1617. William in the second generation was still in Caversham in 1618 when his name appeared in estate papers of his near-neighbour Mr Lybbe of Hardwick, these suggesting that he, like his father, was in the business of property and of lending money.[27]

A coat of arms at the Old Rectory

The year 1638 was a significant one at The Old Rectory because the date was carved into a newel post at the top of a flight of stairs, with a hound's head carved on reverse of the post. Above the staircase was a plaster moulding with the initials W, A and I, forming a triangle with the A at the base, and a second connected moulding showing a coat of arms. The design of the coat of arms consists of two crossed implements, perhaps swords or knives, and the heads of three hounds (talbots) wearing collars and showing their teeth and tongues. Talbots are not uncommon heraldic figures and they can represent loyalty or may simply illustrate an interest of the holder, or symbolise a family surname. These items together, date, hound, arms and initials, suggest that the Alexanders were still at the house in 1638. There is no evidence of any right of Alexander to bear arms but this might have come from a female line. The register of St Peter's, the parish church, in which a marriage between William and someone with the initial 'I' or 'J' might have been recorded, has been cut at some time, leaving a gap where the entries for the year 1638 would have been. The significance of the date remains a mystery. The death of Mr William Alexander is recorded in the Caversham burial register in 1654 and that of 'Mris Joan Alexander' in 1661 but while they may have been in the parish at these dates they were not necessarily still at the Old Rectory.

The Browne family who succeeded the Alexanders at Caversham Rectory were also known to be Royalists and Catholics and had connections with not just one, but with two, of the Gunpowder Plotters. George Browne of Shefford, knighted in the early 1590s, was related by marriage to Robert Catesby and directly to Lord Montague, whose servant Guy Fawkes had been. Catesby had warned Montague not to go to the opening of Parliament.[28] Because George Browne died in 1615, with no mention in his will of property in Caversham (and because it seems that the Alexanders may still have been there in 1638) it is most likely to have been his son George (1590–1664) who later occupied the house. This son was the child of Sir George's second marriage to Mary Tyrwitt. There were also three daughters of his first marriage to Eleanor Bruges, all of whom were mentioned in his will. One of the girls, Joanna or Jane, joined the Companions of Mary Ward, a group of women founded on Jesuit lines in 1609 who worked with the poor and who established

The mouldings of arms of the Alexander family above the staircase and the newel posts, the further one with the date 1638 on the near side, were taken from the Old Rectory by a later owner and incorporated into his new house on the same site.[29]

schools for girls. Mary Ward (1585–1645) was from an outlawed and persecuted Catholic family who believed that she was called to start an active order for women although the church at the time saw women only as able to marry or to enter the enclosed religious life. The Companions worked in Europe and sent members back to England to work under cover with Catholic families.

The house at Caversham passed by succession to John Browne (1628–80), son of George and his wife, Eleanor Blount.

Endnotes

1 Mary Kift *Life in Old Caversham* (Reading, 1980), p 10.

2 J B Hurry *Octocentenary of Reading Abbey* (1901) p 41; H E Butler (ed) *The chronicles of Jocelin of Brakelond* (1949) p 69–70. The story of the deeds and transgressions of Henry of Essex was inserted into Jocelin's chronicles by the hand of someone who had heard the story from Jocelin himself. H Morley *Trial by Combat* 1918, Reading Museum object 1931.279.1, painting located at the foot of the main staircase.

3 F Gordon Spriggs *The history of the Church of Greyfriars Reading* (published privately, 1963), p 12–3.

4 Kift p 56, 62.

5 J Malpas *Caversham Park and its Owners* (published privately, 1997), p 11–15.

6 The National Archives [TNA], E 40 3176 Demise by Henry VII to Peter the abbot and the convent of Notley of the site of Caversham Manor.

7 N F Ticehurst 'The Swan Marks of Berkshire' *Journal of the Berkshire Archaeological Society* vol 36, 1932, p 62.

8 I Yarrow *Berkshire* (London, 1952), p 96. The author refers to accounts in the PRO (now TNA) as his source. The Brigham family had their own chapel at the east end of the north aisle of St Peter's Church and this passed later to the Vanderstegen family. Rent was being paid to the church for its use as late as the 1940s.

9 F Thacker *The Thames Highway* vol II (David and Charles, reprinted 1968), p 228–30.

10 Thacker vol I, p 54–55.

11 Berkshire Record Office (BRO) D/EX 326 2b Part of map, 1863.

12 J M Guilding (ed) *The Records of Reading: Diary of the Corporation* vol II 1603–29 (1896), p 23. In a list of rents Widow Salter was assessed for a mead plott and Mr Burningham for a tenement and hopyard at Caversham Bridge.

13 C F Prichard (ed) *Reading Charters, Acts and Orders* 1253–1911 (Reading and London, 1913), p 17, 34–35, 45–47.

14 Mary Kift, personal communication.

15 Sarah Markham *John Loveday of Caversham 1711–89* (Salisbury, 1984), p 2; Reading Local Studies Library [RLSH], RH/NW Sarah Markham and Godwin Arnold *The Gazebo and Caversham Court, Reading* (no publication data) p 8; TNA, C43/8/163 Mylward *alias* Alexander v. Brigham; C2/Eliz/B25/42, Brigham v. Alexander *alias* Milward 1558–1603.

16 N Pevsner *The Buildings of England: Berkshire* (Harmondsworth 1966), p 110. *Corpus of Romanesque Sculpture in Britain and Ireland*, electronic archive website http://www.crsbi.ac.uk/crsbi/frbesites.html (16 September 2001).

17 *Victoria County History A History of the County of Hertford: Parishes: Bushey*, vol II (1908), p 179–86.

18 TNA, C43/8/163 Mylward *alias* Alexander v. Brigham; C2/Eliz/B25/42, Brigham v. Alexander *alias* Milward 1558–1603. 'Parsonage' here is the revenue for the upkeep of the incumbent of the church.

19 TNA, C3/280/51 Lane v. Mylwarde Oxford 1596–1616; C3/255/78 Alexander *alias* Millward v Lane Berks 1591–96.

20 Markham and Arnold, p 1.

21 TNA, C/3/253/66 Wellden v. Alexander and C3/231/6 Alexander *alias* Millwarde v. Weldon Berks 1591–96.

22 This case appears in many websites where it is cited as an example of what can happen when a lawyer fails to set out a case concisely and clearly. One site states that Mylward v. Weldon, (1596), was first reported in G Spence *Equitable Jurisdiction of the Court of Chancery* (Philadelphia, Lea & Blanchard 1846).

23 TNA, PROB 11/99 will of Richard Alexander *alias* Millaward of Caversham gent.

24 TNA, STAC 8/131/1 and /2 Earle v. Mylwarde *alias* Alexander, Smythe and others, 1603–25 and Earle v. Mylwarde *alias* Alexander, Salter, Campion, Coles and others 1603–25.

25 *Calendar of State Papers Domestic James I, 1603–10* vol 16, November 1605.

26 TNA, PROB 11/119 William Alexander of Caversham 1612; PROB 11/69 Richard Alexander of Herts 1586; PROB 11/173 Augustine Alexander gent of Reading 1636; PROB 11/130 Katherine Alexander *alias* Mylwarde widow of Caversham 1617. Information on Katherine's family was found on David Nash's website on Berkshire history and the use of this is acknowledged with thanks.

27 Oxfordshire RO [ORO], E1/2/1D/11 Lybbe papers: Manor and farm of Elvedon 1618.

28 Tony Hadland *Thames Valley Papists from Reformation to Emancipation 1534–1829* (published privately 1992), p 61.

29 BRO, D/EX 965/13, photograph of staircase of the house that replaced the Old Rectory. The newel post and mouldings are now in Reading Museum. The background colour to the arms is light blue and the hounds are white with red collars and tongues.

2 Commerce, civil war and settlement: 1600–1750

Commercial activity

Reading's earliest connection with bargebuilding and barge traffic is probably too far back to trace but there is a tradition that King Alfred had a barge made in the town. There was certainly private passenger traffic from London in the 1600s, the visit to Knollys by the Queen of Denmark being an excellent example, and a regular weekly public service was operating in 1637 between Queen's Hythe in London and Reading, from where smaller local boats could take travellers further upstream. It was also possible to hire a waterman and a boat to do the journey and this would have been a sensible and safe alternative to road travel, certainly before the introduction of the public coach services in the 1750s.

The development of the river as a commercial highway ran way ahead of the introduction of controls to manage its overall navigation and to keep a balance between the needs of the mills, the fisheries and bargemen. An Act of Parliament in 1350 addressed the problem of weirs and fisheries obstructing navigation. An early Commission in 1624 applied only to the Upper Thames between Oxford and Burcot; it had the power to make the river navigable and to open, prepare and build any weirs, locks, turnpikes and towpaths that were needed. By 1630 it had accomplished its purpose of making this part of the river properly navigable.

While it is known from wills and deeds that fisheries and ferries were regarded as assets that could be bought or sold, there is not much evidence of their cash value, certainly not in the Reading area. It is therefore particularly interesting to find among papers of a Hampshire family that the Caversham manor, mills and ferry were in 1631 funding an annuity of £56 which was granted by Thomas Emerson of Lincoln's Inn to Edward Manning of Shropshire in trust for Emerson's wife Mary. There are no known other local connections with these people but an Edward Manning was a witness to the will of William Alexander in 1612.[1]

Although there was plenty of through traffic at Caversham Bridge, and it remained an important way in and out of the town, the hub of waterside commercial activity in Reading was not there, but where it had been since the time of the Abbey, at the town centre mills and wharfs on the Holy Brook and the Kennet (where The Oracle, Mill Lane, High Bridge, Duke Street and Kings Road now stand). This is where the town's food and fuel came in and from where its produce left. Two of the first men connected with the waterside to appear in records are John Thorne, fisher of St Laurence, and John Winter, bargeman of St Giles Parish. For both of them the trade terms used as identifiers in 1587 are now misleading.[2] A fisher was then a fishmonger, who at this date would have been selling freshwater fish, and bargeman was a very general term that more usually denoted a crew member but here was used for a bargemaster or owner. That the Kennet side was the centre of activity is clear from the number of stories in the town's records about incidents and offences that took place there and because it was here that movement controls were put in place during the plague of 1625 to prevent the spread of the disease. This was distributed by rat fleas initially and by person-to-person contact once established. Orders were made forbidding boatmen to bring passengers or goods into the town and bargeman John Atkyns was required to remove two women whom he had taken into his house.

Another story in the records, concerning William Bourman, a wharfinger in 1632 at High Wharf, and William Conwaye, master of the *Dooves* of Reading, is interesting because it gives an insight into both the cargo and the crew. There were eight in the crew and they had unloaded 17 barrels of beef for Sir Henry Wallop, to find the next day that there were only 16 barrels left. However one of the bargemen, Edward Terrant, had been found to have joints of beef in his house and so was suspected of the theft. His defence was that of damaged goods; the lid had come off the barrel and the joints had fallen out. Crewmen, Richard Hill and William Hackett came from Reading; Thomas Fowler was from Maidenhead; Henry Lasher from Wargrave; and Phillip Parry from Twyford.[3]

The will of Abraham Edwards, Waterman, of St Giles, Reading, proved in 1639, provides the first evidence of how the barge businesses on the Thames and Kennet were operated. A barge and its cargo were expensive items and the journeys were risky because of delays and damage. The formation of shared ownership or partnerships distributed the risk and perhaps made it easier to accommodate customer requirements. The purchase of a small share in a boat could be a way into a business for a newcomer. Abraham said in his will that John Bradford already had one quarter of his barge and he now bequeathed to him a further share. This redistribution of the shares might have been a means of keeping the business running to the benefit of the testator's

wife or young children. A partner with a small share might pull out, or feel that in the new circumstances he was working for a small return, but a partner with a more substantial share would now perhaps feel that it was in his interest to keep the barge trading.[4]

One of the reasons why the commercial activity remained on the Kennet and Holy Brook, and not close to the bridge crossing the Thames at Caversham, was that they offered between them more channels for waterpower and milling and also that the ground between the town and the bridge was very low-lying and wet. The Vasternes, (the land now between Vastern Road and Caversham Road) was drained by ditches and was not easy to cross. In 1631:

> Mr Henry Atkyns in the behaulf of himself and others made request to the Town Council 'to have the goodwill of this Company by waye of benevolence towards the making of the causeways betwixt Cawsom bridge and the Vasterne. And the Company did then give *xii d* a piece voluntarily towardes the well doing thereof.[5]

Despite the money being provided to make a road between the bridge and the town, it was another 100 years before there was one there which was above water level.

Civil war

Then in 1642 Reading was caught up in the civil war and because of its strategic location between Oxford, where the King had his headquarters, and London, where the Parliamentarians had theirs, it was particularly unfortunate in being held and besieged by both sides in turn. The road bridge at Caversham was central to taking and holding the town during the civil war for both Royalists and Parliamentarians and the Thames was an important route for getting supplies to both sides.

The war began at Nottingham on 25 August 1642 and the King marched to Shrewsbury, then to Oxford and from there towards Caversham. Among his supporters along the riverside were Blount of Mapledurham, Alexander of Caversham Rectory and Lord Craven who had by this

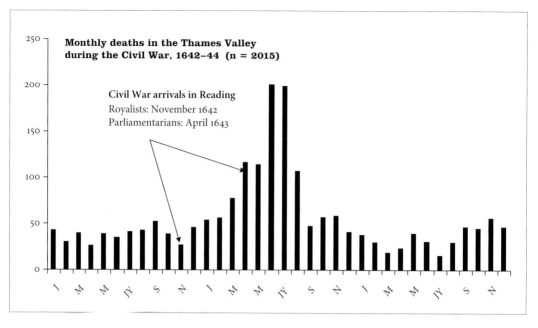

Graph of 2015 deaths in the Thames Valley during the Civil War showing the peak in 1643.

time succeeded Knollys at Caversham Park. Lord Craven's support for the King was valuable. He was a soldier who had been knighted and created Baron Craven in 1627 for military services to Prince Rupert of Orange and had fought on behalf of the King's sister, the Queen of Bohemia, in an attempt to restore her kingdom to her. He also contributed substantially to the financial costs of the war. Charles I stayed at Caversham Park during the fighting. On 3 November the King ordered the Mayor and Aldermen of Reading to make Caversham Bridge strong enough for the passage of his army by eight o'clock on the next morning, and on 4 November he crossed the bridge and led his troops into Reading to form a garrison of two thousand foot and horse soldiers. This force stayed in the town for nearly six months preparing for attack. Ammunition and arms were brought in by barge and pebbles were dredged from the river and put into wicker baskets that were stacked to form defensive positions for the guns.[6]

The whole area suffered pillaging and requisitioning of food, crops, wood, tools and horses by encamped soldiers, and destruction of mills

and bridges. Elsewhere on the river Abingdon, Wallingford and Henley were also involved in the war. The civilian death rate from diseases such as typhus spreading from the army camps, and from the consequences of deprivation, was unprecedented. The graph shows the extraordinary increase in deaths that occurred in 15 parishes along the river whose parish burial registers continued recording during this difficult time. The parishes were Abingdon St Helen and St Nicholas, Basildon, Bisham, Caversham, Cholsey, Henley, Pangbourne, Radley, Reading St Giles and St Laurence, Sonning, Sutton Courtenay, Wargrave, and Windsor. The moving average for 1643 (the number of deaths that might have been expected in these parishes), calculated over a 25-year series of figures, was 347. Actual deaths in the peak year of 1643 were 1144. The moving average for just the two Reading parishes was 152 but the actual figure in 1643 was 529. Both Caversham and Sonning suffered deaths that year in numbers well over normal. If the register of Reading St Mary had not ceased recording during the war the mortality figures would have been even higher. There are only very small numbers of soldiers' deaths in these figures; they are almost entirely civilian.[7]

On 13 April 1643, the Earl of Essex left Windsor with a Parliamentary force to attack Reading. He approached the town on its western side, seized Caversham Bridge, and laid siege to Reading. Essex also attacked and pillaged Mapledurham House because its owner, Sir Charles Blount, was a Catholic and also a Royalist. Essex beat down the steeple of Caversham Church, where Royalists had a cannon, and raised the drawbridge at Caversham Bridge so that a Royalist relieving force from Oxford could not enter the town from that side. (Later research has suggested that Essex came from completely the opposite direction and that it was St Giles Church that was damaged.[8]) The officer of the relieving force went on to Sonning, from where he managed to send 600 musketeers and a supply of ammunition up river to Reading in boats. It is also said that supplies of flour for the besieged forces were sent upstream from Sonning Mill. Essex placed batteries along the riverside to prevent supplies arriving through that route again. The garrison was on the point of surrender as the King's forces drew close and a thousand Royalist musketeers led by King Charles and Prince Rupert met the Parliamentary guard at Caversham Bridge.

However, as they crowded upon the narrow bridge they were an easy target for the Parliamentarians who lined the opposite bank of the river. The Royalists failed to force their way across the bridge. They withdrew up the hill, followed by victorious Roundheads, leaving many dead and wounded. On 26 April the garrison surrendered and the following day mustered to march out with the honours of war. Horse and foot passed through the ramparts and took the road by Caversham Bridge past St Peter's Church, to Oxford. The soldiers of Essex stood ranked ready to enter the captured town. Looting broke out among the Parliamentarians and the wagons and weapons of the retreating garrison were plundered, as was much of the town as they entered. There was an epidemic (the cause is not known) among Essex's troops soon after the occupation.[9] The troops were marched

out again across the bridge to a healthier site on Caversham Hill and Essex settled himself in Craven's home at Caversham Park. The Royalists retook the town in October 1643 and established a garrison there and it was reported that there was plague in the town that year. There was further pillage and requisitioning of food and the town was finally taken again by the Parliamentarians in 1644. Some parishes in the county then suffered a further round of high deaths in the winter of 1644/45 when the war was over and although there is no information about any particular disease, the local population must have been at a very low ebb.

The bargemen may not have suffered as much as other businessmen in Reading and Caversham because the troops on both sides needed supplies of ammunition, food and fuel during both occupation and siege and all had to be transported, whether they were pillaged, requisitioned or bought. Of course the barges may also have been requisitioned. The river was the route by which the wounded Parliamentarians were transported by barge away from the fighting. When the town began to rebuild after the war all the heavy materials must have come in by river and there would have been work again. After the war, in 1646, Reading made a five-year agreement with John Hancocke that he would for five pounds 'repair and maintayne the Drawbridge Bay [of the bridge] and the Long Bay on the north side in all tymber and carpenters' work'.[10]

The King was once again at Caversham in 1647 but this time he was being held at Lord Craven's home at Caversham Park while the Army Council met to decide its next move. After the King's defeat Craven's estates were confiscated by the Parliamentarians, his house reduced to ruins and his woods felled. Craven's estates were returned to him by Charles II at the restoration of the monarchy and he was awarded an earldom. He became guardian of the illegitimate daughter of Prince Rupert and he was also a Privy Councillor. He did not return to Caversham Park.

In the period after the war the London market was the main influence on the cargoes that were carried by the bargemen working from Reading or travelling through Caversham. Beech wood from Buckinghamshire went to London for furniture, timber from Reading went to build merchant ships, malt went from Reading and also came through from upstream. Cheese from Gloucestershire and cider from Herefordshire were put onto the river as far upstream as Lechlade. In the other direction all the towns along the river imported salt, oil, groceries and tobacco from London. Defoe reported that in 1649 there were 8000 cassocks and breeches, 7500 yards of broadcloth, 8000 shirts, and 8000 pairs of shoes and stockings that came up river to Abingdon to be sent from there to Bristol by road and then on by sea to Ireland. All this trade, even when it was only passing through Reading and Caversham, brought money into the area from lock and bridge fees; every barge needed casual labour to haul it to the next area and each crew needed food and supplies. There was no Sunday traffic on the river during the Puritan period except for going to church or in the case of an emergency and this was strictly enforced until the Restoration and the prohibition stayed in place for another 200 years. However, although the early Commission had been successful in improving navigation in the reaches immediately below Oxford and although the river was such a major highway, there was no central control over the Upper Thames until the formation of a new Commission in 1694.

King's Meadow

A map of the town showing the wartime defences in 1643 is an early source which identifies the meadow land in the triangle between the Thames, the Kennet and Reading Abbey as 'His Maiesty, his meadowe'.[11] When Henry VIII had seized the abbey lands in the area they had all become Crown property.

While much of this land was then leased or sold, one piece remained in royal ownership and this still carries the name it had in the seventeenth century: King's Meadow.

The Old Rectory: the Lovedays

The lease of the Old Rectory, the house alongside St Peter's Church, and two adjoining farms changed hands twice in fairly quick succession. Sir John Browne, son of George, sold the lease in 1665 to Richard Jones. One of the previous tenants had added to it a summerhouse with a boathouse beneath and a weather vane on it carrying the date 1663. The estate then passed from Richard Jones to Thomas Loveday, a member of the Company of Goldsmiths. His descendant, Sarah Markham, writing about his move to Caversham, said:

> He settled on the old parsonage house at Caversham, ideally situated on the river he knew so well and within fairly easy reach of London; for Thomas may have had the idea of establishing a gentleman's seat in the country (in common with many others who having made their fortunes, had joined the general exodus) but he was still a man of business and kept his London properties until he died.[12]

Thomas did spend most of his time in London but when he died in 1681 he was buried at St Peter's Church. His widow continued to live at the Old Rectory or Old Parsonage, and more about the extent and management of the property emerged during her tenancy. A neighbour, Dr South, who held a lease for Caversham Priory, also from Christ Church, Oxford, complained that Mrs Loveday was paying less than he was although her estate was larger. He said in support of his argument that she had, as well as the house, summerhouse, orchards, tithes and glebes, another house with a walled garden, barn, stable, coach house, pigeon house and yards which she let and that she made money from the sale of fruit from her orchard. This orchard held 60 apricot trees and there were peaches and nectarines on the walls at the side of the house. The tithes and glebes were payments based on local property made by parishioners to the church or clergy but in this case they were attached or impropriated through the contract with Dean and Chapter of Christ Church to the Rectory and its occupiers.[13]

Sarah Markham told another story about the

slight rivalry between Dr South and Mrs Loveday that adds to the history of this part of riverside Caversham. Soon after she was widowed, a regiment of soldiers arrived in the area, probably from the army of James II, and required to be quartered in local houses and inns. Dr South complained to her that the soldiers in his house had been noisy and troublesome and so was not pleased to hear that she had approached the Commanding Officer, saying that as a widow with female servants she would not wish to have soldiers in her house, but that she would be happy to take as many officers as her house would allow. As a result she was allotted the Commanding Officer himself and he was a very considerate guest.

Even if the Lovedays were not troubled by the soldiers in Caversham, there were groups of travellers crossing the river and passing their gate so frequently in 1675 and 1676 that they cannot have been unaware of them. The Poor Law system of the time permitted support to be given to those in need only in their parish of birth or of accepted residence and those who became in need away from home had to make their way back to their own parish, helped by small contributions from churchwardens or from overseers of the poor in the places they passed through. St Peter's Church, close to a major river crossing, saw more than its fair share of travellers in need. Almost every line of the churchwardens' accounts for 1675 records payments to individuals and to companies of up to a dozen travellers together. Thirty-nine travellers were given help in June 1676 alone. Each person was given about 3d to see them on their way. Many of those coming through were seamen, perhaps just paid off at the coast and returning home after action in the naval battles of the last of the Anglo-Dutch wars.[14]

Mrs Loveday's son Thomas married in 1703 and came to live in Caversham in 1709. Thomas had a son John in 1711 and died in 1720. John was brought up by his mother and grandmother and went to Reading School as a dayboy when he was six. The family fortune was secure enough for him to live in the style of a gentleman. He went to Oxford and came back to begin a life of travel,

study of antiquities, book collecting, social visits and entertaining, all of which he recorded in his diaries. One of his entries in typical style, and interesting because of its reference to the site of the Chapel of Our Lady, was about comments made to him by the mayor, John Watts in 1731:

> Alderman Watts said that when Causham-Bridge was last built-up above half a year since, they light upon the old Foundations of the bridge and upon a Stone with an ancient Inscription which workmen let slip; that the Road before [was] at Norcot Scower; that a Chappel was upon Caversham-Bridge dedicate to the Holy Ghost, as says Queen Elizabeth's Charter; that the Chappel of our Lady was at Benwell's, Caversham Farm.[15]

John wrote in his diary of visits to, and visitors from: Grove House; Hardwick House; Englefield House; Mapledurham House; Caversham Park and Caversham Farm. Two of his friends were Charles and Elizabeth Cadogan of Caversham Park. After the Restoration Lord Craven had sold the 1000-acre Caversham estate with its 240-acre deer park to the Earl of Kildare. He in his turn sold it in 1718 to William, Baron Cadogan of Reading, who demolished the old house and replaced it with a huge mansion, one of the most splendid houses in the country, with extensive landscaped gardens which went down to the river.[16] It then passed to his son Charles, second Baron, and his grandson Charles Sloane, third Baron and first Earl Cadogan. Caversham Park became the property of Charles Marsack in 1783.

John Loveday died in 1789 but the house stayed in the family until 1799 when the lease was sold by his son to William Blackall Simonds of Reading. Farms that were part of the Loveday holdings were offered at the time of the sale to the Stevens family who had been renting them but William Simonds, Major Marsack of Caversham Park and Robert Deane of Reading were all in the market to buy them.[17]

Caversham Mill

Caversham Mills in the 1500s were part of Francis Knollys's estate. There is a long gap until the next recorded ownership in 1690 when they had become a separate enterprise, the information coming from the will of Thomas Cart[w]right, miller of Caversham.[18] Thomas and his wife Hannah had four children, Thomas, Edward, Charles and Elizabeth (later McCorley) and when he died in 1690 his son Edward became the miller. The word 'miller' in his description could have meant either that Thomas was the owner employing a miller or that he was involved in managing the milling himself on a day-to-day basis and employing mill workers. He was almost certainly the owner with a lucrative business, with rights over the flash lock and control over the water level on the river attached to the ownership.

Millers formed business networks with farmers, maltsters, brewers, mealmen and barge owners and were in a position to make investments within their community and Edward was no exception. He was named as friend or executor in the wills of three Caversham mealmen and he, with a baker and a mealman, had a business arrangement with the Lybbe family at Hardwick, a big estate upstream from Caversham. These connections suggest that the Cartwrights were in the flour business and that the Caversham mill was a corn mill and not a fulling or cloth mill. Both kinds of mill were on the original site but the cloth industry in Reading had by now almost disappeared so there was no demand for local cloth to be strengthened, thickened and washed by being pounded in a mill.

Edward's will, proved in 1729, listed his land holdings at Checkendon, Caversham and elsewhere. There was no male heir in this second generation so the family property passed in 1729 to Henry Cartwright and George McCorley, nephews of the testator. There was a further transfer of the estate and money out at interest to Henry and his son Edward in 1742 when Elizabeth, widow of the older Edward, died in 1742. When Henry died in 1760 there was no mention of the mill; he was a gentleman with extensive property in Caversham and a vault in the church for his resting place.

The fisheries

There had been both fisheries and a ferry attached to the Caversham Manor estate when this was owned by Frances Knollys in 1552. After a gap of about 200 years there is now information about the extent and ownership of some of the fisheries in the town, although not about the ferries. Fisheries, fishing rights over defined areas, were valuable. Owners could rent them out or could use them to provide food for the table or for sale. They were important to the economy of the town because they provided employment and trade. Most of the coarse fish were considered edible, especially pike, while trout and eels, as elvers or adult fish, were popular food. The value of fishing rights at this time is clear from the financial and social status of those who held them. In 1723 a lease of some of the former abbey holdings was sold to Anthony Blagrave of Southcote and to John Dalby, steward of the Borough of Reading.[19] Three years later Dalby's name appears in exchequer records in connection with fisheries and meadows at the Ort (now Kings Road and London Road) and elsewhere in the town (King's Meadow and the area between the station and the old Huntley and Palmer site). In this extract from the document describing Dalby's holdings 'piscary' simply means connected with fishing:

Fishing rights included the setting of wicker traps to catch eels.

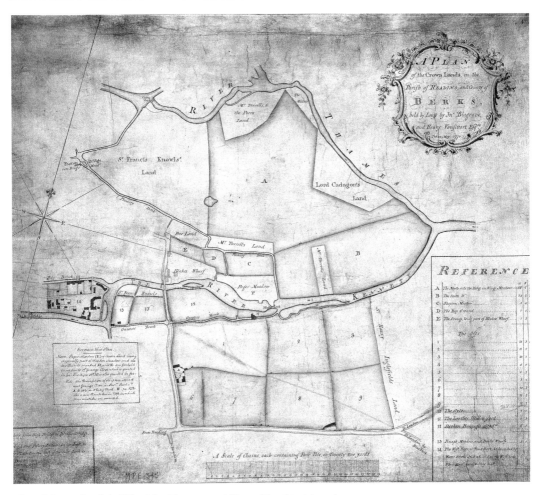

Plan of Crown lands held by John Blagrave and Henry Vansittart (1770).

… piscary and fishing in the River Thames in Reading belonging to the cellarer of the late monastery of Reading, piscary and fishing called the Pool under the lock in Reading, and piscary and fishing above Reading called the Fishing of Kennet, piscary and fishing at Caversham Bridge, piscary and fishing at Gunter's Brook.

In 1749 John Dalby (second generation, the first John having died in 1720) and Anthony Blagrave were named in connection with the ownership of the same lands and fishing rights. By 1770 Dalby's share in the lease had been sold by his widow to Henry Vansittart of Shottesbrook, MP and Governor of Bengal, and the other part was in the name of John Blagrave.[20] A map of former Crown lands made to illustrate these holdings shows the position of fisheries on the S-shaped length of the Kennet from High Bridge (present day Duke Street) to Blake's Bridge (Chestnut Walk – Homebase) and also immediately below Caversham flash lock on the Thames. A footnote to the map says that 'Casom Lock' fishery extended eastward to the Kennet and to the west of the lock beyond Caversham Bridge to Comb Bank (where Cow Lane and Littlejohn's Lane now are), although the map does not extend this far. Sir Francis Knollys, Lord Cadogan and William Turrell also owned parts of the site of the former Crown land (King's Meadow), the miller had a small area of it opposite the mill and some of the site was Poor's Land, an area allocated during enclosure to be rented or cultivated for the benefit of the poor of a parish.[21]

William Havell's painting of *Old Caversham Bridge from The Warren* showing the White Hart on its right.[24]

Improved road access to the bridge

The road which led to the bridge on the Berkshire side (Caversham Road) was in places below water level before 1724 and when the river level rose so that the flash lock could be worked (which could be as often as twice a week), the road flooded so that even the horses had to swim and in winter the road was impassable for days. John Loveday, living on the Caversham side of the river, became a weekly boarder at Reading School in 1718 to avoid the difficulties of travelling daily.[22] The road was remade in 1724 after the mayor, John Watts, raised the money by public subscription.[23]

Thomas Freebody, occupier of a private wharf and stables at the White Hart, Caversham Bridge, on land owned and leased by the Corporation of Reading (the site of the Crowne Plaza), was in a position to make use of the better road. The wharf may even have been set up because of the new trading opportunities created by the improved access. He was competing with the Kennet wharfs, with the built-in disadvantage that barges bringing goods up from London to his wharf had to be hauled up an extra reach beyond Kennet Mouth and had an extra lock to go through, and a bridge to pass under, with the added cost of the tolls for the lock and the bridge. Thacker said it took 45

men to haul a barge the 30 miles from Windsor to Sonning and another 18 men for Sonning to Blake's Lock on the Kennet. No bargemaster would add to his costs and his time by travelling further upstream, unless they were offset by some advantage to trade such as the new road.

The Freebody family

The story of the Freebody family at Caversham Bridge starts with the baptisms of the children of William and Mary Freebody: Susannah (1723), Thomas (1724) and James (1728) in the Caversham parish register. There are Freebody references in that register from about 1670 onwards but these are the first for this particular group. William's will in 1767 described him as a Mapledurham fisherman. The term 'fisherman' at this time signified a professional who earned a living by selling his catch.

The son Thomas moved to the Berkshire side of the river to run the wharf and this is partially dated by the entries in the Reading St Mary's register of the baptisms of his children, Thomas (1748/49) and Lydia (1749/50). Thomas died in 1751, aged only 27. He left to his young son Thomas 'the house wherein I now dwell by the name of the White Hart at the foot of Caversham Bridge with the Wharfe House, stable, two meadows of pasture ground with a garden thereunto belonging, and

A fishing punt with the kind of equipment and traps used by William Freebody.

likewise the other gardens and an eyott lying on the other side the way' and to his daughter Lydia, still a baby, 'the house and garden standing on one side of the gateway'. His will refers to his lighter boat as part of his estate but it does not mention any of the working equipment that would be expected in a wharf. His father William and his brother James were appointed trustees for the children and so it is possible that other functions of a wharf were owned elsewhere in the family or by a partner and were therefore not mentioned in the will.[25] The Freebody family story can be filled out a little more from the will of William, the fisherman, in 1767. His three surviving children, James, Hannah Warwick and Elizabeth Soundy were his main beneficiaries, with his fishing boats, nets and tackle passing to his son James and to his son-in-law John Warwick. Apart from the nets, he might have had fish traps or grig weels which could be baited and placed or fixed anywhere in the river and which were mainly, but not entirely, for eel fishing.

Endnotes

1   Hants Records Office [HRO], 5M50/27/2714 Southwick and Norman Court Estates, copy of deed of covenant dated 26 April 1631.

2   TNA, PROB 11/70 will of John Winter or Wynter and of John Thorne 1587.

3   J M Guilding (ed) *The Records of Reading: Diary of the Corporation* vol II p 23, 242, 245, vol III (1896), p 165. The theft the following-year of half a bushel of rye from fields in Caversham by Terrant's wife Margaret and his daughter Marye was also described in the records.

4   TNA, PROB 11/181 Will of Abraham Edwards Waterman of Reading, 19 August 1639. Edwards could have become a member of the Company of Watermen by apprenticeship or because his father was a member. His membership did not restrict the way in which he traded.

5   A L Humphreys *Caversham Bridge 1231–1926* (Reading, 1926), p 18.

6   David Disbury *Beef, Bacon and Bag Pudding: old Berkshire in the Civil War* (new edition Norfolk, 1998), p 40.

7   J Dils 'Epidemics, mortality and the Civil War in Berkshire 1642–46, *Southern History* vol XI, 1989, p 40–52. Permission of Mrs Dils to use figures to create the graph from work done by an extramural class led by her is acknowledged with thanks.

8   M C Barrès Baker *The Siege of Reading: the failure of the Earl of Essex's 1643 spring offensive* (eBookslib, Ottowa 2005), p 230.

9   Disbury, p 47.

10 Guilding, vol IV, p 237.

11 RLSL, LMC 579, Map of Reading 1643.

12 Sarah Markham *John Loveday of Caversham 1711–1789: the life and times of an Eighteenth-Century onlooker* (Michael Russell, 1984), p 2.

13 The status of the incumbent of the parish was determined by who received the tithes. When entitled to the whole tithes of the parish, the incumbent was called a rector. He was otherwise a vicar. At Caversham where the tithes were impropriated to a layman, the incumbent was a perpetual curate.

14 Berkshire Record Office [BRO], DP 162 St Peter's churchwarden's accounts, 1672–77.

15 Markham, p 49. Henry Benwell lived at Caversham Farm.

16 Robert Pearman *The Cadogan Estate: the history of a landed family* (Haggerston Press, 1986), p 49.

17 RLSL, RH/NW Sarah Markham and Godwin Arnold *The Gazebo and Caversham Court, Reading* (no place or date of publication), p 5.

18 TNA, PROB 11/399 will of Thomas Cartright miller of Caversham 1690; PROB 11/628 will of Edward Cartwright miller of Caversham, 1729.

19 C Slade *The Town of Reading and its Abbey* (Local Heritage Books, 2001), p 38.

20 TNA, PROB 11/576 will of John Dalby of Reading Berkshire, 9 November 1720. Dalby's will makes only very general reference to lands, tenements and hereditaments in Caversham.

21 TNA, Exchequer records E 367/4251 (1739/40), /4744 (1749), /5502 (1770/71), /6837 (1726), /7122 (1749) and map MPE 1/345 (1770).

22 Markham, p 9.

23 W M Childs *History of the town of Reading* (Reading, 1905), p 188.

24 Reading Museum, William Havell *Old Caversham Bridge from the Warren*.

25 TNA, PROB 11/795 will of Thomas Freebody of St Mary, Reading, 1752.

3 Navigating the Thames and Kennet: 1700–1750

The Kennet opened to Newbury

The Kennet Navigation Act of 1715 allowed the building of an 18-mile-long canal from Reading to Newbury. It followed the line of the river in part but new cuts were made with pound locks at Southcote and Fobney in 1723. In the early days of the extension of the navigable Kennet to Newbury, the Corporation and the traders of Reading were afraid of the competition that this would bring them, not least because of the cost implications of a horse being able to pull a greater load on the canal than it could on the fast-flowing river. They thought that their position and importance would be threatened, so much so that the Mayor, Robert Blake, led townspeople in damaging the locks as they were built and a Henley barge coming down from Newbury was stoned by 300 people when it reached Reading. The bargemen of Reading shared these fears and in 1725 expressed them very forcibly in a letter to Peter Darvall or Darvill, a bargemaster of Maidenhead, who had taken a boat up beyond Reading to Newbury:

> Mr Darvall wee Bargemen Of Redding thought to Acquaint you before 'tis too Late Dam you if y work a bote any more to Newbury wee will Kill you if ever you come any more this way wee was very near shooting you last time wee went with to pistolls and was not too Minnets too Late, the first time your Boat lays at Redding Dam you wee will bore hols in her and sink her so Don't come to starve our Fammeleys and our Masters

for Dam You if You do we will send you short home for you have no aceation to come to teak the bred out of Oure Childrens mouths …[1]

The fears of the Reading bargemen about loss of trade were unfounded and traffic increased in both places. However the greater the economic activity in a town and the more routes into it, the greater is the risk of disease being brought in by outsiders. This had been recognised in the era of the plague when controls were put in place during outbreaks. By the eighteenth century plague had died out and the disease that was now most feared was smallpox; it was endemic, there was a high death rate and it left the victims who did recover with pock-marked skin. Smallpox was epidemic in London in 1729 and high burial rates spread westward into parishes along the Thames and Kennet during the spring and summer. There were peaks of deaths in Windsor in April, Reading in May and Thatcham in August. The recorder of the parish of St Giles in Reading, the parish on the Kennet through which all the barges passed, specifically mentions smallpox as a cause of death that summer and John Loveday at the Old Rectory said in his diary that the disease was active in the town in August.[2] The first graph overleaf shows how similar were the patterns of high monthly death in the three Reading parishes together and in Thatcham in the summer of 1729. The second graph shows the severity of the summer mortality in the Thames Valley in 1729 compared with the

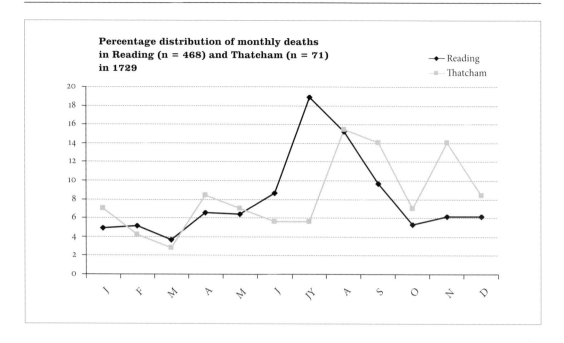

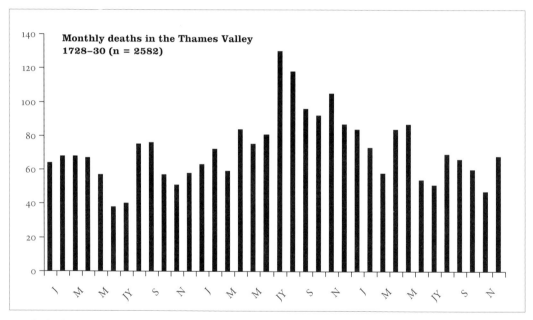

Graphs firstly to show similar monthly patterns of death in 1729 in Thatcham and Reading and secondly to show the increase in deaths in the Thames Valley as a whole in 1729 when there was smallpox in Reading and elsewhere in the area.

previous and following years, demonstrating that it was a crisis year.[3]

There is one way in which smallpox was spread that is worth examining in the context of the Thames and Kennet Valleys in 1729. The raw material for papermaking was cotton and linen rags and these were collected in London by scavengers and itinerant rag and bone men, or by the poor in times of sickness in return for poor relief, and stored in warehouses ready for distribution.

The main occupation at this time at Thatcham on the Kennet was papermaking. The miller of the Sheffield mill at Thatcham, Richard Fry, as well as being a papermaker, was a rag merchant with warehouses at Bull Wharf, Queenhithe on the Thames in London. One of the cargoes that came up by barge from London to Reading, and then on to Thatcham along the Kennet to the paper mill, once it was navigable that far, was rags and old clothing that had been collected by scavengers in London. There were also paper mills at Bray, Cookham, Hurst and Ufton. Rags were also spread on fields to rot and provide a source of organic material.

There was a risk in handling old rags because smallpox could be transmitted indirectly from viruses shed from scabs into clothing, where they remained active for up to a year, and the London cast-offs might contain clothing or bedding from victims. If the rags were infected, then those most at risk of catching and spreading smallpox would have been bargemen, waggoners and employees at the paper mill: the burial register says that the wife of Richard Fry, the paper miller and rag merchant, died in September 1729. While one cannot, at this distance in time, prove a connection between smallpox in London and Reading and high death rates in Thatcham and elsewhere in the region, there is a case to be made for the navigable waterways being one route for the transmission of the disease and for the cargoes of rags going to the paper mills being the carriers of it.

Working practices on the Thames

The working conditions of bargemen at this date were difficult and a first-hand account of the problems they encountered is found in evidence given to a government committee by a Reading bargeman who would have been working on the canal at the time of the Darvall incident. The evidence of this bargeman, William Pearce, given in 1750, contains information about the cargo he carried, the relationship between its weight and its volume, the capacity and dimensions of his boats and something of the costs and charges he incurred in transporting goods from Reading to London. As well all this detail he reports on the very poor conditions of the banks and towpath and the navigational difficulties arising from the opposing needs of the millers and bargemen each to have a good flow of water for their work.

A review of working practices will set the scene for William Pearce's evidence. There was no central control over the Upper Thames until the formation of a Commission in 1694 which had the power to sort out abuses and to settle carriage rates. There was no continuous solid path for towing and gangs of 'halers' or 'haulers' pulled the boats and mostly waded along the foreshore if the wind was not right for hoisting a sail. The most efficient way to tow a heavy load in a straight line is to have it directly behind whatever is pulling it but this was just not possible with a barge in midstream hauled by men or horses on the bank. (The change from men to horses as haulers took place during the mid-eighteenth century.) A compromise was to position the haulers on the towpath well ahead of the load but the pull exerted by them was still to one side and so the bargemen had to steer or to pole the barge all the time to correct the course and to hold it straight. At the same time the barge team were navigating the natural bends in the river, with or against the flow of the river, avoiding shallows and watching to see that the rope between barge and bank was clearing all the obstructions in its path. They also had to pass teams coming in the opposite direction but on the same side of the river. When horse-hauled boats reached a bridge, the horse had to be unharnessed and taken around the bridge and down to the water the other side. A light line was then floated from the boat on one side of the bridge to the crewman on the bank on the other side, or from crewman to boat, depending on the direction of the current, and with this the towline was taken under the bridge and the horse reharnessed so that the boat passed under the bridge. If a horse stopped pulling, the barge lost steerage and would float on, even overtaking the harnessed animal and, at worst, pulling it into

VIEW on the THAMES from CAVERSHAM BRIDGE near READING BERKS.

View on the Thames from Caversham Bridge near Reading drawn by W Havell and engraved by John Pye, *c*1830. The engraving shows ornamental gardens on the right, perhaps those of the Old Rectory, and demonstrates the difficulties of navigating a horse-drawn barge round a bend in the river.

the river, so any damage to the towpath or the bank which caused it to stop or to divert from its course, was a matter of concern. Equally, anything which altered the pace of the river flow, diverted it, or which caused an artificial build-up or drainage of water, was a problem to the bargeman.

A weir marked a change of level between stretches of the river and, to prevent the water from one reach cascading down to the next one, a moveable barrier was built across it. The head of water that built up on the upstream side was controlled by this barrier. When a barge wanted to cross the weir, the river level could be allowed to build up and part of the barrier lifted so that it could shoot across the weir on the 'flash' of water that ran through the gap. This rush of water continued on downstream, stirring up the riverbed and eroding the banks; other traffic or moored vessels felt the effect of it as it passed.

In 1750 the condition of the river for navigation purposes had become so bad that a petition was made to Parliament by 'Gentlemen, Freeholders, and others, of the several Counties of Middlesex, Surrey, Bucks, Berks, Oxford, Gloucester and Wilts … and other Persons interested in the Navigation of the Rivers of Thames and Isis … ' to see what could be done about it. This petition was brought before a House of Commons Committee so that the powers of the Commissioners could be examined together with all the pieces of legislation which governed the navigation of the upper Thames by barges, boats and lighters.[4]

The committee members called William Pearce, bargemaster and resident of Reading, as a witness to tell them at first hand about the problems experienced by commercial users of the river. He had been taking barges to London for the past 40 years. He would have been working from the wharfs on the Kennet rather than from Caversham and this is confirmed from his reference to Sonning as the first lock he encountered on his journeys, but the story he told to the committee about his working conditions would have been one familiar to all river users. These are the main points from his evidence to the committee:

… the Banks in several Parts of the River have been washed away; insomuch, that he knows several Places which were (in the Memory of the Witness) used for Paths for the Horses, and are now Ten Foot under Water: This disobliges the Navigators to take fresh Ground for their Towing-Paths; and the Owners of such Ground force them to pay what sums they think proper, for the Liberty of Towing:

That he apprehends such Decay of the Banks is to be attributed to the Sett of the Stream, and not to the Track of the Horses, or Towing of the Barges.

That the Owners of the Locks have rendered the Navigation more dangerous, by letting the Sills, or Bottom of the Lock, where the Tackle is fixed, in order to shut it, lie too high; and from not shutting or drawing their Locks in a reasonable time:

That the Witness had a Barge in great Danger of sinking, about Six Weeks ago, by running against the Sill of the Lock; by which she broke of all her Steerage: And other Barges have received considerable Damage at the same Place:

That the Lock where this Damage was done, had been newly laid, and was placed higher up the Stream; and by that means was more prejudicial to the Navigation than formerly; though it had always been bad. But, being asked the Question, he said, That the placing the Lock in that manner was convenient for the adjacent Mills.

He further said, That the Barges now in Use draw no more Water than those used 40 Years ago; that those Barges were as wide as the present, but not quite so long; and that the largest of the modern ones would carry 300 Quarters of Malt more than those formerly used: That the Barges draw four Foot Water; but by putting up what they call Wash-boards, they can load them so as to draw Two Inches more; and he believes it has always been the Practice to put up Wash-boards; that he had them up at the time he received the Damage, as aforesaid; nor does he think the Navigation safe without them; but at that time his Barge did not draw more than Four Foot Water; nor was it his largest Barge, he having One that could carry 1,400 Quarters of Malt; whereas that which was damaged, would carry no more than 900: That 10 quarters of Malt weigh about Twenty-five hundred Weight; so that the largest Barges will carry 3,500 Weight, and are 125 or 126 Foot long, or thereabouts; but the length of the Barge does not render the Navigation more dangerous; on the contrary, he apprehends a short Barge to be in greater Danger than a long one:

That the Navigators pay greater Prices for passing the Locks, than formerly; that at the First Lock on the Thames at Sunning, the full-sized Vessels, which used to pay no more than 7s 6d now pay 12s 6d and the lesser Vessels in Proportion; that there has been nothing done to the Lock, to cause this Increase of the Duty, it being rather in a worse Condition than formerly:

But unless the Navigators will comply with the Demands of the Occupiers, the Masters of the Locks won't supply them with Flashes of Water in the dry Seasons. Being asked the Question, he said, That the Bargemen had sometimes sent their Servants to pen and draw the Locks, on such Occasions; but that those Proceedings were unwarrantable. He further said, That a Barge would often lie aground, and other Barges running foul of her, would frequently obstruct the Navigation of the River; but if, when there are many Barges in Company, they were obliged to keep in a right Line, one after another, it would prevent that Inconvenience:

That the Price of Water-Carriage is already advanced 1s for every Twenty-five hundred Weight; which is about 10 per Cent:

And if the said Act should not be continued, and some further Regulations made, it will be greatly detrimental to the Navigation of the said River.

While William had plenty to complain about, his evidence does reveal that there were other vested interests on the river besides those of the bargemen: landowners who charged for the horses to come onto their land to get past a fallen river bank, lock owners who would not co-operate with bargemen to produce a sufficient height of water to get the barges across the weir, and the mill owners for whose benefit the lock had been re-sited. Although he does not mention them, there were also fishermen who wanted a position near the weir for their fish traps so that the flow of water generated by the change of level would provide their catch. The larger and heavier barges now in use were as much the cause of the damage as the level of the cill or siting of the lock. The cill was part of the 'flash lock' system for holding and lifting the barrier. The significance of the discussion about whether these heavily-laden vessels sat lower in the water than earlier craft becomes clear with the knowledge that the depth they drew was critical in assessing how much clearance there should be over obstructions and how much head of water should be built up to generate sufficient flash to carry a 70-ton barge containing a valuable cargo across a weir. The obstruction to traffic of grounded barges was in no-one's interest. The evidence showed above all that navigation and river management were difficult and highly-skilled work and that both were in need of some regulation.

The Thames Commission

The result of William Pearce's evidence was that the House of Commons Committee agreed the need 'to bring in a Bill for the better carrying on and regulating the Navigation of the Rivers of Thames and Isis, from the City of London, Westward to the Town of Cricklade, in the County of Wilts'. The legislation came into being between 1750 and 1812 as The Thames and Isis Navigation Acts. Both the bargemaster and owner were made responsible for any damage done by their boats or by their crews to cargoes, fish, fowl, pounds, locks, weirs, bucks, dams, floodgates, bridges, land, trees, meadows or ground. Much had been made in the evidence about the depth of water that a fully-laden barge could draw and the act required any barge drawing more than 3ft to be marked with a white line.

If a barge drew more that 3ft 10in its master would be liable to double charges at the lock and could be required to lighten his load. Every barge had to have two inches 'of clear board in the shallowest part of the gunwale or solid side of the said barge boat or vessel above the surface of the water'.[5]

The Commission set up in 1751 was a large one with about 600 members who were landowners or civic officers and although it had powers to regulate the river, it could not improve it. However by this time there was an interest in building canals to by-pass rivers and this created a further pressure on the river authorities to make some improvements to navigation and so the first Commission was replaced in 1771 by one with salaried officials and, most importantly, with powers to acquire land and to carry out improvements. The most important of these was the replacement of flash locks with pound locks, but close behind in usefulness was the development by the Thames Navigation Commissioners of the towpath system, whereby they bought land and built paths alongside the river, establishing ferries where the path had to change bank.

Endnotes

1   M Hinton *A History of the Town of Reading* (published privately, 1954), p 129.

2   Sarah Markham *John Loveday of Caversham 1711–1789: the life and times of an Eighteenth-Century onlooker* (Michael Russell, 1984), p 47–8.

3   The aggregated data on mortality was collected during an extramural class led by Mrs Joan Dils, with whose permission these figures are used.

4   'Thames and Isis navigation petition' *Journals of the House of Commons* (1803 reprint) vol 26, 1750, p 30.

5   Acts relating to the Thames and Isis Navigation passed in the 24 George II and the 11, 15, 28, 35 and 52 George III, London 1838.

4 Barges and bargemen in Reading: 1750–1820

Barging communities

Mary Prior proposed that there were settled communities of bargemen along the Thames wherever a tributary or a canal joined the main waterway. In an analysis of the community living at Fisher Row in Oxford she found it tight-knit and intermarried, with businesses passing from father to son, trade and family closely linked. After the Oxford Canal opened in 1790 the community absorbed some canal boatmen through marriage but they were generally an entirely separate group from the river men, living afloat in their distinctively-decorated narrow boats, and carrying different cargoes. Prior saw the river barge community in Oxford as part of 'a linear colony stretching the length of the Thames'. It had working contacts (bargemasters with the employers and bargemen with the employees) with millers, lock-keepers, carriers, carters, wharfingers, publicans, wood-mongers, timber merchants, horse-keepers and bow halers. This chapter explores evidence about the barging community of Reading, shore-based around the wharfs of the Kennet near its junction with the Thames, and shows some of its practices and activities in the context of a tight community with wide contacts as described by Prior at Oxford.[1]

A ropemaker winds a finished line on to a frame from a long row of posts that have supported it during its manufacture.

Business practices

Three overlapping sets of information about working practices emerge from the wills of local bargemasters working the Kennet and the Thames in the eighteenth century, and two of them are concerned with the continuation of business and family after the death of the testator. Wills refer to the types of partnerships or shared interest in boats and barges which existed between owners and which have already been mentioned in connection with Abraham Edwards in 1639. The wills of William Camplin (1739) and William Paice (1775) each left any shares or interest in vessels, boats or barges held at their death to their sons. This suggests that investment in a share of a boat was not a static arrangement and that they knew that arrangements existing when they made their wills might have ceased or been replaced by others by the time they died. John Biggs (1762) left his barges and equipment to his wife and son as tenants in common so that they could carry on his business in partnership for their mutual benefit. The second theme in the wills of this group was the practice of appointing friends as trustees to continue to run the business or to invest sums of money, sometimes quite substantial ones, on their behalf for the benefit of children, grandchildren and children of kin. William Paice left money in trust for his grandchildren; Robert Bowsher (1820) for his sister and children of kin; Robert Mills (1814) for his son during his minority; and Samuel Biggs (1776) put all his barges, boats, tackle, cloths, punts, lines and rigging in trust for his wife and son. The trustees of John Biggs (1804) were instructed to sell his barge and tackle for the best price they could get for the benefit of his wife.[2]

The third set of information in the wills is that of the equipment needed for loading and protecting the cargo and for moving the barge. The term 'tackle' that both Samuel and John Biggs used would have included ropes and pulleys that were part of any loading or lifting equipment on the wharf or in the boat. Lines, or ropes, were expensive because they had to be made to take the entire strain of the load during towing. They could be as much as 200 yards long and weigh up to 6 cwt. Samuel Smith (1773) left his implements-in-trade to his wife. The wills of William Camplin, the first John Biggs, Matthew Lovegrove (1746) and John Plumridge (1784) between them add to the equipment list: sacks, tar cloths (tarpaulins), cables, sails, masts and poles.[3] Plumridge left his hilliards or balances for weighing meat and his fishing tackle to Edward Stone of the Market Place. An earlier source (1634), a complaint about a theft, adds some smaller, more portable items to the equipment list: 1 hitcher, 1 pole, 1 locke, haulf a chayne and a shovle.[4] An advertisement for the sale by auction of the *Britannia*, a 70-ton newly-built Thames barge, said that it came com-

plete with standing tackle, side cloths and a fitten cabin.[5] No will mentioned horses, the inference being that these were not owned but hired as necessary. A 'final' request from the wills of the bargemen comes from William Paice, a man who knew the value of a good piece of timber, who asked that his grave should be lined on the earth side with four-inch-square heart of oak!

The will-makers among the barge community also had properties which they had rented out. This does not imply that all bargemen were wealthy but that ownership of property makes it more likely that a will be written. The following are examples of the extent or location of their holdings: Charles Truss (1731) the west side of London Street; William Salter (1746) several properties in Sivier Street (Silver Street); William Ward (1776) a freehold in Whitley, 2 messuages (house with land and buildings) on the west side of London Street, leaseholds at the corner of London Street and Mill Lane, houses, gardens and yards in Mill Lane, other undefined tenements and messuages; James White (1842) Katesgrove Lane, Sydney Terrace (Oxford Road), wharf buildings in St Giles and houses which he had built.[6]

While floods, droughts and damage to boats and to goods were unavoidable risks, there were other elements of the trade which could be controlled. One of these was the pick-up of cargoes carried by the bargemen, which had to be well organised and subject to agreements on both-sides. A single producer of grain for malting or for flour, a maltster receiving barley and sending out malt, a miller or a grain dealer might have a number of customers who would rather let them, the producers, have the problems of bulk storage and spoilage and who would take delivery only of sufficient for their immediate needs. A supplier, unless he had his own barges, therefore needed reliable transport arrangements for his goods if the customer was to get deliveries on time. An agreement drawn up in 1751 between four Reading bargemasters, one of whom was Charles Truss, and 40 mealmen from Reading, Caversham and Sonning, all on the Thames, and Burghfield on the Kennet (each place had a mill or mills) shows

Barges waiting to go through a pound lock.

how the system could work. The bargemasters agreed to provide enough vessels to carry the mealmen's produce to London and they would charge eight shillings per load of wheatmeal or flour and eight shillings per 80 bushels of pollard or 100 bushels of 'broad brann'.[7] They would not use hooks for loading or unloading so that they did not tear holes in the sacks and they agreed to bring the sacks back free of charge. The agreement was to run for three years, the bargemen to load the mealmen's goods to the exclusion of other material, and there were penalties on each side for non-performance or for using other vessels.[8]

Speed of deliveries depended on whether the bargemen worked by daylight only or whether they worked long hours on a 'fly boat' system with a double crew and a change of horses. Thacker gives a figure of 3 days in 1770 for a barge of 200 tons to travel from Reading to London, supporting this with detailed timings and costs in terms of wages of regular employees, hire of extra men and horses at various places, provisions, tolls, winches and lock fees.[9] Bargemen had regular stopping points at wharfs, such as Freebody's Wharf at Caversham Bridge, where they could stay overnight, stable their horses, pick up messages, fuel and food, and where they could store equipment. Agents at these places represented both the bargemen and the industries dependant on water transport. The pick-up and delivery points for the cargoes would have been at wharfs where there was easy road access for the wheeled vehicles that would take the goods on to their destination.

The wills of bargemen show that shared ownership of boats was common and the reasons for this, apart from the continuation of the business, were that a barge and its cargo were expensive items and that the journeys were risky because of delays and damage. The formation of shared ownerships or partnerships distributed the risk. The story of what happened to a barge owned by Richard Cobb of Reading in 1769 makes some of these issues very clear. The barge, loaded with malt, set out from Reading to London and arrived at Chertsey on Friday, 20 January. There it sank with its cargo. It was not lifted until the following Tuesday, 24 January, by which time the malt was spoiled. If Cobb was the sole owner then the loss of trade was entirely his. Whether he was responsible for the loss of the cargo would depend on the agreement he had with its owners. The cargo was made up of malt from eleven different owners, ten maltsers, mainly from the Kennet Valley, and one brewer. The maltsters were John Soundy of Henley (100 quarters of malt); Thomas May, Brimpton (60 qtr); Sarah Carter, Englefield (40 qrt); William Mosedale, Stanford Dingley (60 qtr); John Yard (80 qtr); Charles Butler (100 qtr); Thomas Hunt (66 qtr); Joseph Young (40 qtr); William Wicks (60 qtr) all of Reading; William Goddard, Oakley Hants (45 qtr); and brewer Edward Collings of Richmond (135 qtr). If this cargo, with so many pick-up points, was typical then the bargemaster with more than one vessel at his disposal would have an easier time in handling the requirements of all his customers than one with a single boat.[10]

The reason this story has been recorded is that duty had been paid on the malt and depositions were taken from all the cargo owners about the quantity of malt involved and from Henry Lewis, the bargeman, about the whole incident so that a claim could be made for repayment of the duty. Malt is the raw material of beer. It is barley which has undergone a controlled germination at a malting to the point where its starch has changed to a sugar, and which is dried to stop the process, and perhaps roasted to give colour to the brew. It has to be ground in a mill before it is used for a brew. A quarter of malt produces approximately four barrels of beer. Any government wanting to impose a tax on alcohol introduces it early in the production chain and it is then passed on to the consumer at the time of sale. Both malt and hops were taxed in the eighteenth century, hops more highly than malt. If the malt did not reach the stage of becoming beer, very strong evidence of what happened to it had to be produced before the tax could be refunded.

In mid-century the Thames was primarily a commercial highway and the bargemen were not the only business users of the river. There was a weekly passenger service from London taking four days to come up to Reading, and travellers could continue upstream for a further two days to Abingdon or they could travel up the Kennet to Newbury. The return journey, being downstream, was quicker. Although there were some who used the river for pleasure they were not significant in numbers.

Improvements to the navigation

The year 1770 was another significant date in river management because the Thames Act of that year gave the Thames Commission the right of compulsory purchase from riparian (river bank) owners of the land for locks and weirs, and the power to order pound locks to be built to replace the flash locks. Caversham came within the Commission's district covering the stretch between Boulters and Mapledurham Locks. Sonning's pound lock, three miles below Caversham, was built in 1773 and Mapledurham's, four and a half miles above it, in 1777. Caversham's flash lock was replaced by a pound lock in 1778. A horse towing path was built in 1778 just upstream of Caversham Bridge. It passed through Freebody's Mead and then through Freebody's Wharf, continuing 'to pass at the back of Purley Church so as to avoid Mr Waldridge's orchard and yard' and, after that diversion, on to Mapledurham.[11] Another Thames Act in 1795 gave the Commission more powers for the compulsory purchase of land for towpaths along the river but the powers did not include the right to acquire land where there was a house, garden or orchard close to the river. This limitation severely restricted the practical value of the Act.

It was about this time that the first of the Treacher family began what was to be 90 years of service as surveyors for the Thames Navigation. John Treacher was a carpenter from Sonning who began working for the Navigation in 1773. By 1786 he was in charge of building the pound locks with John Clark as surveyor. In 1791 Treacher was appointed General Surveyor for the upper district of the Navigation, and in 1795 he became General Engineer of the whole Navigation. He

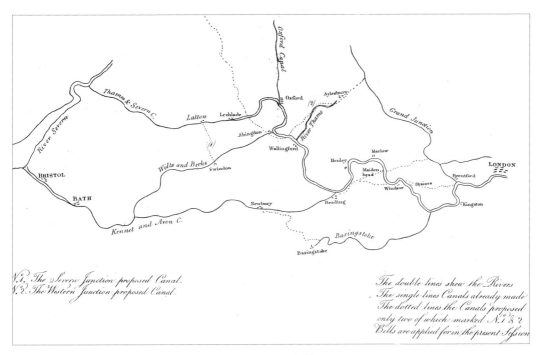

Plan to show the proposed Severn and Western Junction Canals.[14]

The canal system

was followed in these roles by his son John, who was appointed General Surveyor of the whole Navigation as well as being the surveyor of bridges for Berkshire. The family also built and maintained bridges for private owners. A third generation, George Treacher, became Assistant Surveyor in 1824 and General Surveyor in place of his father in 1836. George's death in 1836 brought to an end the family association with the Thames Navigation Commission.[12]

The canal system

In Reading town centre two more locks were installed on the Kennet: County in 1775 and Blake's on the new cut in 1802. The Thames and Severn Canal opened in 1789 and the Oxford Canal in 1790. The opening of these two canals allowed coal to be brought to the Thames Valley from Somerset and from the Forest of Dean, causing a dramatic local fall in price, a fall that was equally dramatically reversed when the Oxford canal froze in 1794/95.[13] Although Reading had always had connections with Oxford directly

along the Thames, this new link extended the connection far beyond into the Midlands. The Wilts and Berks Canal at Abingdon, opened in 1810, linked the Thames directly with the Kennet and Avon near Bradford-on-Avon and indirectly with the North Wilts Canal and with the Thames and Severn Canal. Downstream, Reading had access to London, the English Channel and the east coast. The town also had access via the Kennet to Newbury and direct access to the Kennet and Avon Canal and Bristol. This part of the inland network allowed cargoes from Ireland or from further west to be brought into the country through Bristol rather than having to travel round the coast. Reading was, in effect, an inland port. It was far more efficient, and therefore cheaper, to tow a barge on a canal than it was on a river because the canal was narrower and straighter and relatively free from current.

There were proposals to cut new waterways (dotted lines on the plan above) which would divert traffic from the Thames. A link between the Thames and Severn and the Wilts and Berks canals would cut out the need to travel round the Oxford loop and a link (the Hants and Berks canal) between the Kennet and Avon and the Basingstoke waterway would reduce traffic between Reading and Windsor. The Monkey Island canal was planned to run from the Kennet at Reading through Sonning and Twyford to Bray. On the other hand Reading bargemen might have gained from a link from the town to the Grand Junction or to Brentford. All the proposals were defeated when they came before Parliament.[15] The map (page 35) is taken from a plan dated 20 February 1811 and submitted to the Committee of Commissioners of the Thames and Isis Navigation and the reverse of the document has an extra interest in the hand-written estimates on it of £60,000 for building the Latton – Swindon link. This figure covered all the cutting and earth work, nine locks, bridges, aqueducts, culverts, stopgates, towing paths, collection and lock houses and damage to land.

Barges and bargemen

The bargemaster was the owner and often acted as merchant as well as carrier. The bargemen formed the regular crew, and the bow haulers or halers were casual labourers employed to tow the barge. Boats of 60 tons capacity were crewed by three men and a boy or an apprentice but the larger boats, of up to 100 tons, needed five or more men. A short list of vessels registered in 1795 gives the requirements in the table above for manpower and these are roughly in line with the figures from other sources.

There is very little information about barge-builders in Reading in the eighteenth century. Kennet side was perhaps more valuable as a wharfage and boats were built elsewhere. Two names only remain, those of George Bennett who died in 1803 and Richard Clement who died in 1796. Clement was also a timber merchant at Boult's Wharf. However there is local information about how a new boat was commissioned and built. An agreement made on 17 July 1795 between David Burgess of Sutton Courtenay, boatbuilder, and Joseph Sills, wharfinger of London and agent

Boat capacity	Crew
128 tons	1 cost bearer, 5 men and a boy
87 tons	1 cost bearer, 3 men and a boy
85 tons	1 cost bearer, 3 men and a boy
60 tons	1 cost bearer, 4 men
30 tons	1 cost bearer, 2 men

Table to show the relationship between boat capacity and crew size.[16]

to the Thames and Severn Canal proprietors, to build a barge, shows that such arrangements were formal and binding and that they covered all the material used, the dimensions and technical specifications to be achieved and the delivery date. Although the builder was an Oxfordshire man, he was building a Severn barge, 87ft 6in by 11ft 9in with a jointed rudder, a variant of a West Country barge for the canal and Severn River: it was 'in all respects to be built and finished in a good, substantial and workman like manner with good sound timber free from sap and in every other respect as West Country barges are generally made'. In this case the boat was to be safely delivered on or before 17 October next, three months from the date of the agreement and payment of £165 was to be made on completion. In the quotation below the '& &' signs are simply shorthand for 'and the rest' or 'etcetera'.

> … the Britten and hatches to be of the best yellow deal of the usual thickness properly laid down with usual pump holes cupboard & & with uprights compleat; caventrees to be made of heart of oak and to be made to shift; The chine plank 3 inches thick, the hoof to be of oak. The Huddies of elm, ten knees on each side, three beams, that is to say two in the storage and one under the forebeam; The cups in her bottom and swims to be properly lined, the colling to be nine feet and a half from the end. The ironwork to be found and provided and sufficient clamps fixed by the said David Burgess with chime plates from end

Waterway	Upstream limit	Length (ft)	Width (ft)	Draught (ft)	Tonnage
Thames	Wallingford	128	18	4	170
	Abingdon	112	20	4	135
	Oxford	87	17	4	100
	Lechlade	88	12	4	65
Kennet	Newbury	109	17	3ft 10in	128
Kennet and Avon	Newbury to Bath	73	13ft 10in		
Western barge		*128*	*18*	*Max 4ft*	*200*

Upstream limits for barges of different sizes with the dimensions of the Western barge given for comparison.[18]

to end and round the hoof and made good and substantial and of proper size and strength … a fore windlass and a fire hearth properly lined with iron to be fixed in the usual places …[17]

Barges were built for the waterways they were to use. They were built with variations of length and draught so that they could navigate the bends on each river or canal, get into locks and get off shoals when they ran aground. The West Country barge that Joseph Sills refers to as the standard to

which he wants his Severn barges to be made was the usual type of boat on the Upper Thames. They were flat-bottomed boats, the underwater part built from planks of elm and the upper parts from oak. All the underwater joints were caulked with strands of fibres and the whole boat was painted with pitch to keep it watertight. They were stable and easy to load and they could also be floated off shoals more easily than a boat with a keel. The disadvantage was that they were more difficult

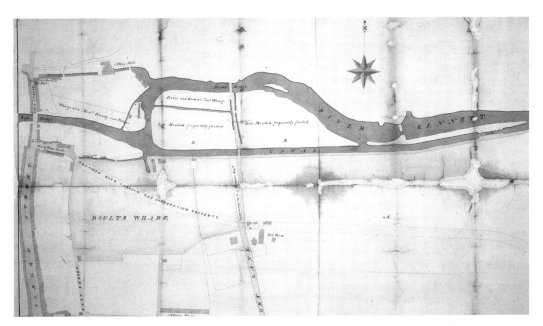

Map by R Billing, Reading 1829 showing town centre wharfs with names of owners, canal cuts and River Kennet. Boult's Wharf and Blandy and Palmer's were on either side of the canal at Duke Street Bridge and Provis and Brown on the river running parallel.[19]

to control than a keeled boat when being towed. They were solidly built to carry the rudder and the bow was pointed. The design had developed from an earlier Western barge where the bow was squarer but the term is often used as a general one. Barges built in Reading and Pangbourne in the eighteenth century for downstream owners in the coastal trade were different again in dimensions: flat-bottomed, 54 to 60ft long, 16 to 17½ft wide and 4½ to 5ft draught.[20]

The table above (page 37) shows the upstream and tonnage limits on the Thames for barges of different lengths and widths at the end of the eighteenth century. A Newbury source quotes 200 tons to Kingston, 80 tons to Reading and 60 tons on up to Oxford.[21] These limits dictated the journeys that bargemasters could arrange. If a Reading man took a cargo down to London in a Western or West Country barge he could only return with a cargo as far as Wallingford. If his load was for Oxford he would have had to offload it at Wallingford into a smaller boat. In practice bargemen probably worked regularly to and from the same point to minimise these problems. There would have

been similar variations of barge for every river and on each canal as it was built. The difference between the sizes of the Thames boats working up to Reading and the smaller boats required for the Kennet and Avon between Newbury and Bath was an issue for barge masters in the early days. The register of barges made in 1812 shows that Reading owners had by then a range of barge sizes so that between them they could carry loads of between 66 tons (Benjamin Williams's *Halford*) and 133 tons (William Blandy's *Adventurer*). This suggests a degree of specialism in the runs they made and the cargoes they carried.

Commercial activity along the Kennet generated a need for wharfs and so for wharfingers. The trade term, like that of miller and bargeman, covered owner, owner-manager and manager of a wharf, any of whom might also have acted as agent or commissioner or shared business interests with customers. Early references are to William Bowman in 1632 and to Simon Dye who was near High Bridge in 1638. The name of Robert Blake, son-in-law (as was Charles Truss) to Edward Wilder senior, bargemaster, is now perpetuated

The Kennet at Southampton Street looking towards Seven Bridges Wharf, *c*1820.

in Blake's Wharf (present day Homebase) and Blake's Lock. He was a substantial landowner and his will in 1727 referred to the messuage and estate where he lived with the wharf, waters, lock and fishing, lands, pasture, meadow and other property in Reading. At this date the lock would have been a flash lock, the pound lock being built in 1802. Other major figures along the wharfs were William Terrell and William Buy who held a lease inherited from his father in 1687 for properties divided into eleven units in the Sivier Street (Silver Street) – London Street area for which the rent was 36 shillings and two fat capons or two pounds of refined sugar. Edward Osborne had property in Duke Street and a mortgage of premises in Market Place.[22]

In 1801 there were barge owners or companies running services most weeks from Reading to Queenhithe in London (Mr Clements, Mr Biggs and Mr Mills & the Reading Company) and one going through Caversham about once a fortnight on its way to and from Oxford (Messrs Dodd, Law and Co). John Man and William Blandy ran the Reading Navigation Company from Blandy's Wharf at High Bridge.[23] Newbury barges were going most weeks through Reading to Kennet Wharf in London. The names of Bosier, Kinner and Lewis, Bristow and Beeston were added over the next few years to the Reading list and Beasley and Williams to those going through Caversham

to London. The Kennet and Avon Canal was completed in 1810, connecting Bristol, Bath, Newbury and Reading with London. In 1812 there were just two barges trading from Caversham, a mill boat of 28 tons owned by Robert Deane, and the *Britannia*, 81 tons, owned by William Freebody. There were ten more barges trading from Reading and the twelve boats were the local contribution to a total of 157 horse-drawn barges registered above London.[24]

Barge transport was dependent on weather and river conditions and so deliveries were not reliable. The *Britannia* sank in 1815 but William Freebody did get his lock toll remitted. (Freebody died in 1820 aged 54.) There were 12 weeks of snow and ice from December 1813 until March 1814 when the river and the canal froze and boat traffic stopped completely, prices rose, fuel was short and bargemen and coal-heavers were deployed to shovelling snow in Duke Street and London Street. The 28-ton mill boat and the mill business were only a very small part of the property of Robert Deane of Caversham at his death in 1822. He had a farm at Burghfield, a coppice and timber, freehold houses in Reading, freehold house and land in Caversham and sufficient money to leave £10,000 to his daughter and £5,000 in trust for his son Henry. He had a half share in Caversham Mill which he left to his three children, Robert Micklam, Henry and Elizabeth.[25]

Endnotes

1   Mary Prior *Fisher Row: Fishermen, Bargemen and Canal Boatmen in Oxford 1500–1900* (Oxford, 1982), p 199–202.

2   TNA, PROB 11/695 will of William Camplin 1739; PROB 11/1012 William Paice 1775; PROB 11/877 John Biggs 1762 ; PROB 11/1557 Robert Mills 1814; PROB 11/1631 Robert Bowsher 1820; PROB 11/1351 John Biggs 1804.

3   BRO, Berkshire Archdeaconary Wills, D/AI/95/154 Matthew Lovegrove 1746;

D/AI/110/47 John Plumridge 1784.

4   J M Guilding (ed) *The Records of Reading: Diary of the Corporation* vol III (1896) p248.

5   *Reading Mercury* 26 March and 2 April 1832. The description comes from advertisements for the sale by auction of the boat to take place at Maidenhead.

6   BRO, Berkshire Archdeaconary Wills, D/AI 130/70 Charles Truss 1731; D/AI 124/158 William Salter 1746; D/AI/141/159 William

Ward 1776; D/AI/165/ 117 James White 1842; D/P 96/6/42/ 1–19 William Ward, deeds of property in London Street, 1753.

7   Pollard was bran sifted from the flour or a fine bran containing some flour.

8   F Thacker *The Thames Highway* vol II (David and Charles, reprinted 1968), p 232, quoting Reading Corporation records.

9   Thacker p 235. The author gives a detailed list of the cost of a three day journey to London from Reading of a barge of 200 tons.

10 BRO, R/JQ/1/7, Reading Borough Court of Quarter Sessions 1769.

11 P Chaplin *The Thames from Source to Tideway* (Whittet Books, 1988), p 30.

12 This information has been taken from the introduction to the section of the BRO catalogue covering the records of the Thames Navigation Commission and the business records of the Treachers.

13 J R L Anderson *The Upper Thames* (London, 1970), p 195.

14 BRO, D/ELV/ B3/14 Plan to show the routes of the proposed Severn and Western Junction Canals.

15 Basingstoke canal. Petition of noblemen, gentlemen, clergy, freeholders and others in the counties of Southampton and Surrey' *Journal of the House of Commons* (1803 reprint) vol 36 p 720–1, 1778. This account contains discussion about gains and losses to trade throughout the area if a navigable waterway was built to link Basingstoke and the River Wey in Surrey.

16 BRO, Q/Rpa 1: List of vessels registered under the Boat Registration Act 1795.

17 BRO, D/ELV B3, Agreement to build a barge, 17 July 1795. H Household *The Thames and Severn Canal* (Alan Sutton, 1983), p 121. The proprietors of the Thames and Severn Canal were trying to expand business by ordering

boats and arranging for barges to berth at Sills' London wharf. Joseph Sills was appointed superintendent of trade from an office in Upper Thames Street.

18 D C Wilson *The making of the middle Thames* (Bourne End, 1977), p 143.

19 TNA, MPI 1/790/5 Map of Kennet and wharfs.

20 R C Jarvis 'Eighteenth Century London Shipping' in A Hollaender and W Kellaway (eds) *Studies in London History* (London, 1968), p 409–410.

21 Penelope Stokes *Going with the grain: the story of Doltons 1792–1992* (Doltons, 1992), p 22. Barges operating out of Newbury and carrying grain, timber and coal, were locally built and were wider than the usual canal narrow boats. They were flat-bottomed and round-ended and the largest of them required a crew of six men and a boy armed with a pole to keep the boat in the navigation channel.

22 TNA, PROB 11/848 will of William Terrel 1759; PROB 11/615, Robert Blake 1727; PROB 11/14/07, Edward Osborne 1804; PROB 11/558 William Buy 1717; Guilding vol III p 434 Simon Dye 1638; Guilding vol II p 123, 242, 245, vol III p 165 William Bowman 1632.

23 Adam Sowan ed. *The Stranger in Reading* (Two Rivers Press, 2006), p xvii.

24 BRO D/EX 1457/1/130, Register of barges on the Thames re-measured by order of the Commissioners in August and September 1812. Of the Reading owners, Law had three barges (*Friend* 70 tons, *Stroud* 70, *Old London* 71) Richard Mills had two (*Venture* 84 tons and *Mary Anne* 132) and five others each had one (Robert Mills *Beanshell* 70 tons, William Blandy *Adventurer* 133, Benj. Williams *Halford* 66, John Bristow *Industry* 132 and Saml Kimmer *Jubilee* 131).

25 TNA, PROB 11/1688 will of Robert Deane of Caversham 28/7/1824.

5 Steam power on river and rail: 1800-1850

New technology

The development of steam power at the beginning of the nineteenth century to drive barges and tugs, and to run engines for the mills, changed working practices on the river completely. At the same time it allowed the development of pleasure boats, steam launches and passenger steamers, and consequently the development of boatbuilding and boat-hiring businesses to provide the boats.

The first experiment to work a barge against the tide with a steam engine took place in 1801. 'The moment the engine was set to work the barge was brought about, answering her helm quickly, and she made way against a strong current at the rate of two and a half miles per hour.'[1] A steam barge passed through Reading on 25 September 1813 on its way from Bath to London and it returned on 22 October, 'having been engaged to carry passengers &c from Richmond to London but the Lord Mayor would not permit it as it would deprive so many watermen of employment. It consumes two bushels of coal a day and travels at eight miles an hour.'[2] Various sources would suggest that this was the *Richmond*. Steam-powered boats appeared widely on the Thames in about 1814. A French boat carrying linen, en route from France to Bristol, was at High Bridge on the Kennet in 1816. One local company saw the commercial possibilities of steam: Parsons of Newbury applied in 1818 for permission to navigate free of toll a boat with a steam engine on board, probably a tug, for towing loaded boats.[3]

River management

With increasing traffic and changing technology there was a continuing requirement for active management of the river. Consideration had to be given to working conditions of those who managed the weirs and locks because they were busier than ever and their work was essential to the control of water level and the safe movement of river traffic. In 1816 The Thames Commissioners bought land on the north side of Caversham lock from John Weldale Knollys for £45, for a lock house and garden, and in 1819 they purchased two further pieces of eyot land on the north side for £200.[4] One piece was in the possession of William Johnson and handwritten notes on the left of the 1815 plan of the land shown overleaf say that the eyot, called Blandy's Eyot, belonged to a minor for whom Chas Shepperd Esq was acting as trustee. The notes on the right say that the committee recommended the purchase of the piece of 12 poles marked A, that it believed part B belonged to the Commission and that part C, 20ft by 15ft, was where the house was to be built. This plan is valuable because it shows the site of the old flash lock as being in the mill stream beyond the present weir and so a point of possible contention between the miller and the bargemen.

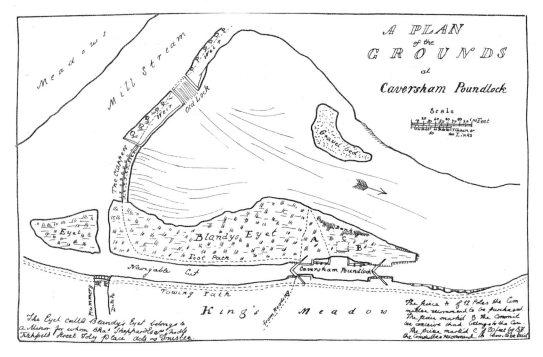

Plan of the grounds of Caversham pound lock (1815) showing also the position of the old lock on the mill stream.[5]

The house and garden were built alongside the pound lock in 1819.

A surprising aspect of river management was the introduction in 1826 of a timetable for the downstream movement of the 'flash'; surprising because pound locks had been installed on most of the river. However there were locks above Oxford, and at Cookham, Bray and Boveney below Reading, that still had not been modernised. For barges using them, the old system of waiting for water to build up so that they could cross a flash lock was still in use. The wait was a potential cause of delay and the effects of the water as it went through the locks caused difficulties in navigation below them. To address these problems a timetable was published so that river users would know at what time the surge of water could be expected to arrive in their area. The flash took 70 hours to travel from Lechlade to Sonning and the first lock was drawn each Sunday at 2pm and each Wednesday at 5pm, reaching Caversham the following Wednesday at 10.30 am and on Saturday at 1.30 pm, moving on to reach Sonning an hour and a half later.[6] The timetabling

of the flash was useful to those carrying out work on the river because they could schedule it, and any necessary lowering of water levels, to fit between the surges of water. In 1832 the Thames Navigation, with work to be done, put a public notice in the local press to say that a wane would be run (presumably water levels lowered and the flash controlled) at Shiplake, Marsh (Henley), Hambleden and Hurley from Monday 11 May until after the passing of the flash on Saturday 23 June, during which period there would be no passage through Marsh pound lock.[7]

In nineteenth-century Reading the waterways were central to the economy. Suttons were trading as corn and seed merchants, and both Simonds Brewery (one of fifteen in the town) and Huntley and Palmers were flourishing businesses needing coal and grain. Supplies of coal were available to these companies, and to the gasworks, by river via the Wilts and Berks Canal joining the Thames at Abingdon; their raw materials, wheat and barley, were brought from farm to mill or to maltster by barge, and flour and malt brought to the factory or brewery in the same way. The finished products,

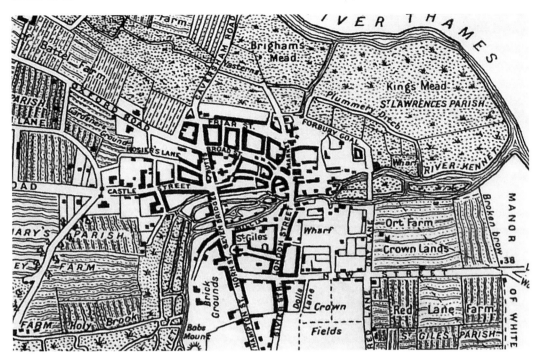

The centre of the Borough of Reading 1813.

biscuits and beer, could be delivered anywhere on the waterways or exported to the British colonies via Bristol or London. All three companies had direct access to wharfs on the Kennet. Local grown or imported timber for building or for fuel could be delivered to, or sent from, public or private wharfs, and bricks and tiles from kilns at Reading and Caversham could be distributed throughout the country. The owner of the Old Rectory sent chalk from the quarry behind the house to Bristol.[8]

There are many more entries for barge companies in Rusher's *Reading Directory* in 1828 than there had been in 1801 and a greater degree of commercial activity is suggested by the increased number of towns they delivered to, and by the number of wharfs in Reading and in London at which barges would pick up and drop off goods. By 1835 boats did not go just once a week but instead they went 'regularly' or 'frequently' from Reading to Queenhithe and Triggs Wharfs in London and via Oxford to Bristol and Birmingham; they went from Newbury, now picking up at Huntley and Palmer's, Williams'

Commercial, Blandy and Palmer's and Gasworks Wharfs, and delivering to Steel Yard, Hambro, Kennet and Queenhithe Wharfs in London.[9] The office for the Kennet and Avon Canal Co was at their own wharf in Bridge Street.

It is fortunate that, just at the time that the barge activity was at its peak, the register of one of the town's three parishes, Reading St Laurence, gives the occupation and residence of the people whose events it is recording between 1817 and 1837.[10] Although this is only a partial sample of the parish population it does show that the boatbuilders, bargebuilders, bargemasters and bargemen who were bringing their children to the church to be baptised were living in Broad Street, West Street, Friar Street, Kings Road, Abbey Wall and by Abbey Brook (around present day Abbey Square and Chestnut Walk). The 1841 census confirms, by the numbers of bargemasters, bargemen and millwrights living there, that the centre of activity was in and around Kings Road and Kennet Side in St Giles Parish. The names of Reading bargemen identified in national and local sources have been listed in an appendix (see page 196).

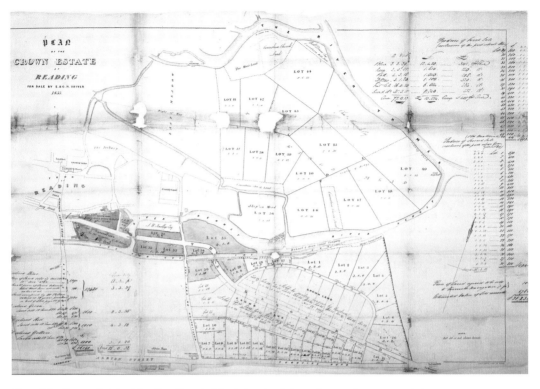

Plan of the Crown Estate at Reading for sale (1832) showing lot numbers and acreage and place-names.

Not all the river traffic was goods; there were passengers as well. In March 1832 it was reported that a party of emigrants set out from Caversham to make the first stage of their journey to their new country by river. While the identity of this particular group has not been followed up, the *Berkshire Chronicle* during that month commented on the rage for emigration among the labouring classes (it was a time of agricultural unemployment) and the great risk it carried to those who set off without knowing anything about the need for labour, the wage rates or the dangers in their chosen country.

On 24 March the paper reported that 100 ships were fitting out in the Port of London to carry emigrants. The *Reading Mercury* in the same month carried an advertisement from Mr Manford Nott, Market Place, Reading, which said that 'every information may be obtained free and passages secured on moderate terms to North and South America, Canada, Quebec, The Cape, Van Diemen's Land, New South Wales and Swan River.' [11]

In 1832 notices appeared in the national and local press to announce the sale in more than 50 lots of 50 acres of the Orts Estates, Crown lands in the Borough of Reading, the auction to be conducted by Messrs Driver of Whitehall on 21 November.

The estate extended from the Thames, through King's Meadow to the Kennet and canal cut, and extended to both sides of Orts Road and Kings Road to London Road. It thus had great commercial potential. The sale details referred to waterside premises, valuable building sites for shops or breweries, wharfs, warehouses, dwellings and villas. This sale was in anticipation of the business that steam technology would bring to the town centre. Parts of King's Meadow opposite Caversham Mill were excluded from the sale: these were the Poor's Land (see page 21) and two plots belonging to Robert Deane, the miller, and an adjoining plot of Caversham Church land.[12]

Brunel's bridge taking the
railway over the Kennet.

Competition from the railway

The 1840s were a period of expansion in the
town. The work available in the factories brought
people in and new houses were built in Reading
and in Caversham to accommodate them. Social
and public health needs were addressed with the
opening of the Royal Berkshire Hospital, Reading
Gaol and the Reading Cemetery. The railway
came to Reading in 1840. Brunel had worked on
the Sonning Cutting during 1839 and had brought
the Great Western Railway line from Paddington
to Reading, with Reading station opening in
1840. The GWR had purchased the land for the
station from the Knollys estate, with the newly
established Haslam's appointed as the agents to
handle the sale. The track followed the line of
the river into the town, Brunel's brick bridge
taking it across the mouth of the Kennet.[13] From
there it cut through land between the two rivers,
leaving the Kennet and its wharfs to the south
and the Thames and King's Meadow to the north.
Together, the map of Crown Lands below, showing the amount of land taken by the railway, and
the image overleaf of the Great Western Railway
train crossing the Kennet going towards Reading,
show the impact of the arrival of the new technology. Reading was further connected to London
via Wokingham in 1849 when a link was made
with the South Eastern Railway by the Reading,
Guildford and Reigate line, and again in 1856 when

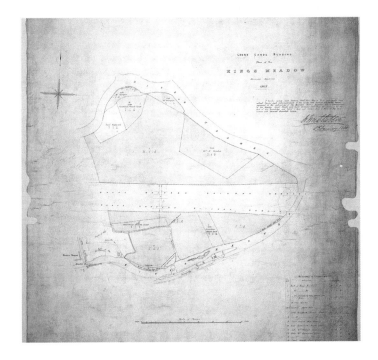

Plan of Crown Lands at King's
Meadow (1865) showing field
boundaries and acreage and the
path of the railway through the
centre.[14]

the London and South Western Railway opened from Waterloo to Wokingham. The adjoining stations for the two lines were no more than a mile from Caversham Bridge and less than that to the nearest river bank. Robert Ray, a former bargeman and lock-keeper of Maidenhead, welcomed the coming of the railway as an alternative to river transport. He said that navigation on the river was 'bad, uncertain and dangerous' despite the construction of pound locks. It was regularly interrupted by frost, drought, floods and repairs, and bargemen could be responsible for making good loss or damage to cargo. He thought that the proposed GWR line from London to Reading would be highly beneficial to all the towns along it.[15]

Entrepreneurs in the 1840s thought that using steam vessels to pull existing barges was the means by which river traffic could be revived although they recognised that there were obstacles to be overcome, one of which was the negative attitude of bargemen and riparian owners to the changes. In 1844 the Kennet and Avon Canal Conveyance Company wrote to the Thames Navigation to ask whether there would be any objection to its proposal to build three small iron steamers of 12-horsepower and to put them on the Thames for use between Reading and London. The power would be provided by a disc engine, already in use on the Grand Junction Canal, which would have a screw on each side of the bow to provide ample power without raising a wash to damage the banks. The running costs would be only half of those of using horses.[16] The prospectus of the Barge Steam Towing Company issued in 1849 stated that its purpose was the introduction of steam power in lieu of horses in the towing of barges, trows or scows to compete successfully with the railways. It also made the point that steam vessels for towing barges had not been used so far in the upper part of English rivers because it was a commonly held view that a vessel could not be built which would not lose power in shallow water. The prospectus set out evidence that the market for its proposals was there. It gave a count of barges passing through the upper Thames in February

1849 with the following figures: through Marlow 1 barge (100 tons total), Henley 4 (250 tons), Reading 16 (895 tons), Wallingford 1 (50 tons), Oxford 1 (56 tons). Such 30-horsepower boats as the company proposed to build would have the advantage of the newly discovered electric light so that with lamps and batteries installed they could travel day and night.[17] It was only in this same year, 1849, that an earlier prohibition on the use of locks on Sundays between 6am and midnight was overturned on the basis that the Thames was a public highway and that there was a right of access along it at any time.[18]

Steam barges did gradually replace the horse-drawn vessels but they did not revive trade. Even though in 1850 Huntley and Palmer's biscuits still went by river and agricultural machinery was sent from Reading Iron Works, river transport continued to decline. The Thames Navigation Commissioners found themselves in a very difficult financial position in the early 1850s because the reduction of trade on the river had reduced their income, but the remaining trade had lengthened the working week of its employees with Sunday and night traffic, and had increased the need for riverside management. The steam vessels, being faster than the old horse-drawn boats, created a wash that damaged the banks and stirred up the mud. The Commissioners were just as keen as the development companies that trade should revive and they decided that, as a stimulus to trade, barges travelling between Abingdon and Windsor could pass without tolls during the year 1851. The following year they were forced to reduce the wages of lock-keepers although allowing some to keep the tolls from pleasure boats. Two years later the Caversham lock-keeper lost his wages altogether although he was offered the occupancy of the lock house, a wooden building put up in 1819, and the tolls from pleasure craft.[19]

This difficult time of re-adjustment continued into the next decade. The Katesgrove Iron Works in Reading was a producer of steam engines, notably the Barrett, Exall and Andrews's horizontal fixed engine, which had won a prize at the Royal Agricultural Society Meeting at Chester

View of Reading from the Great Western Railway embankment at Kennet Mouth c1840. Drawn by William Fletcher and engraved by W Newman.

in 1858, and an illustration of which headed the firm's note paper. The company wrote in 1860 to George Treacher, civil engineer and surveyor at the Thames Navigation, to report that it had built a steam barge as an experiment and its success would depend on the results it could show to the trade. The company wanted to know whether any adjustments could be made to tolls and other charges to help to restore trade to the river.[20] It was a losing battle and the waterways gradually

lost what advantages their extensive network gave them as the railway companies continued to build both main and branch lines. The Huntley and Palmer's site was very close to the main railway lines on the east of the town and eventually a spur line was built to connect the factory directly to the railway.

In its early years the railway succeeded with passenger traffic better than it did with heavy and bulky goods traffic because of the costs involved,

Talbot's timber yard at Caversham Bridge with barges alongside.

An osier break used to strip bark from willow stems.

and so for coal and timber the barge trade retained the advantage of its inland distribution network. Commercial activity on the wharfs on the Kennet continued for coal, timber, wine, corn and salt merchants, millers and boatbuilders. The railway company bought the canal in 1852. The weighbridge wharf was in Kings Road and, to give an example of the variety of ancillary trades still alongside the river in 1865, there were at the Kennet and Avon Co and Bear wharfs alone an agent, a blacksmith, a vet, a bargebuilder and timber merchant, with millwrights, engineers, boilermakers, and beer sellers nearby. Dunton and Sons, a company now remembered for its gypsy wagons, was at High Bridge Wharf in 1874, trading as 'coach and cart wheelwright and general smith'.[21] Huntley and Palmers bought Blake's Wharf in 1867.[22] The Reading Iron Works still had coal delivered from Somerset via the Somerset Coal Canal in 1870 and there were coal, timber and bargebuilding wharfs at Caversham Bridge at this date and later. Simonds Brewery continued to send beer to London by river into the 1880s. Reading Borough Council built a sewage pumping station at Blake's Lock in 1873, using bricks from Collier's brick works at Grovelands.[23] The railway had no interest in keeping the canal working and so the waterway gradually deteriorated and finally became unusable.

Osier growing: one trade unchanged

Alongside all the new working practices there was one old trade which remained unchanged in style and which flourished to fill the need created by the railways for hampers and baskets for freight and for passenger luggage. This was osier growing, and it may well have been as old an occupation on the river as fishing, since the need for fish traps, baskets, wattle and hurdles existed as far back as there was settlement. Osiers or withies are single stems of willow, a plant which grows well in riverside ground.

The tithe apportionment maps and lists of the 1830s and 1840s are good sources of information about land ownership and occupation and whether the land was being cultivated as meadow, woodland, arable or osier beds. The big landowners in the Caversham area had their own osier grounds so that their estates were self-sufficient in all the traps, containers and fencing materials they needed, but they leased out other grounds and there were also independent osier growers. George Donkin of Wyfold had an eyot under osiers and withy beds occupied by William Wittington. Crawshay, the Welsh ironmaster at Caversham Park, had osier beds on the Thames occupied by Thomas Freebody, who was a fisherman at Caversham Bridge. William Blackall Simonds, at what is now Caversham Court, owned the Griffin public house and also had in hand the osiers growing on the eyots nearby. The trustees of the mill estate had a withy eyot near the mill. One of the biggest osier grounds was a meadow on the Reading bank (now The Promenade, Richfield Avenue), upstream from the bridge and owned by Robert Deane, Edward Tubb (the miller at Caversham) and Mary Young. This was also occupied by Thomas Freebody. Jeremiah Breach was cultivating osiers or withies, both on his own account and as occupier of Dean Micklem's land, on eyots at Caversham. Mary Taylor was another owner with an osier eyot in hand. A Reading bargemaster from Blandy's Wharf, Jeremiah Whitehouse, had two pieces of land close to Caversham Bridge, Ten

Acre and Hither Meadows.[24]

Osier cultivation had a number of advantages as an occupation. It required minimal investment in stock, tools and labour. An osier bed could be productive for up to 50 years and could yield 3 tons an acre. In the Somerset Levels it was estimated that 8 acres of osiers could support a family.[25] The seasonal work combined well with fishing, provided female employment and could be extended into basket-making, to fill the increasing demand (there were four basket-makers in the town in 1842) from rail transport.[26] The river was a means of transport for the osiers and other willow products.

The first step in cultivation was to put willow cuttings into prepared ground. In the following years shoots were coppiced or cut back near to ground level so that in a good year 15 or 20 straight, unbranched light and springy stems would develop from the original shoot. After leaf fall in November and before sap movement in spring these stems (which were the osiers or withies) were cut with a sickle, cleaned and boiled. If the rods were to be brown the bark was left on but if they were to be light brown then the bark had to be removed. Others were kept over winter and peeled in the spring to produce white stems. The rods were then dried, sorted for size and bundled up for sale. The willow shoots could be left growing for longer if larger or thicker rods were needed. The Kennet Valley and the area just upstream of Caversham produced hoops for barrels and sent them by barge to London.[27]

Another use for cut green shoots of willow was 'spiling', a technique of weaving into wattles or hurdles, which was adapted to strengthening stream or river banks or for giving protection against flooding. If stakes were driven downwards into the river bed along an eroded bank then shoots could be woven between them to form a fence and the landward side backfilled with wood or earth. The willow stems were very tolerant of the water and would root and increase the strength of the bank.

Endnotes

1 F Thacker *The Thames Highway* vol II (David and Charles, reprinted 1968) p 204.

2 William Turner *Reading seventy years ago: a record of events from 1813 to 1819* (John Read, 1887) p 1.

3 Thacker p 167.

4 BRO, D/EX/1457/1/92/27 Letter from Mr Cooper dated 21 April 1854 to G Treacher of the Commissioners sending to him a copy of the plan of the land involved from the conveyance of the time. The first piece of land was 40 pole and the other two were 3 roods 8 pole and 2 roods and 35 pole respectively. The copy is no longer with the letter.

5 RLSL, BC HQ, 'A plan of the grounds of Caversham Pound Lock 1815' *Guide to the records of the Thames Navigation and the Thames Conservancy* (Berkshire Record Office, 1978), p 8.

6 Thacker p 175

7 *Reading Mercury* 21 May 1832.

8 RLSL, RH/NW Sarah Markham and Godwin Arnold *The Gazebo and Caversham Court*, Reading (no publication data) p 15.

9 Directories name Mills, White, Humphrey, Gillet & Hedges, Williams and Laws on the Reading to London and Reading to Oxford runs in 1828 and Packer, Drewe, Bloxham, Lamb, Blandy & Palmer, Shaw & Co in 1835. There were also many barges running between Reading and Newbury.

10 BRO, DP97/1/1 St Laurence, Reading, baptism register.

11 *Reading Mercury* 26 March 1832.

12 TNA, MP1 1/791 Plan of Crown Estate at Reading (1832); *Reading Mercury* 19 November 1832, p 1.

13 Brunel's bridge is now a listed structure.

14 TNA, MPE 1/1120 Plan of Crown Lands in Reading (1865).

15 TNA, RAIL 280/92 Evidence of Robert Ray, millwright of Maidenhead, on the inconvenience of the Thames Navigation 1835.

16 BRO, D/EX 1457/1/91/29 Letter from J C Shaw to the H Graham Esq Clerk to the Commissioners of the Thames Navigation.

17 BRO, D/EX 1457/10/15 Prospectus of the Steam Barge Towing Company, 1849.

18 JRL Anderson *The Upper Thames* (Eyre and Spottiswood, London 1970) p 197.

19 John Kemplay *The Thames Locks* (Gloucester, 2000), p 12, 34, 44–45, 49–50.

20 BRO, D/EX 1457/1/92/36 Letter from Katesgrove Iron Works to G Treacher Esq.

21 Janet Keet-Black 'The Reading Wagon' *Berkshire Family Historian,* September 2002.

22 BRO, D/EX 1092/9/1-7 Deeds of Blake's Wharf 1863–76.

23 The building still exists as Blake's Lock Museum and as a restaurant. Part of it is still pumping sewage.

24 BRO, DP 98/27/A, St Mary tithe award plot 5, Caversham award 605, 605a, 627, 628, 489, 480, 482, 534, 600.

25 C J Cornish *Naturalist on the Thames* (London, 1902), p 121; J L Jones *Crafts from the Countryside* (David and Charles, 1975), Ch. 10: Basket Osiers.

26 The basket-makers were John Cook, High St; J Duckett, Bridge St; William Davis, Union St; and Richard Gomm, St Mary's Butts.

27 P Preece 'Buscot Coppice, Bradfield' *Berkshire Old and New* No. 9, 1992, p 33–40.

6 Caversham people and places: 1840–1870

Changes ahead

In the early 1800s the view from Caversham Bridge was little changed from the beginning of the previous century. Upstream on one bank there were meadows and eyots liable to flooding and under osier production, and a long sweep of natural terraced woodland on the other. This reach continued past the Fishery Islands at Chazey Farm to Norcot Scours, Kentwood Deeps, the Roebuck Ferry and the village of Purley and finished at Mapledurham lock, weir and mill. In the foreground, close to the bridge, there was the White Hart Hotel on the left hand side and the first buildings in Bridge Street, the Griffin Inn and the houses in Buck Side on the right, with St Peter's Church and its tower behind them. Beyond this small cluster of buildings and in front of the church was the Old Rectory, almost 300 years old by this time. Downstream from the bridge the ferryman's cottage was on the central island, with a parchment factory and a few other buildings on the left. There was very little else until one reached the mill, the lock and the lock-keeper's house.

The scene was to undergo substantial changes between 1840 and 1870, with a new bridge and new access to the river, and be transformed around the bridge and on the downstream Berkshire bank by commercial development between 1870 and 1900. It was to lose the landmarks of the White Hart Hotel and the Old Rectory. This section of the riverside story looks at some of those changes and at the comings and goings of businesses along the waterside in the nineteenth century. It also records the beginning of leisure activity on the river as fishing became popular, and the beginning of spectator sport as crowds turned out to watch the first regatta.

The story of the people and businesses on the river becomes easier to put together from the 1830s onward because the civil registration of births, marriages and deaths began in 1837, the decadal censuses began in 1841 and records of burials in the new cemeteries run from the 1840s. Maps and lists were compiled for the tithe and enclosure activities; the local press was well established and providing the names of people who took part in events. And of course in this century there was photography, with Francis Frith and Henry Taunt taking an interest in the river; Joseph Green and later his son Alfred, in business in Bridge Street, Caversham; Dann Lewis in London Street; and by the end of the period Philip Osbourne Collier, living on the Berkshire bank opposite Fry's Island.

The Old Rectory

The original house on this highly desirable residential site (Caversham Court) had been occupied since 1799 by William Blackall Simonds a brewer from Reading. He had taken over from Loveday the lease granted by the Dean and Chapter of Christ Church, Oxford.

Simonds married Jane May in 1783, daughter of Daniel May, the miller at Pangbourne. His brewery had been started in 1785 in Broad Street and re-sited in Bridge Street in 1789. A family home was designed for him by John Soane in 1790 alongside a brew house, new offices, and stables. The move to the Old Rectory in 1799 made the brewer's home quite separate from his workplace. He also had a London address at 40 York Street, off Baker Street.[1]

When William Blackall Simonds took over the estate from Loveday, the house had been unoccupied for seven years but was in reasonable order. Along with it were stables, barns, a coach house, housing for cart horses, piggeries, kitchen garden and a separate dwelling with wash house and brew house. The immediate estate was about 78 acres. The lessee was required to pay the stipend of the perpetual curate at St Peter's but in return had the profit from fees for services and from Easter gifts. The agreement also included glebe lands and tithes of the entire parish of Caversham, which were described in a survey at the time of sale as 1200 acres of arable land and 250 acres of greensward. At the time when enclosure of land was under review the Clerk to the Dean and Chapter suggested that Simonds might consider lessening the tithes in return for some of the common land that might be enclosed, but he was most unwilling to do so. He said that there was not sufficient commonable land available to redress the balance. He offered instead to sell the tithes to the owners of each property within the estate but, as he could set a prohibitive price that would effectively stop any sale, the offer was not helpful. The old documents relating to the estate were brought out and these showed that in 1773 there was far more tithable land in Caversham, a further 2443 acres, than the amount that was described in the survey made when Simonds bought the lease of the estate. He had more tithable land than he had paid for because the more recent survey at the time of sale had not defined it correctly. The Dean and Chapter sought counsel's opinion. John Skynner

of Lincoln's Inn said in 1812 that

> It is most evident that the Dean and Chapter, through the misconduct of their agent, have made a most improvident bargain but the mere inadequacy in the consideration does not furnish any grounds for impeaching it. The purchaser was not bound to disclose to the Dean and Chapter or their agent any information respecting the extent or value of the property, which ordinary care on their part would have equally supplied to them. But in this case there really seems reason to suspect that some undue representation on the part of Simonds led to concluding the treaty upon terms so injurious to the interests of the Dean and Chapter, and under this impression, and considering the great value of the subject of dispute, I cannot but recommend a Bill to be filed by the Dean and Chapter for the purpose of setting aside the sale. At the same time I think it very doubtful whether, under the circumstances stated, there may not be a deficiency of evidence to establish fraud against the purchaser.

A case was brought in Chancery by the Dean and Chapter in 1817. The agent, Richard Davis, who had made the survey for them, said that he thought he was making a general description, not a detailed list. It was shown that Simonds, the purchaser, had invited Davis, the vendor's surveyor, and his wife to make his house their home while the survey was being made. It was implied, but could not be proved, that there had been some agreement between them or that Simonds had deceived Davis in some way. The case was dismissed and Simonds continued to hold the tithes for the parish. As a result of this William Blackall Simonds, and later his heir Blackall, were allotted a substantial number of awards when the land in Caversham parish was enclosed.[2]

By 1840 the striped house had been pulled down, although perhaps not entirely, and replaced by a new one.[3] This was a large gothic-style building in stone, fronted by a gateway set into a solid tower decorated with turrets and crenellations. The ornamentation continued round the house at roof level and there were tall conspicuous chimney stacks. The staircase and hall from the old Tudor house, and the Alexander coat of

Blackall Simonds' house viewed from the tower of St Peter's Church.

arms, may have been incorporated into the new one. However David Nash Ford says that both William Blackall and his wife Elizabeth had arms and that these are shown along the borders of Thomas Pride's Map of Reading (1790) to which the brewer was a subscriber. Thus any idea that his son may have adopted or introduced the Alexander arms to gentrify his new house would seem to be ruled out.[4]

The main reception rooms faced south over the terraced garden and the river. The gazebo and the stable block were retained and a yew hedge surrounded the kitchen garden on the side nearest the church. Fishing rights from Caversham Bridge to Taylor's Ait at Mapledurham went with the property, as did eel bucks just downstream from the garden.

In 1841 the house was occupied by Edward Vines, a solicitor of independant means, and his wife and children, although still in the same ownership. Blackall died in 1845. From this time on, the Simonds name appears frequently in the story of the riverside as its members held office in many of the local sporting clubs and societies. The family were generous in offering the use of their gardens alongside the winning post to regatta committees on racing days.

Caversham Park

This estate came on the market again in 1832 when it was put up for sale by Charles Marsack, a former member of the East India Company, and its auction was advertised in the *Reading Mercury*. It had at this time to be sold in its entirety with four farms, the Black Horse public house near the chapel in Peppard Road, houses and cottages and extensive rights of fishery. The estate did not find a buyer until 1838 when it was bought by William Crawshay, a Welsh ironmaster.[5]

Riverside families: fishermen and watermen

The Freebody story was left in the previous century at the point where where one member of the family, Thomas, had moved from Caversham to the Reading side of the river and had died young, leaving the wharf and the White Hart in trust for his two small children, Thomas and Lydia. The child Thomas reached adulthood to marry Sarah Lewington and to have eight children but died in 1780 aged 31. Sarah remarried and although she and the children may have moved away from the river at Caversham, the tenure of the White Hart remained in the family. In 1839 Ann Freebody was

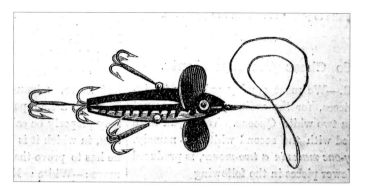

An artificial fish lure as it appeared in the *Boy's Own Paper* 1884.

the occupier of the public house and of a garden plot and Bridge Pightle meadow, all owned by the Corporation of Reading.[6] In the 1841 census it was a Mary Freebody with a daughter Lydia who was named as resident there but this seems to have been a mistake and the name should have been Ann. A trade directory entry in 1843 and the 1851 census both name Ann as occupier. She died in 1855 leaving her leasehold and personal estate to her daughter Lydia Elkin, then Mrs Woodroffe.

There was another branch of the family that descended from William, the fisherman of Mapledurham, this time via his son James who inherited all his fishing gear. James's grandson, Thomas Freebody, already introduced as an osier grower and fisherman, was living in one of George Donkin's properties on the Caversham bank in 1839. The term 'fisherman' at this stage probably described someone who sold some of his own catch for bait or for the table and who took others out to enjoy a day's angling, providing the boat and the bait and making sure they took home a reasonable catch. This is supported by a description of him in his will as a boat proprietor. He and his wife Mary, née Pitman, had a large family and brought three of them to be baptised at St Peter's Church in 1820 and another two in 1827. After Thomas's death Mary continued the business also under the trade description of boat proprietor. She was the first of several women in the Freebody family to manage the business alone.

Another waterman on the same side of the river was Richard Lyford who combined the trade with beer selling. A waterman, unlike a ferryman working a regular service between two points, would have poled a punt, providing a 'taxi' service for people and goods, perhaps also acting as a lighterman for the barge trade. Lyford and his wife Lucy occupied a house, beer shop and garden belonging to Caversham landowners, the Vanderstegens. Thacker described him as good-tempered and obliging, but an ill-conducted publican who kept the inn by the bridge.[7] Lyford died intestate in 1843.[8]

Advertisements in the local press for fishing tackle illustrate the diversity of styles and methods of fishing that were current in the 1830s. The sport at this date was still very much an upper class activity. H James at the Golden Salmon in Gun Street, Reading, was an ironmonger and fishing tackle manufacturer. His stock, with its selection of nets, might have appealed to the professional fisherman taking large catches for food or bait rather than to the sportsman. He offered rods and silk, hair and hemp lines, floats, baits, gut and flies, and also landing, spoon, bait, casting, flue and drag nets. William Ravenscroft in Minster Street in 1842 was also a fishing tackle manufacturer. Manford Nott, already introduced as advertising arrangements for emigration from his warehouse premises at the corner of the Butter Market and King Street, (near present day Barclay's Bank, King Street), had a more sophisticated range of equipment for sale which might have appealed to retailers or specialist anglers. He offered the best and common rods, to be used with fine silkworm gut, silk eight-plat, trolling hair and cord lines. He also had artificial minnow and dace and salmon flies, trout spinning and jack tackle, paternosters (weighted fishing line with jointed attachments for hooks), limerick (type of hook for trout) and trout hooks, carp floats, and cork trimmers (floats for pike fishing) for private waters. Nott's stock had been taken over from his predecessor in the Butter Market and it may have been offered as a one-off rather than as a regular retail service.[9]

The first regatta

Reading is fortunate in having two stretches of water long and straight enough for competitive rowing, one above Caversham Bridge and the other on the Dreadnought reach below the lock. When Reading Regatta was held in August 1842 on the upstream stretch, arranged at only a month's notice, it was intended that it should be the first of a series of annual events. It was the hottest day of the year, and, by early afternoon, Caversham Road was crowded with coaches, omnibuses and flies as the spectators arrived; the innkeepers' booths on the Reading side of the water were attracting crowds and Mr Poulton of Duke Street in his marquee was doing good trade in the heat with soda water and lemonade. Crowds were watching from all along the Warren. There were just two competitions, a sculling race and a cutter match for coxed fours, but heats were rowed for each so the programme lasted most of the day and ended with a 'funny match'. This was not, as might be thought, a crowd-pulling fun event such as walking a greasy pole but a race for a category of clinker-built sculler. The *Chronicle* thought something like donkey racing was needed to keep the crowds amused during the gaps between the races, but on the whole it approved of the day.

The following year the event was called the Reading and Caversham Regatta and this time it was held on the wettest day of the year. The committee had raised funds to offer a Caversham Challenge Cup (value 40 guineas) for crews within the districts of Oxford and Windsor, a Reading District Challenge Cup (30 gns) for amateur coxed fours within an 18-mile radius and a Ladies Presentation Cup (10 gns) for amateur scullers. Some offence caused by comments in the *Chronicle* had caused Henley crews to boycott

the events. At this date rowing club members from the professional or landed classes, professional watermen and local 'artisans' all competed together: there was no class distinction and no separation of amateur and professional oarsmen. The Caversham crew in the Reading Cup (G Donkin Esq, J Freebody, T Simonds Esq, C Hutchinson Esq steersman), were missing one of their regular members, the Caversham waterman Richard Lyford, and so they rowed at a severe disadvantage.

The final race, a watermen's purse, was a punt race. This form of racing was a sport which had been developed by fishermen using their fishing punts for competitions between themselves. It was also popular at Eton until it was stopped by the headmaster in 1852. Bets would be placed on these races and they were notorious for their rough and tumble, for jostling and cheating and for deliberate fouling. When punt races between local watermen became part of the regatta, their reputation had to be changed and the punters had to comply with racing rules. It was agreed that a competitor could be disqualified if an appeal against him was made to the umpire about any deliberate interference with another competitor. As a result of this, the race for the watermen's purse was awarded against Peter Freebody because of an alleged foul, a decision which had serious consequences the following year. In the evening of regatta day there was a prize giving at the Griffin and some of the crews went off to enjoy themselves at the Elephant in the Market Place.

The bad weather of 1843 had blunted enthusiasm for the regatta and in 1844 it was again organised at short notice. It did not attract the numbers of the 1842 event and one of the races was spoilt by a competitor catching his oar in weeds that should have been cleared from the course and another by an oarsman catching a crab. This year the local crew of the *Billie Stewart* rowed at full strength, J Wheeler replacing the late Richard Lyford. At the end of the day Mr Tagg, the umpire, was waiting in the umpire's galley to go up the course for the Town Challenge Cup when an attack was made on him and his crew by Peter Freebody, disqualified

A Thames punting champion.

Punt racing developed into a sport on its own on some reaches of the Thames under the guidance of the Thames Punting Club. Ned Andrews, a fisherman to be introduced again later in this story, was the winner of the first professional punting championship in 1877. A professional, as in rowing later, was anyone working in or about boats whose physical development and familiarity with the river was seen to give them an advantage over a university or club crew. The sport of punting did not develop on the Caversham reach as it did elsewhere because the river bottom was not suitable and because the river was very deep below the bridge. A description of the best path to take down when punting down the Thames was compiled in 1907 and it explains how bad it was on the regatta course:

> The reach down to Tilehurst is very beautiful and good shoving. At Keel's Boat-house below Tilehurst station it gets muddy and down to Caversham Bridge the bottom is as bad as it can be. Then the shoving is right bank as far as Caversham Lock. After leaving Caversham Lock shove across to Deans Farm, then down the left bank to opposite mouth of the Kennet; from there it is bad until reaching the island; left bank below the island and good shoving to the bend; across to barge walk side and keep on to the lock.[11]

the previous year, who was ferrying passengers in a punt from the Reading to the Caversham bank.[10] Mr Tagg fended off a blow from the punt pole but the ferryman first hit the boat with the wooden end of his pole, then holed it with the metal end. The crew made for the bank as quickly as they could and Mr Tagg tried to take his attacker into custody but he was thrown into the water and, because he was a non-swimmer, had to be rescued quickly. Two days later Freebody appeared before Henley magistrates to face charges of wilful damage to the umpire's boat and of the attack on the umpire. He was fined for both offences with a penalty of 4 months in prison and hard labour if he failed to pay.

It was difficult for the committee to sustain popular enthusiasm and to collect subscriptions to finance an annual regatta, even with the help of the Caversham supporters, especially without a local rowing club to maintain interest, and after a couple more years the event lapsed.

Families of Thames fishermen involved in punt racing took to punt hiring and boatbuilding as new trading opportunities when the occupation of fishing lost its importance. In Berkshire the boat businesses of Wyatt of Wargrave and Ned's firm, Andrews of Maidenhead, began that way and of course Freebody of Caversham followed the same route.

Riverside families: millers

Caversham Mill and the mill barge were owned by Robert Deane until his death in 1824 when he was 69. He was a mill owner rather than a miller and it has already been said that he left a half share in Caversham Mill to his three children jointly. His son, Robert Micklem Deane, a sub-

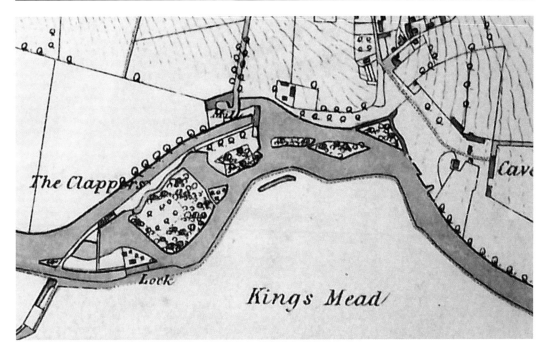

Extract from map of Reading 1863 to show the pound lock, the site of the old flash lock between the lock island and the next one (View Island) marked as a dark strip and the mill sluice on the backwater close to the mill.[12]

stantial landowner living at Dysons Lodge, was throughout very specific when he wrote his will in describing the one-third share of that half of which he was disposing. What is most interesting about this will, proved in 1840, is that it says that the mill and lock were in single ownership. Robert Micklem Deane described his

> equal undivided third part or share of or in that freehold messuage mill lands lock freehold and other hereditaments situate and being [in Caversham and in Reading] and commonly called or known by the name of Caversham Mill and also that lock there on the river with the appurtenances thereto belonging unto the said James Winch Grave [of Kidmore End] and Charles Marsh Deane [of Winchester].

The original connection between mill and lock at Caversham was with the flash lock, in the centre of what is now the weir and the Clappers Footbridge. The pound lock had been built on the far side of the river from the mill, between King's Meadow and Blandy's Eyot, long before 1840. It was built by the Thames Navigation and passed to the management of the Thames Conservancy.

The eyots had been sold by John Weldale Knollys to the Conservancy in 1815. There is no established connection between the Deanes and the pound lock. The lock referred to in the will was therefore the old flash lock, still used to control the flow of water past the mill. Deane's beneficiaries were his wife and his sons, Robert and Charles, but the bequests were heavily qualified in terms of marital status and age and of what could be done with the one share in connection with the other two shares.[13]

Robert Micklem Deane, like his father, had been a mill owner and not a miller and so his death in 1840 may not have brought any change at the mill itself. In 1841 Edward Tubb, father and son, were millers living at Caversham Mill and one of them had been overseer of the poor for Caversham with John May in 1836.

Just as the distinction between mill owner and miller can be blurred, so can that between self-employed miller renting the mill and the employee mill worker when the term 'miller' is used in the census or parish register for both of them. In Lower Caversham all these men were

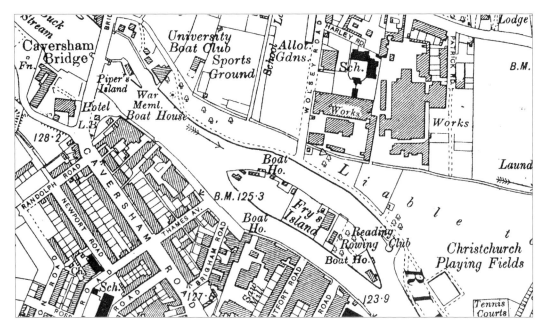

Extract from map of Reading 1932 to show the position of Fry's Island relative to the White Hart Hotel (Crowne Plaza) and the site of plots immediately below the bridge both of which were occupied by John Fry.[14]

described as millers: Henry Leach (1815); George and William Evered (1827–28); James Sawyer (1838); John Bayley, James Parsons and William May (1841).

In 1851 the mill was occupied and worked by John Hicks and in 1861 by John Chalmers with Edward Bradfield, Richard Matthews and George Lawyer of Caversham all probable mill employees. John Champion was the miller living at Caversham Mill in 1861. A report in *The Times* on flooding in 1869 provides incidental information about his occupation, stating that the house by Mr Champion's mill was inundated. In 1871 John was 75 and still working as a master miller employing six men. The Mill House was occupied by another miller, John Curtis.

John Champion's son, Joshua, who worked with him in Kent in 1851, moved to Reading by 1861 to work one of the town mills, was working in Surrey in 1871, finally returned to Caversham by 1881 to live in retirement, age 57, at Thames Bank.

Until the 1840s grain had come into the mill by barge and the meal had left the same way, but milling was a changing trade. Steam power,

which had taken the barge trade from the river and put it onto the railway, was now the new motive force for milling. Water power was unnecessary and production no longer needed to be alongside a river.

Fry's Island

It was not easy to find information about the ownership and occupation of the big island, marked on late nineteenth-century maps as Fry's Island. Until this time the island had no name. It now looks as if Fry may have been found and ownership established, although the two are unconnected. The tithe map and list of names of those occupying and owning each piece of land in the parish of Reading St Laurence in 1839 say that this island, together with Great and Little Brighams Meads, the Dairy Homestead, the Vasterns, Withy Eyot just above the lock and part of King's Meadow were all owned by John Weldale Knollys. It would seem therefore that these pieces of land, like Lock Island sold by Knollys in 1815, were part of the original Caversham Park estate, but not sold on when the main part changed hands. The occupier of part of King's Meadow was Charles Poulton and the occupier of all the rest, including the island, was Robert Clarke.

The Vastern and the Brighams Meads and the island were all cultivated as meadows (an area extending to the present day railway station) and the presence of a dairy homestead (the present day Harris Arcade, Station Road) does suggest that they were used for cattle grazing and milk production. It had been part of the island puzzle that when a new occupier took possession in the 1890s he was soon able to hold tennis and country dancing parties without site clearance but if it had been grazed this would explain its open state. There are also stories that the new owner ferried cattle across in a punt and again this would fit in with its use as grazing land.

The same set of tithe records identifies John Fry as the occupier of two riverside plots, 2 rods 12 poles in size, just downstream of the bridge. One of these was described as garden and wharf and the other as garden and both were owned by Reading Corporation. These plots were quite separate from those at the White Hart public house where Ann Freebody was the occupier until her death in 1845, although they too were all owned by Reading Corporation. A change of occupation at the White Hart took place sometime between then and 1850. In that year John Fry, a widower of St Mary's Parish, son of John Fry and Mary (née Reeves of Tilehurst) of Burghfield, married Ester Peters of Reading by licence at St Giles and the certificate gives his occupation as innkeeper and his address as Caversham Road. His actual address was revealed in the 1851 census as the White Hart Hotel. He (age 60) and [H]ester were there with a daughter from John's earlier marriage and a niece. In the next census ten years later John Fry and his wife were living on board the *Queen of the Thames* moored on the Caversham bank near the bridge and the enumerator, not sure whether to count the couple in the parish figures or not, made a special note on the first page of the notebook about him. It said that the *Queen of the Thames* was a pleasure boat used in the season for excursions and in the winter months

as a dwelling.

There is still no link between this John Fry and Fry's Island but, given the established pattern of land being owned by one person, leased to another (the occupier) and then rented out by the leaseholder to yet another person, it still may be found that he was for a time the tenant of it. Perhaps he moored the *Queen of the Thames* there at some time. It seems too much of a coincidence that the Fry with a wharf and a public house just across the water, a mooring on the Caversham bank and an association with the area for at least ten years was not the one for whom Fry's Island is named, especially since map-makers attached the name to the island in the second half of the nineteenth century. Robert Clarke, the man who was leasing from Knollys the island, and the meadows opposite, has yet to be identified.

Riverside families: bargebuilders

The Talbot family made its first appearance on the waterside in the 1850s and was established there by the 1860s. This was a family whose strong presence in the business life of the town was to continue for more than a century. Robert Talbot, who was born in 1777 in Pangbourne, moved to Shadwell, London, and later to Lambeth. One of his sons was apprenticed to a shipwright and two others, Richard and Edward first appear in Caversham in 1854 when *Billings Directory* lists them as being bargebuilders in Rotherhithe and in Caversham. Richard was about 40 and Edward in his late 30s. They took over the site occupied earlier by John Fry, downstream of the bridge on the Berkshire bank. By 1861 Richard, then a timber merchant, was established with his family at Bridge House, Caversham, and three of his sons Charles (17), George (19) and Frederick (16), all born in Rotherhithe, were in the business with him, the first as a bargebuilder and the other two as clerks. This family business is an excellent example of a combination of merchant, carrier, transport and wharf being managed within one venture. A timber merchant with family connec-

A barge at Talbot's wharf before 1871 with the old bridge in the background and the turrets of the Old Rectory and the tower of St Peter's Church behind that.[15]

tions in the London docks, and with the enterprise to build barges to bring the trees by river to a wharf alongside his own yard, was set to succeed because he could cut both his costs and his dependence on others. By the end of the decade entries in *Kelly's Directory* describe Richard as an English and foreign timber merchant as well as a bargebuilder and coal merchant while Charles was a bargebuilder, both of Caversham Road, and George a coal merchant at Great Northern Wharf, Caversham Road, but the enterprise was essentially one unit.

Thames Conservancy

The financial position of the Thames Navigation had become very serious during the 1850s as the barge trade and income from tolls declined while the need to control and manage the navigation increased. In 1857 the Thames Conservancy took over the river downstream from Staines. In 1865 the point was reached where the powers of the Commission were examined by a parliamentary select committee and witnesses with knowledge and practical experience of the river were called

to give evidence:

> It was concluded that the maintenance, management and navigation of both the Upper and Lower Thames should be under one body. The existing Commissioners are not a corporation and therefore open to personal liability claims, their constitution is out of date and they have no power over tolls levied on the river since the majority of locks and weirs are owned by individuals. Maintenance has not been carried out and dangerous embankments have been erected by individuals in the reclamation of land. Expenditure is exceeding income, with creditors waiting to be paid, and overall traffic is being lost as a result. It is recommended that the Board of Thames Conservancy takes over responsibility for the River, pays off all existing creditors with the aid of Parliament, maintains separate accounts for the Upper and Lower Thames and ensures that all tolls in future go towards work on the river.[16]

These recommendations were put into practice in 1866. All the locks, canals and works were transferred to the Thames Conservancy and compensation was paid for all privately-owned works taken over. The Conservancy was given the power to purchase land that was required for further works. It could control navigation, approve the erection of any structure in or by the river, carry out maintenance and ensure the safety of the river and its users. The Conservancy did not acquire the soil or bed of the river above Staines. That remained with the riparian owners who each owned the river bed to the centre line. There was an awareness at this time of the damage to the river from pollution and in 1866 the Conservators served notice on the authorities at Reading that they were to stop sewage and other pollutants from being discharged into the water.[17]

The new bridge

Until 1869 the two halves of the road bridge were different in construction, a division that marked the boundary between Reading in Berkshire and Caversham in Oxfordshire. The Caversham half of the bridge was supported by small stone arches which limited the size of boat which could pass under it and the Reading side, built of wood, had better clearance and in earlier times had been constructed as a drawbridge. A ferry operating just below the bridge was a cheaper means of crossing the river for those who had a wide load or who did not wish to pay the road toll. The ferryman's cottage, in fact a substantial three-storey house, abutted the bridge on the downstream side. Reading was a growing town with a railway, factories and a working population living in new residential areas and the bridge, and the poor roads leading to it, were now inadequate. Reading and Caversham had to co-operate and move with the times. The Caversham Bridge Act of 1868 defined the liability of Oxfordshire and of the owners of Caversham Park estate for costs of rebuilding and maintenance and made barge owners responsible for damage caused by their boats. The construction of a new bridge began. It was an iron bridge, of the same construction all the way across, which could support bigger and heavier loads and whose structure gave clearance to bigger boats. The supporting pillars were driven into the riverbed by a screw action using

a capstan, a method which replaced the old pile-driving process.

Work on the bridge was delayed by flooding in February 1869 after heavy rain the previous month. King's Meadow, including the race course, the footbridge to Caversham, the public bathing place, Reading Cricket Club building, Talbot's timber yard, Kennet wharfs and the rear of houses in King's Road were all under water. The house of the Knight family at the mill was in the middle of a vast lake.[18]

The big event in connection with the construction of the iron bridge was the spectacular move of the ferryman's house. This was resting on the old stone bridge and it either had to be demolished to make way for the new structure or it had to be moved. Over the years the distance which it was moved has increased with the telling of the tale from 8ft to 25ft, and the human-interest story of Mr Piper and his family staying in the building during the move has been added and has stuck firmly. The contractors were Messrs Head and Co and they worked with Mr Woodman, the Borough Surveyor, to make sure that the three-storey house was fully supported and braced. It helped that the house was square in section. The walls of the basement were rotten and so they were removed and a new framework put in their place. This was surrounded by a cill underpinned by roller plates between which were iron rollers. The engineers used hydraulic and screw jacks to move the structure and in two and a half hours it had been shifted 8ft without so much as a broken window.[19] There is nothing in the press reports to support the story of the Piper family being moved with it. The opening of the bridge in 1869 gave better public and commercial access to the river and marked the beginning of the great boom in pleasure boating at Caversham.

The opening of the new bridge without a road toll brought about the end of the ferry that had been there in one form or another for more than 500 years, putting Mr Piper out of a job. When the photograph overleaf was taken the new bridge was in place but the stone part of the old one had not yet been removed, so the year was

Mr Piper taking a loaded ferry across to the Caversham bank in about 1871 with the new and part of the old bridge behind it.[20]

probably 1871. At first glance the photograph looks as if the ferry was making a routine crossing but that is not so. It was a staged event for a professional photographer under perfect weather conditions: the man at the bow is holding the boat in place with his pole and the reflection of the boat is so clear and unruffled that it cannot have been making any forward movement at all. Perhaps it was a photographic record of the last crossing with some of the regular users on board, like the milkman delivering for Mr Muire of Mapledurham Dairy.

Endnotes

1 TNA, PROB 11/1839 will of William Blackall Simonds.

2 BRO, DP 162/26A and 1A Caversham enclosure awards on line, www.berkshirerecordoffice.org.uk.

3 Secondary sources suggest that the new house at the Old Rectory was designed by Augustus Pugin but this has not been confirmed from any primary sources.

4 David Nash Ford's May family history website at www.mayfamilyhistory.co.uk.

5 *Reading Mercury* 25 June 1832.

6 BRO, DP 98/27/A plots 1–4, St Mary tithe award 1839. Owner Mayor, aldermen and burgesses of Reading. Plot 1 Bridge pightle (meadow), 2 Garden plot 3 White Hart Public House 4 White Hart meadows.

7 F Thacker *The Thames Highway* vol 11 (David and Charles, reprinted 1968), p 233.

8 D Barratt, J Howard Drake, M Priddey (eds) *Index to Probate Oxfordshire 1733–1857* (Oxon Record Society), vol 61, 1997 p 117. Thomas Freebody boat proprietor Caversham 1847 will and affidavit 226.376; 260/1/76; Richard Lyford waterman Caversham Bridge 1843 Bond, affidavit 112.115; 285/4/3. Admin. to wife Lucy on 21/10/1843.

9 *Reading Mercury* Advertisement for H James 18 April 1831 and for Manford Nott 4 July 1831.

10 *Berkshire Chronicle* 24 August 1844. The J Freebody and W Freebody named among the racing crews could have been the brothers of Peter, sons of Thomas and Mary.

11 R T Rivington *Punting on the Thames* (published privately, 1983), p 27 and 68–9. This book has instructions on building a Thames punt in appendix 3.

12 BRO, D/EX 326 26 part of map, 1863.

13 TNA, PROB 11/1930 Robert Micklem Deane 1840. Graves and Charles Deane are mentioned several times in the will and may have been the owners of the other two shares in the various properties.

14 RLSL, OS map of Reading 1932.

15 RM, REDMG 50/82, Talbot's Wharf at Caversham Bridge.

16 House of Commons, *Select Committee on the Thames River* sessional papers, vol XII, paper 399, HMSO 1865.

17 *The Thames Conservancy 1857–1957* produced by the Conservators, p 11.

18 *The Times* 1 January and 3 February 1869.

19 *Berkshire Chronicle* 30 January 1869 and *Reading Mercury* 30 January 1869.

20 RM, REDMG 1931/118/1, the final crossing of Piper's Ferry.

7 Changes, real and perceived: 1860–1880

Before and after the fishing regulations

Steam power had taken the trade from the horse barges, and steam barges had been replaced by rail transport. The great boom in pleasure boating was beginning and in Reading this followed the opening of the new bridge in 1869. Working men had leisure time and access to cheap rail travel and many of them came to the river to fish. The wealthy anglers who had had the river to themselves up to then, and the professional fishermen who went out with them, were now aware of the changes because they curtailed their privileges.

The anglers and the fishermen had an event and a date on which to fix this sense of change: a legally enforced closed season introduced in 1869. A classic book on angling, published in 1912, is *The delightful life of pleasure on the Thames and an angler's perfect sport* by a Berkshire man, James Englefield. Its subtitle is: *Before and since the fence months were legalised in 1869*. This book gives a vivid picture of fishing before 1869 and an appreciation of the size of catches anglers were regularly taking from the Thames for sport, and only incidentally for consumption. It sets a scene against which to see the changes that took place. Englefield describes the increased use of the river by the new anglers who had arrived on the scene since the coming of the railways. With the old-style anglers still fishing and the new ones taking

their share, the river was being overfished. As well as the large catches that were being taken, poaching was rife, nightlines were set, and landowners rented out their fishing or used it themselves. In recognition of the need for change, the Piscatorial Society had been founded in 1836 and the Thames Angling and Preservation Society in 1838. In 1869 much needed new controls were brought in to stabilise fish stocks. In addition, the 'fence' months, closed seasons for fishing, were introduced, and were to be strictly observed, to protect spawning adult fish from capture. For Englefield and for later writers it was as if these controls had brought about the social changes that were happening along the river.

Englefield began fishing when he was seven and said in the preface to his book that he continued for over eighty years. His enthusiasm for the sport began while he was at school in Reading in about 1840 'under the able tuition of Mr Charles Havell, who had then left a leading position at Dr Valpy's celebrated Grammar School and set up for himself at Kendrick House in London Road'. When his father came to visit him at school and to take him out, they stayed at the George Hotel, fitting in some fishing together on the Kennet or on the Thames downstream towards Sonning or upstream at Caversham. Sometimes, when they took a fishing punt, a friend of his father's, William Silver Darter, came with them.[1]

Englefield later lived in Wargrave and in

Maidenhead, so many of his observations about angling are drawn from his experiences on the Thames in Berkshire. He was a regular contributor to *The Field* under the name of Red Quill. It is from these articles and a diary of his catches that his book was compiled. Writing about a time in the 1860s before the controls were introduced, when he was concentrating on fishing for roach and catching 8 to 10 dozen a day, and even 13 dozen on one occasion, he described the surroundings in which he fished without interruption:

> … one might fish all day in the middle channels of the river without having once to shift the punt, for the steam launch was unknown on the Upper Thames, and the one up-and-down journey was taken weekly between Reading and London by a lumbering steam collier called *The Sons of the Thames*. There were also large black barges occasionally, drawn by four or more horses in single file, and led by the bargee, carrying a whip. He also had a cabin at the stern of the barge, where cooking was done for each day by his wife; and they slept there in peace under the glittering stars.

So in these pleasant surroundings he could enjoy his sport for 17 hours at a stretch, for days at a time, the excitement keeping him going, as he sought to break a previous record. Englefield's catches were quite legal and quite acceptable at the time and he describes some of them: he caught 10

A barge pulled by horses in single file, the bargeman and his wife in the cabin, just as described by James Englefield.

brace of chubb in a few hours, 15 dozen gudgeon on one day, 28 pope on another, 145 perch in two days and 18 jack in flooded conditions in 1864 by spinning with dead bleak. (Jack are young pike although sometimes both terms are used interchangeably. Pope and bleak are lesser-known river fish.) Each of these catches was the result of a single day's sport for a man whose primary interest was fishing. He became known as one of the most successful of Thames anglers:

> … making big catches of any and all sorts of fish by the usual as also the advanced methods of bottom fishing generally in swims previously ground baited … The ground baiting was effected by throwing in overnight several quarts of worms cut into small pieces … or lobworms enclosed in balls of plastic clay …[2]

He often had with him a professional fisherman, someone like Thomas Freebody, who handled the boat, advised on the best places to try, provided the bait and put it onto the lines and landed the fish. A fishing rod by this time had a loop at the end to hold the horsehair line and a reel to feed it out and take it in. On the occasion when the jacks were caught the fisherman, Ned Andrews (already mentioned as a punting champion), had come to Englefield a few days before and suggested that the conditions would soon be just right for spinning and that this would be better sport than live-baiting. He brought the boat, fully fitted for the day, to Englefield's landing stage on the morning of 3 February 1864 and took him to a suitable anchorage. The river was high and running fast. The fishing line was weighted with shot and it carried 'five or six swivels and a flight of hooks consisting of four triangles and a lip hook'. A freshly killed bleak was impaled along its length and in its lip by the flight of hooks. This bait, when the line was cast into the fast water, would spin like a live fish to lure the jack. If the water had been quiet the bait could have been towed behind a boat, but this too became illegal under a Thames byelaw not long after the fence months were introduced. Englefield's agreement with the fisherman was for a crown for his trouble and one shilling for every jack killed over 2lb in

A professional fisherman ready to help his patron land a catch.

weight and for every one caught after the first five, but this time he was paid a sovereign. This system of payment was an encouragement to the fisherman to produce results but, if he was wise, he kept the numbers under control so that his patron was left with unfulfilled ambitions and the feeling that he still had something to achieve on the next outing.

James Englefield was also an eel fisherman and he rented water in which to lay eel baskets or wells. He baited them with gudgeon which he had caught himself with a net and set them on the river bed in the evening weighted with bricks, hoping not to draw the attention of poachers to them. The basket was just under 5ft in length and widening from a funnel-shaped neck to base. He trapped over 400 eels in three seasons, some of which went to his dining table.

The fence or closed seasons in the Upper Thames were defined by law in 1867 (and introduced in 1869) as from 10 September to 31 March inclusive for salmon, salmon trout, and trout, and from 14 February to 31 May for pike, jack, perch, roach, rudd, barbel, bream, chubb, carp, tench, grayling, gudgeon, pope, dace, crayfish, bleak and minnow. Fishing was permitted only between the beginning of the last hour before sunrise and the end of the first hour after sunset. Young specimens were protected by regulating the size of nets to be used. The mesh of nets used by professional fisherman had to be more than two inches and small fry were only to be taken for bait and only

in a cast net with a sack no more than 14 inches deep. Size limits were defined for all species (and again these are 1867 figures and the measurement was from the eye to the end of the tail): pike 12in; tench 8in; barbel 12in; grayling 9in; perch 6in; or any salmon of less than 4lb or any salmon trout or trout of less than 1lb.[3] The use of crayfish nets, grog wells for eels and eel bucks or stages were excluded from regulations. It was particularly hard for Englefield that while private waters were exempt from some of the controls, the fence months applied to all waters and directly affected him and his upper class social group.

The reference to grayling in the Thames is an indication that the waters were still clean since the presence or absence of this fish is recognised as a pollution indicator, the equivalent of the canary in the coal mine.[4] It had been reported in 1810 that the introduction of the flushing water closet, discharging sewage into the Thames, was the cause of the beginning of the disappearance of salmon but since the new legislation specifically mentions them, they had not yet completely gone.[5]

When the new regulations came in, there was a period of grace before prosecutions were brought but there were incidents of fishermen still using large nets and in 1870 it was time to make an example of someone. That year a charge of illegal fishing was brought against Thomas Aust for using a net 13yd in circumference in the Kennet at Reading. William Johnson, a river-keeper, produced the net in court and Mr Riesman for the Thames Conservancy said that nets of 5yd were the largest allowed for taking bait. Aust said in his defence that he thought the Conservancy had no jurisdiction above the Six Bells (presumably a well-known public house and landmark) but he was fined 10s and costs and the net was cut through the middle in the courtroom, as the byelaws required, so that it could not be used again.

Englefield catches his reader up in a debate about fishing for trout by spinning with bait or by fly-fishing. This was for him very much a 'before and after the controls' matter but it was not as simple as that. The issues it raises were part of the changing social scene and explain some of

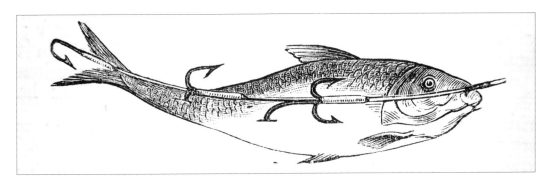

A fish impaled along its length to be used as bait. The illustration appeared in *The Boy's Own Paper* in 1884.

what was written about trout fishing in the next century. To look briefly at the debate it seems that there were two accepted ways of catching trout in a sporting manner: spinning and fly fishing. The first of these was similar to spinning for jack, using a smaller fish impaled along its length as a bait. As the angler cast the line into the water, the bait would spin, catching the light like a live fish, and act as a lure to the trout. This species, it was believed, fed only once a day so there was skill needed to identify a likely time and place. The sport needed a well-stocked river to be successful. The season for spinning was very short, confined to May and June, also because of the feeding habits of the trout. By July it could gorge on the shrimp hatch and was not interested in chasing bleak. In the second sporting way of catching trout the angler used a rod to cast an artificial fly at the end of a line to mimic the action of a live insect in or on the water. The rods in use at this time were heavy and not easy to use and this inclined anglers towards spinning as a method for a successful catch.

Patrick Chalmers, another well-known author who lived and fished at Goring, writing in 1932, brought to the trout fishing debate the issue of social class. He said that the Thames did not seem to attract the same class of fisherman as in the palmy days (1865) when his father was angling.[6] Then every riparian village had its professional fisherman and important centres had four or five of them, each with a lucrative clientele and a waiting list. Now, Chalmers said, the new light-weight fly rods and the improved ways of travel had taken

these anglers elsewhere and, as a result, the old Thames skill of spinning for trout was being lost. While tackle had improved with new materials for rods and lines and more sophisticated reel design, the real change was one of social class. The man like Englefield, with a house on the river bank, who rented water from a local landowner, and who had leisure to spend days on the water, and who had money to pay fees to his fisherman, hire a boat and buy expensive equipment, had had the best of the river. He was moving elsewhere – Red Quill himself moved on to fly-fish for trout on 16 other rivers in England, Scotland and Wales, including the Kennet and the Lambourne.

Chalmers said that a new race of trout fishers (the 'army of bank anglers') had appeared since Red Quill's day, anglers without professional aid or personal knowledge, whom he called 'danglers, not anglers'. They were taking their share of the water and the fish stock. Red Quill (James Englefield) himself had said that in the part of the season when the fish were feeding on the shrimp hatch, scores of good trout would come to a sad (and unsporting) end by being caught by live bait on leger (weighted) tackle and the army of bank anglers would enjoy good sport. However, instead of the idyllic solitude that Englefield had enjoyed in his fishing punt, these new anglers in punts and on the bank would have to contend with the

> … continual and increasing disturbance of the river from the wash and hurry and turmoil caused by hundreds of steam launches and the endless procession of every description of floating craft, from the light canoe, dinghy or outrigger, to the

'Continual and increasing disturbance' caused by the newcomers enjoying the river.

lordly, much decorated or hotel-like houseboat. Its banks will then also be thronged by gaily-dressed and joyous holiday makers, merry and loving couples towing boats along, horses also drawing skiffs and houseboats, and by an innumerable host of spectators – especially at the locks; by idlers, loafers and roughs.[7]

Trout became less common in the Thames and C J Cornish, writing in 1902, attributed its scarcity between Reading and Abingdon to increased use of the Thames tributaries which were its spawning grounds.[8] The skill of spinning for trout was lost too. Englefield and his contemporaries did eventually try restocking the river with trout fry but they found it difficult and expensive. It was left to the angling clubs of the 1880s and 90s to buy adult fish from breeders and to put them into the Thames. The trout stock did not again reach a level where, for Red Quill, fly fishing was worthwhile.

Changing times: the first of the boat-letting businesses

By the time of the 1871 census Mr Piper, the barge-builder and ferryman, had died and the cottage at Caversham Bridge was occupied by Selina Piper, a widow aged 37 and a boat proprietor. Photographs of the cottage (see page 60 and 62), variously called Ferryman's, Waterman's and Fisherman's, before and after the new bridge was built, show some skiffs and canoes tied up outside the house

Willow Grotto, home of the Freebody family.[9]

and so there was some kind of boat business operating from the island, the very first evidence of a boat-letting business in the area. Pleasure boating had already arrived elsewhere on the Thames as a result of increased leisure time and the arrival of new kinds of boats, but this was its beginning at Caversham.

The Freebody business was also at the bridge in 1871 although it had been at the Parsonage Meadow at the time of the 1861 census. It was being run at both dates by Kate (Kitty) Freebody. In 1865 she was an allottee in the Caversham enclosure award.[10] She was the daughter of Thomas and Mary who, as a widow, had traded as a boat proprietor on her own. Kate, who had been a dressmaker, took over from her mother and also ran the business alone. The nature of her trade is not known but it certainly became boat-letting in the 1870s. Her older brother Thomas James had died when he was 25 and another brother, Peter, who was still a waterman, was living in Castle Street in 1861 with his nephew Thomas,

apprenticed in the bootmaking trade. It was this apprentice who would ultimately take over from Kate. Her site opposite Piper's Island was given the name Willow Grotto in the 1871 census.

The opening of the bridge and the improved access to the areas alongside, brought with it new businesses and new people. Whether Bill Moss or Edward Cawston opened up first at the bridge still has to be discovered but either way it was close-run. Bill Moss made his first appearance in the area in 1871 when he, a 23-year-old boatbuilder from Greenham, married the widowed Selina Piper.[11] Bill moved into Waterman's Cottage with Selina and took over the business. Edward Cawston was born in Lambeth in about 1841 and he trained there with Searle's, a company with a very high reputation who had boat yards at Lambeth, Eton, Henley and Oxford. He brought his wife Sarah and his daughter Louisa to the Caversham side of the bridge between the 1871 census date and 1873 when the company's first advertisement appeared alongside that of Bill

W. MOSS

(late E. F. PIPER)

**WATERMAN'S COTTAGE
CAVERSHAM BRIDGE**
BOATS HOUSED · BOATS TO LET
Good accommodation for Boating,
Fishing and Pleasure Parties.

Fishing punts ✳ Fishermen ✳ Live Baits
Ginger Beer, Lemonade and Soda Water

E. CAWSTON.

(from SEARLES)

BOAT BUILDER
CAVERSHAM BRIDGE
On the Oxfordshire side of the bridge

**BOATS AND CANOES OF EVERY
DESCRIPTION BUILT TO ORDER**

Boats housed or to be let by the week, day or hour

GINGER-BEER, LEMONADE &c

Moss in Henry Taunt's publication, *A new map of the river from Oxford to London*.

So here were the two newcomers offering their services by advertisements, reconstructed here to display the mix of font size and type faces typical of the date. Both were offering boats to let. Cawston was advertising his connection with Searle's and making a point of mentioning canoes, which were his speciality. He built the Rob Roy, a wooden canoe rather like a kayak, decked over except for the cockpit, which John McGregor had

invented in 1865 to be strong and light enough to be lifted out and carried over land during long journeys. Moss was using the goodwill of the late Mr Piper and although his trade was boatbuilding, he was using a new opportunity in the market by offering fishing to his customers. The army of anglers did not fish entirely from the banks: some needed boats and bait and sometimes a tutor or an advisor to fish with them to make sure they had a good day's sport, and after the fence months had been introduced there were still

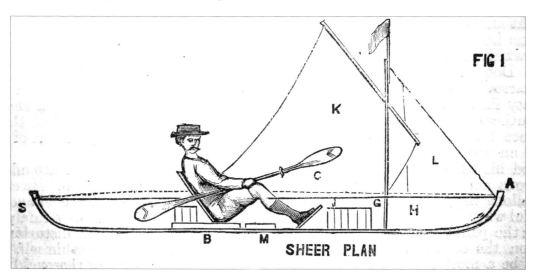

The sheer plan of the Rob Roy canoe, the speciality of Edward Cawston, illustrated an article in *The Boy's Own Paper* in 1884.

some anglers in the James Englefield style whose status was improved by having a professional with them. The rates of pay did not rise much after Englefield's time. Patrick Chalmers said in 1932 that it was as well for a beginner to employ a fisherman to learn where to angle and where not to. He advised a figure of 10s for the day, with 15s if it was a good day and a sovereign if the man netted a big trout. He confirmed that fees included the bait and that the angler paid for the beer and the afternoon tea.[12] Where Bill Moss learned his skills as a fisherman is not known but he came from a boatbuilding family on the Kennet and must have been apprenticed locally so it is likely that an interest became an occupation.

Continuity among the changes

Downstream on an island near the mill (present day View Island) there was in 1871 a family connected with two very old skills. William Knight (69) and his wife Eliza (59) were osier or willow-rod growers and their widowed son Henry (38) was a basket-maker and cane worker who also had premises at 167 Friar Street. William combined osier growing with gardening. Henry's brother Edward and his 13-year-old son George completed the family. These trades require little equipment and are generally low in investment costs but of course they have to be supported by sales and deliveries. Suitable sized rods for making a basket have to be soaked in water to make them pliable and left overnight for the moisture to penetrate and it helps the weaving process if the working atmosphere is humid. The basket-maker can work directly on the floor or without a workbench although some used a lapboard to support the piece they were making. The size and design of the basket would dictate the working conditions. The essential requirement was that knives, shears and a tool to knock the woven area down the upright spokes were all to hand. There were three other local basket-makers, George Bristow and Richard Gomez in St Mary's Butts and D Cook in High Street. The Knights were still at View Island as two households in 1881. Eliza

A basket made by the one of the Knight family.[13]

was a widow and Henry was a rod grower with his son George, the basket-maker. Henry William Knight, basket-maker at Caversham Mill Fishery, was declared bankrupt in 1891 and it seems that he left the site that year.

The barge trade still had a presence on the river for carrying heavy cargoes 30 years after the railway came to Reading. Talbot's Wharf was on the towpath on the Berkshire bank and just downstream of the bridge and alongside were the firm's timber yard and bargebuilding sheds. Richard Talbot was now 58 and described in the census as an English timber dealer and barge builder employing 30 men and 9 boys. He was still living in Bridge House in 1871. In his family of 13 children, 10 were boys, most of whom were employed in the business or in the same sector. In 1881 his son George Talbot, then 39, continued his coal merchant's business and advertised various grades of domestic coal (Best Wigan, Cannock Best Deep, Best Cobbles and Kitchen Nuts) regularly in the *Berkshire Chronicle* as available at Tudor Wharf, Caversham Road. Earlier he had been at Great Northern Wharf. A decade later he also advertised Nixon's Navigation, a suitable grade of coal for the steam launches that passed his door. His brother Charles, age 37, had been a bargebuilder at Algoa Wharf in the same road since 1870. He employed 30 men and 3 boys

in 1881.[14] The various wharf names perhaps just distinguished the various divisions of the company at the bridge rather than indicating that the family had other sites. A couple of hundred yards further downstream on the same side from about 1892 was George Lewis's timber yard and a barge mooring alongside.

Time for more regulations

The pound lock at Caversham was replaced by a new one in 1875 and the weir replaced in 1884. The first management group for the river had been the Thames Navigation Commissioners appointed in 1751 to be responsible for towpaths, locks, tolls, and for regulation of the river and its traffic. Its membership came from landowners in counties alongside the river and included the mayors of the riverside towns. The Thames Navigation Act 1866 transferred the management and jurisdiction of the river from Staines to Cricklade from the Thames Navigation Commissioners to the Conservators of the River Thames, later better known as the Thames Conservancy. Reading Corporation, set to lose its mayoral representation, objected to the Navigation Act. The Conservators were already responsible for the lower reaches and had been since their estab-

lishment in 1857. Now on the upper reaches the Conservators were faced with declining barge traffic, and thus declining income from tolls and charges, but with increasing public demand to use the river for pleasure, pressures from riparian owners who saw their privacy and privilege being invaded, and increasing demand by water boards for water for domestic and industrial use. The Conservators were responsible for the maintenance of the river and its backwaters, tributaries and streams, for the towpath, banks, ferries, weirs, locks and lock tolls, for regulating events, registering pleasure boats, licensing larger boats for public use, and for seeing that byelaws to promote the safety of river users and to prevent pollution were complied with. The Thames Preservation Act 1885 recognised that the time of the river as a commercial highway was over. It was a statement of public rights to use the river for recreation and it was directed towards preserving the river and regulating its use and its traffic for that purpose:

> The Thames is a navigable highway and has come to be largely used as a place of public recreational resort: and that it is expedient that provision should be made that it should be preserved as a place of regulated public recreation.

The shooting of wildfowl on the water, which had become a problem in the 1870s and 1880s because of the danger to other river users, was made illegal by the act. The *Lock to Lock Times* specifically mentioned the shooting of kingfishers in this context on a number of occasions. Registration fees and lock fees were introduced in 1887 for private pleasure boats.

Charles Dickens junior, in his *Dictionary of London* in 1879, set out all the lock tolls which were charged by the class and the length of the boat. For example a steam pleasure boat not above 35ft in length to go through a lock and to return on the same day cost 9d with an extra 3d for every 5ft extra. A small two-oared rowing boat was also 3d, a four-oared was 6d and above four-oars the fee was 9d. A houseboat cost 2s 6d. Any of these fees could be paid annually when the equivalent cost of a 9d daily charge was 40 shillings, a sum

E. A. TALBOT,

Timber Merchant & Barge Builder,

Thames Avenue Wharf,

CAVERSHAM ROAD, READING,

Near the Bridge.

which would have paid for passage through more than 50 locks.

By the 1880s there were about 250 steam launches on the river, and they were regarded by the traditionalists as a nuisance and 'the curse of the river' because of their speed and the wash they created, and because of the attitudes of the newcomers who drove them. The river was no longer the province of the rich. Passenger steamers, available for hire by groups or offering scheduled day trips, catered for the leisure time of all levels of society. These boats were larger than the steam launches and were under the control of professionals, and they did not therefore create so many problems. The Board of Trade appointed surveyors to inspect annually the safety of all steam vessels used by members of the public because of the risks inherent in fire-powered engines in wooden boats and of boilers holding steam under pressure. As far back as 1838 the boat companies on the whole river had joined together to form a professional organisation, the Thames Boat Builders Protection Association, and in about 1889 A H East and A G Bona, the two real entrepreneurs among the local boatmen, and to be introduced later, were the committee members representing the Reading area.

To quote Dickens once more:

On the Upper Thames no steamer is allowed, between Teddington Lock and Cricklade, to run at such a speed as to endanger any other boat, or injure the river bank. No one is allowed to ride or drive on the towing-path, to unload anything upon it, to place any vessel on the shore in front of it, or to take any stones, &c., from the banks. No vessel must remain in any lock longer than time enough to pass through, and if she pass without paying toll, the amount due can be demanded at any other lock before admitting her. No vessel — unless in case of necessity, through strength of current — is to be towed from the bank otherwise than from a mast of sufficient height to protect the banks, gates, &c., from injury.

An article in the *Berkshire Chronicle* in 1891, attributed to *The Standard*, commented on the wear and tear on the locks and weirs by normal water flow, by increased flow following spring rains and by floating ice in winter, as well as by badly-managed barges. It said that 700 men were employed in conservation in summer time and that the river was now essentially a playground. Lock men were mostly chosen from retired petty officers and paid between £30 and £40 a year. The article argued that as the men lived rent-free, already had pensions and could make money from the sale of garden produce in summer and from the minding of boats, they must be fairly well off. Most were officers of the Thames Angling and Preservation Society and, as water bailiffs, performed many of the functions of ordinary police. They patrolled the towpath and the lock houses were the police centres for the river. The article ended with the comment that in a mechanical age

An illustration of Caversham Lock from an article about Caversham and Reading in the *Lock to Lock Times* in 1889.

it was strange to see lock men winding winches and opening heavy gates by hand.[15]

In recognition of the value to anglers of the work of these professionals, the Reading (Waltonian) Angling Association gave an annual dinner to the local bailiffs, lock men and ferrymen and in 1895 the event was held in the Great Western Hotel and it was reported that twenty of them came.[16]

Although non-power boats for hire were registered with the Thames Conservancy, their owners were not required to provide any evidence of their safe construction or design or their regular maintenance. This was brought to local attention on 1 August 1896 by a dreadful accident which happened in the evening of Reading Regatta day, after the racing had finished. The grandstand and enclosure were illuminated and a mimic gunboat was brought up the river to bombard Caversham, the event attracting many spectators. The warden of Reading Boys Home, C J Murdoch, brought about 15 of his boys to see the event and hired from Frederick Schulze of Castle Street a kind of cycle boat with a driver and assistant to take them up the course. The craft consisted of two boats fastened together with a platform on top, surrounded by a guard rail about 2 or 3ft high. In the centre there was a paddle wheel which propelled the whole thing along. The party set out from Bona's landing stage and went up as far as the Fisheries. Coming back down the course at about 9.30pm the craft turned over in a dark spot under a tree near Haslam's landing stage on the Oxfordshire side and Murdoch and four of the boys were drowned. There was a reasonable

number of boats at this point and many people went to help, including Dryland Haslam, so preventing the tragedy from being even greater. Accounts in the *Reading Observer* from eye-witnesses and from the inquest brought out that when the boat, described as a roughashlar, overturned, some of the boys had been trapped under it within the wire-netting guard rail. The rail was fastened with gas piping and so could not be released easily. It was also revealed that earlier in the day there had been an accident to the craft, known locally as the convict boat, when, according to the owner, a punt had gone under one side of the double boat and caused water to be taken in. Water had then been put into the other side to make it level. Bill Moss was called at the inquest and said that he had examined the boat and that he did not think that it was possible for a punt to get under it as described. There was a hole two inches above the water line that had been made by a boat hook or similar object but it had been there for some time. He made the point that the certificate of registration held by the owner since April was no guarantee of safety.[17]

Boat-letting

Sometime between 1871 and 1881 Bill Moss had moved out of Waterman's Cottage and had settled on the Oxfordshire bank alongside the Freebody premises. He was living in Bridge Street, Caversham, between the Crown Hotel and the river, either just behind or beside the boathouse. His wife Selina had died but his daughter Rosie and his son Frederick were both there, as were his step-children Minnie and Frank Piper.

The shorter man in the centre in the photograph of the boathouse overleaf, and outlined against the closed door, is Bill Moss and his name is on the front of the building: 'W. Moss. Boat Builder, Boats Housed'. Above this is an essential item for the trade, the clock from which the hirings were timed and charges calculated, clearly visible to the customer so that there could be no argument. There is no mention of fishing on the sign, and no fishing boats outside, but he was still advertising himself as a fisherman as he had in 1871.[18] There are some skiffs tied up outside and a canoe alongside the shed. The building is wooden and there is a sliding door across the front.

The second photograph of the boathouse shows that Moss and Freebody had very similar stock and were running businesses immediately alongside one another. In 1881 it was still Kate Freebody, daughter of Thomas the fisherman and his wife Mary, and sister of Peter who had competed for the Watermen's Purse, who was managing the business at Willow Grotto. Unlike her neighbours Moss and Cawston, she was not a boatbuilder.

The 1881 census for Caversham gives Edward Cawston's address as Caversham Bridge and his occupation as boatbuilder. It is not clear from this information where his site was. He may have exchanged premises with Moss and have been on the island, he may have already been on the Berkshire bank as he was in 1885. He may have had two sites. In the 1880s he owned a shallop capable of carrying 30 people.[19] This was a shallow boat that could have more than one set of oars, and which was used as a ferry, a design still seen on the Thames as the Royal Barge. Although he was primarily a boatbuilder he expanded his business into boat-letting and, like quite a few boat yards of that era, he also hired out ponies for towing.[20] His advertisement, which appeared in a local paper in 1885, showed that he understood the need to reassure those new to the river and to offer attractions for all kinds of customers.[21]

Another business opened at the bridge. An Italian, Antonio Giovanni Bona, came to England in 1878. After working at Skindles in Maidenhead

---

E. CAWSTON

BOAT AND PUNT BUILDER

THAMES SIDE, CAVERSHAM RD

Respectfully informs the Clergy, Gentry And Inhabitants generally of Reading, Caversham and neighbourhood, that he has just erected a PAVILION for the better accommodation of his kind patrons.

☞ A new LANDING STAGE has also been made, so that those that are timid can with ease and comfort enter their boats with perfect safety.

Ladies and gentlemen taught the art of Rowing

Fishing punts to be let

Pleasure boats (large and small) let by the hour, day or week; experienced men when desired

Open from 6am and 9 pm Boats on hire from 6d, 9d to 1s per hour

Good Camping Ground Lemonade, Ginger Beer, Soda Water etc

The Caversham 'bus passes the buildings every hour

---

and meeting his wife there, he took over the White Hart public house and transformed the old building into an up-to-date hotel. He was there in 1881, age 29.[22]

Henry Taunt, an outdoor photographer and lover of the Thames, listed the following in 1889 in his guide to the river: 'Boats let and housed: W. Moss, Oxon shore, E. Causton, Centre Island, T. Freebody, Oxon shore, A. D. Bona Caversham Hotel; Fishermen: W. Moss, H. Knight, G. Knight, H. Rush, W. Clark.' The fishermen he named, all earning at least part of their living by this trade, were Bill Moss and Harry Rush, both well-known expert anglers, Henry and George Knight, basket-makers, and William Clark, known locally as 'Watercress Bill'. Another local fisherman, not listed here, was Jack Bright.[23]

Such was Harry Rush's fame as a fisherman that a story about him (perhaps a 'fisherman's

Bill Moss outside his premises at Caversham Bridge.

The premises of Moss and Freebody close together in the backwater behind Piper's Island.[24]

tale' he was still telling) appeared in the anglers' column of the *Berkshire Chronicle* in 1912. This suggested that a chance catch he had made in about 1880 had marked the beginning of trout fishing at Caversham Pool.

A clergyman came to Reading to fish for trout. He was directed to William Kirby who did not really know what to do but he went to Caversham Pool at the Clappers with an old jack spinner and found Harry Rush there in a punt.

Kirby made an attempt at a spin and then Harry took the rod and at the first attempt hooked a 3lb trout. The clergyman was so pleased that he offered to buy the rod, line and fish. The fishermen, according to the story, kept it quiet that this was their first attempt at trout fishing but of course Harry was using an old skill which had been generally lost, as Chalmers had said, since stocks declined and a generation of fishermen left the Thames.[25]

Endnotes

1 J Englefield *The delightful life of pleasure on the Thames and an angler's perfect sport: Before and since the fence months were legalised in 1869,* (London 1912). Darter was a councillor in the town for 45 years and mayor in 1850–52.

2 Englefield, p 7.

3 Charles Dickens (Jr), *Dickens's Dictionary of London,* 1879 quoting the fishery laws of 1867.

4 Information supplied by Michael Wheeler to whom thanks are given.

5 I Currie, M Davison and B Ogley *The Berkshire Weather Book,* (Westerham 1994), p 5.

6 Patrick R Chalmers *At the tail of the weir,* (1932 London, reprinted 1984), p 23.

7 Englefield, p 110.

8 C J Cornish *Naturalist on the Thames,* (London 1902), p 57.

9 This photograph appears by permission of Mrs Jenny Freebody.

10 BRO, DP 162/26/A Kate Freebody, allottee 1865.

11 William Moss, born 8 April 1848, son of Ellen *née* Cornish and George Montague Moss, Bargebuilder, of Stroud Green, Greenham. George Moss was the son of a bargebuilder, Thomas Moss, also of Stroud Green. Greenham has a wharf on the Kennet and Avon Canal.

12 Chalmers, p 31.

13 BRO, D EX 965/68/1–3 photograph of basket made by Mr Knight.

14 Census for Caversham 1881. The family home was in Bridge House.

15 *Berkshire Chronicle,* 12 September 1891, p 7 col 4.

16 *Lock to Lock Times,* [L TO LT] NO. 400, 30 March 1895. Mr Henry Creed was in the chair, Mr W Moss was vice chair and the Association was represented by Messrs Hurley, Butler, Mackrill, Flanagan and F Brown (Hon Sec).

17 *Reading Observer,* 8 August 1896, p 8.

18 S Read (ed) *The Thames of Henry Taunt,* (Allan Sutton, Gloucester 1989), p 100–1.

19 Census for Oxfordshire 1881, Caversham ref. 1489/80/8.

20 P Chaplin *The Thames from Source to Tideway* (Whittet Books, 1988), p 110.

21 *Reading Observer,* 13 June 1885, p 5.

22 Census for Berkshire 1881, Reading St Mary ref 102/42/28.

23 S Read, p 101.

24 RM, REDMG 1975/53/21 Moss and Freebody at Caversham Bridge.

25 *Berkshire Chronicle,* 3 May 1912.

8 Rowing, fishing and baby farming: 1880–1900

The regatta again

In April 1877 there was another attempt at establishing a local regatta. A group of supporters, led by the Mayor, W Hood, and Honorary Secretaries L A R Simpson and George Westall met at the Ship Hotel in Reading and agreed to hold an event at Caversham if a sum of £175 could be raised or guaranteed. One of the first tasks was to get permission from Alfred Paulin of Battle Farm, and occupier of the meadows alongside the course, to use those fields and to put up a stand for spectators and tents for the crews and their boats. When he agreed, provided that a policeman could be present to keep the public out of his other fields during haymaking, a subscription list was opened and in May, when £85 had been promised, a date in July was set for the regatta. The committee members wrote to the local silversmiths asking them to submit examples of cups so that prizes could be selected; they invited Frank Williams to be the umpire, and arranged for a stand to be hired, a brass band and advertising. The event took place and was repeated the following year. By 1879 it had grown: there were singers and minstrels to entertain the crowd of about 10,000, Captain Etheridge of the Thames Conservancy came to control the course and the Queen's Hotel was providing refreshments in the enclosure. Mr Cottrell, now the occupier of the meadows, asked for promises to make good any damage; the com-

mittee presented him with £5 and a silver cup, in addition to any agreed payment, to make sure that he was happy. That year there had been a sharp disagreement with George Westall of Watlington Brewery about the sale of refreshments, and he resigned from the committee in protest.[1]

In 1882 it was recorded that the regatta was doing well as an event and that it was popular with the metropolitan clubs, but its very success was increasing the amount of organisation required and, it must be assumed, the costs of running it. Mr Moss of Caversham was asked if he would provide punts for the starting point and for cutting weeds along the course. Wilkins, the Reading Rowing Club boatman, was engaged to make arrangements about watermen, and Kift asked to arrange everything to do with the police and the money-takers. By the following year the committee was wondering whether it would be better to have a stand built, and they were going to ask Mr Lewis if he would build one if they agreed to hire it for the next three years at £10 per annum. In the event they borrowed one from a sports club. Jackson's of Henley could not supply the umpire's launch, so Mr Bona was to be approached. Mr Wing, local surveyor and architect, was now on the committee.

And so it went on, dates clashing with other regattas, accounts to be audited, tenders to be obtained for printing and supplying refreshments, with expectations always increasing. Reading

Banner headline for an article in the *Lock to Lock Times* for 27 July 1889 on the Reading Amateur Regatta.

Working Men's Regatta had begun on the reach below the lock in 1877, the same year as the Reading regatta had been restarted, but it had been more successful and become an annual fixture whereas the older event was struggling. The first reference in the latter's committee minutes to a drop in subscriptions came in 1885, and by 1887 there was a determined effort to reduce costs, including the value of prizes. Bracher and Sydenham were asked what sort of medal they could produce for £2. The umpire's boat would be Clark and Company's *Thetis* at £5. The next year there was a charge of 1 shilling for entry to the enclosure after 4.30 pm and an attempt to get Mr Cottrell to reduce his charge for the meadow.

Despite all these problems behind the scenes, *Lock to Lock Times* reported the 1889 regatta with some enthusiasm and with a collection of drawings of what was described as plenty of incident:

One of the incidents at the regatta, a junior sculler upset by a girl rower 'as neat a thing as ever was seen'.

the judges' box upset in the water; a scratch crew stroked by the president of a university boat beaten by a local crew; a junior sculler upset by a girl rower 'as neat a thing as ever was seen'; scratch eights, the most amusing event of the day, 'the rowing of the crews being something altogether out of the common'. However in 1889, despite the town band and the fair to attract the paying public, there was a deficit in the accounts and the committee decided to try a special appeal; but by 1891 it had to be admitted that the regatta was not financially successful.

It was decided to approach Reading Rowing Club to see if it would be willing to take over the management and in December it was agreed 'that a meeting of the committee and subscribers be called at an early date in January to consider the advisability of continuing the regatta'.

Bill Moss: water bailiff

Moss was head water bailiff for the district and according to the *Lock to Lock Times* he was well known, and well liked, the length of the river from Folly Bridge to Teddington. He was a great smoker and 'to catch him without his favourite weed would be a clever capture indeed; in fact he is generally supposed to be liable to a heavy penalty if found without it'.[2] As local water overseer Bill Moss was called to drag the river in November

1890 when a collie dog stationed itself on the bank at the same place every day for a fortnight and howled dreadfully. Nothing was found but the incident left people speculating as to what might have happened to its master. In 1891 a boy found a parcel floating in the river at Caversham which contained the body of young male child, thought to have been in the water for about three weeks. At an inquest held at the Griffin a verdict was given of 'found drowned'.

Mrs Amelia Dyer, baby farmer and murderer

The local water bailiffs and boatmen were all alerted when in March 1896 the first of the babies murdered by the infamous baby farmer, Mrs Dyer, was picked up near the Clappers by two bargemen taking a ballast boat up-river. When two more parcels surfaced in April, each containing the body of a strangled child, a major search began. A label on one of the parcels led the police directly to Mrs Dyer, who had been living in Lower Caversham. After the fifth body was found, the search was extended to Norcot Scours because Mrs Dyer was reported to have been seen there. A story handed down says that Moss supplied the boat and boat hook for the searches at Caversham; since he was the head bailiff, this is more than likely to have been true. Newspaper reports make no specific mention of boats but they do describe policemen DC Anderson and PS James making a thorough search of the river bed below the weir with a water telescope after the latter (the *Reading Mercury* says it was PC Vince), patrolling on foot along the Dreadnought

Mrs Amelia Dyer, age 57, baby farmer, was hanged by James Billington at Newgate prison on Wednesday, 10 June 1896, for the murder of 4-month old Doris Marmon, one of the seven children found in the river.

reach in April, saw a seventh body in the river and used the telephone at East's boathouse to ring the police station.[3] It was later shown that Mrs Dyer had disposed of the bodies of the murdered children from the foot crossing of the river at the Clappers, Lower Caversham. She was suspected of murdering about 50 babies in all.

Two boatmen, one named Alfred Botting, who made the discovery of the first of the babies in the river.

The footbridge near the Clappers from which the babies were thrown.

Anglers

This is the 'after' period of James Englefield's fishing life, when there were more anglers coming to fish, pollution was increasing, and fish stocks were falling. Angling societies were now being formed as sporting and social groups with the secondary purpose of encouraging and supporting the regeneration of fish stocks. Bill Moss was founder and president of the Reading Waltonian Angling Society, whose headquarters were at the Moderation Inn near Caversham Bridge.[4] Upriver angling clubs held their own fishing competitions. In 1891 about 30 members of the Waltonians went in small boats to just above Mapledurham lock. where they held a peg-down competition and enjoyed a picnic tea.[5] This seems to have been an annual event. A peg-down competition is one where each angler has an allocated stretch of the bank from which to fish, with a peg forming a marker point from which to measure his fishing limit as set out in the club rules. In March that same year Bill said at the annual dinner that the club was in a flourishing condition.[6]

The army of anglers was now providing work for the professional fisherman like Bill Moss. He advised them, let suitable craft to them when they wanted to fish and perhaps provided equipment. His patron pulled in the fish while he, the fisherman, did the essential work of finding the right spot for him to cast his line. An account of the work of the professional of the period says that it was the custom of the Thames fisherman to arrange parties for gudgeon fishing. These professionals, who had usually inherited their occupation, knew every hole and patch of weeds in the reaches where they fished. 'The party complete, they put into the punt: chairs, fishing rods, two poles armoured with sharp iron spikes and known as rypecks, and a huge rake. The rakes were to stir up the bottom, and to dislodge aquatic insects on which gudgeon feed, as a form of ground baiting.' The rypecks secured the punt on either side in mid stream to prevent it drifting.[7]

There were still glimpses of the old style of fishing. One of Bill's patrons was Miss Simonds, daughter of the brewing family who lived at the Old Rectory, and together in August 1889 they caught about 50lb weight of fish in Mr Witheridge's water. In 1895 the Countess Wilton, with her professional assistant Bob Plummer junior, had a week's fishing in Caversham waters, her ladyship again making her headquarters at Bona's hotel.

A gudgeon fishing party.

Eel fishing

Eels rarely featured in any of the accounts of fishing club catches, perhaps because the clubs were out during the day and eels are generally nocturnal feeders. There is no close season quoted in fishing regulations for these creatures, or minimum length for taking from the water. Increasing pollution during the eighteenth century reduced the numbers drastically. The other edible catch was the crayfish, but this disappeared from the Thames in the 1880s as the result of a disease; despite the Reading and District Angling Association's efforts to restock in 1895 by introducing 5000 new specimens, it has not had a significant presence since that time. The disease was probably crayfish plague caused by a waterborne fungus.

No account of the fishing at Caversham can ignore the eel bucks above the bridge, because they appear in so many Victorian photographs. There were also bucks upstream at the Chazey Farm Fisheries, down at Patrick's Stream and at the mill. Eels are edible and the bucks were a form of commercial fishing for the food market, but eels were also caught by professional fishermen with a set line, a net, a baited basket or even by spearing. The *Boy's Own Paper* ran a series of articles on river fishing in 1884 and 85, one of which described eel catching. The author suggested to his schoolboy readers that laying multi-hooked lines baited with worms on the bed of the river overnight would be the most productive style of fishing. Other night-time methods he described were sniggling, using lines baited with animal entrails, and clodding, attracting the eel towards a piece of lead-weighted red worsted with a light. Spearing eels attracted to a light using a trident with serrated tines was also effective. Bobbing was a daylight technique using a baited needle that caught sideways in the eel's mouth.

The commercial eel bucks were conical baskets made of osier rods. They were fixed on a frame with the wide end, about 10ft in diameter, facing upstream, and they could be lowered into the water when empty and raised out again when

Wooden frames to support eel bucks at the upstream end of The Fishery islands at Chazey Farm between Tilehurst and Mapledurham.

full. There were five bucks at Caversham and at Chazey Farm. Adult eels spend most of their lives in fresh water, and can reach a length of about 3ft. When they are mature they return to the sea to spawn. The bucks were used to catch the adult fish as they migrated downstream in the autumn and early winter. What is less clear is how the fish were marketed, sold, prepared or eaten. One account says there was an eel and pie shop in Bridge Street, but there must have been other outlets for the main seasonal catch. There are reports elsewhere on the Thames of half a hundredweight being caught in one night in 1875 (and that at a time when catches had been falling for decades) and to justify catches of even approaching this size there must have been a ready market and arrangements in place to use them, especially as they had to be transported live. It is likely that London was one destination and rail the means of transport. It is evidence of the scale of change in both catch and market over time that eels were sold in mediaeval times not by weight but by numbers, with 26 eels being one stykke.[8] The young eels, or elvers migrated in the opposite direction to the adults, from the sea where they had been spawned back to fresh water. The adults died in the breeding grounds although James Englefield wrote that if it was warm in March and April and the rivers were full, both young and adult eels would leave the sea and go up the river. The elvers went up 'in myriads', with over a thousand passing a fixed point each minute, looking like a thick cable and

ESTABLISHED 1845.

→R. ✝ AYRES,←

The
Golden Fish,

Cross Street,
Reading.

WHOLESALE AND RETAIL

Fishing Rod and Tackle Manufacturer,

AND TOBACCONIST.

Walking Sticks, Fancy Pipes, Cigars, Snuffs, &c.

Mr R Ayres advertising in *Loveday's Almanack* for Reading in 1895 that he could supply fishing rods and tackle and a pipe of tobacco to complete the day's enjoyment.

within about a foot of the bank. Englefield saw this migration, which is called an 'eel fare', in both the Thames and the Kennet when he was a boy at school in Reading.[9] Elvers taken from the River Wye, about 3ins long and no thicker than string, are pressed into a block and fried, producing something like shredded wheat and tasting like whitebait, but no such information has been found about processing the Thames catches.[10] Elvers from Gloucester were so abundant that they were sold by the cart-load for manure.

Fishery protection

Henry Taunt, Oxfordshire author, photographer and mapmaker of the Thames, described the local fishing:

The river from the Roebuck [Tilehurst] is well stocked with jack, perch and chub. Barbel are to be found at the [Norcot] scours and in Caversham Pool, and gudgeon from Mapledurham Lock all along the scours in large numbers. Jacks are nearly everywhere from Tilehurst Station to Caversham Lock. And more especially in the broad near the Fishery and round the Caversham Islands. Trout are fairly plentiful and will no doubt largely increase, as the Reading Angling Associations stock the river with a large number every year, averaging in weight from 1 to 3 pounds.[11]

He said there were roach and jack from Caversham Lock to Sonning, chub under the willows and dace in the scours at Caversham Hill (now The Warren) and Sonning Oaks. There were also barbel and trout near the pumping station on the Kennet (at Blakes Lock).

The Reading and District Angling Association was formed in 1878. Its prime function was the protection of fisheries through the enforcement of the 1869 act, and a follow-up piece of legislation, the Freshwater Fisheries Bill of 1879, which banned the use of explosives in the river. Its president was Henry John Simonds, and Vice Presidents included Messrs Blagrave, Blandy, Benyon, Palmer and Sutton. It had many subscribers among the local gentry and trade, for example Berry, Crawshay, Simonds, Sutton, Thoyts, Joseph Lawes from the Caversham Mill and Mr Yard,

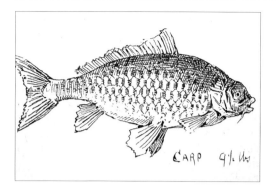

CARP 9½ lbs

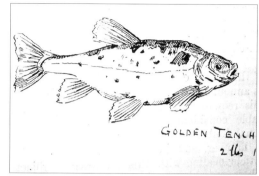

GOLDEN TENCH 2 lbs

fishing tackle manufacturer. In its early years it concentrated on restocking, with the construction of a trout nursery at Caversham, and reference was made in its 1879 report to 30,000 fry of various species of trout and salmon. The trout stew (breeding ground) was closed in 1883 and the fish returned to the river. The Association appointed bailiffs among local professional fishermen on condition that they agreed to a uniform charge when employed as fishermen of seven shillings a day to include punt and attendance, bait to be paid for and the charge for live bait not to exceed 6d per dozen. Local appointments were: Henry Holdway (Reading); Henry Knight and Robert Mills (Caversham); Frederick Knight and Richard Kelly (Caversham and Blake's Lock-keepers). By 1882 the names of William Moss, George Knight and William Clark had been added to the list.[12]

The local paper said 'Reading's [angling club] greatly improved fishing in that district during the first five years of its existence and in fact was said to have kept it alive there'. Its restocking of the river was a success and the Kennet trout that had been introduced were doing well. The Association was presented with some golden carp and secured some 2lb bream, many in spawn, from Huntingdon. The Loddon Fishery (the River Loddon below Twyford and St Patrick's Stream), rented by Reading and Henley Associations, had been improved by the introduction of 200 yearling and two-year trout and by 5000 grayling fry.[13] Members could fish no more than once a week and then only with one rod. In 1890 the Association was said to have been responsible for the improvement of that portion of the

Thames between Goring Lock and Shiplake.[14] The *Berkshire Chronicle* reported the club's continued contribution to the maintenance of fish stocks between 1891 and 1892. It had purchased 50 large trout, heavy in spawn, from Mr Davis of High Wycombe, 28 pike of 3–5lb, 12 dozen bronze carp and quantities of perch, tench and rudd. The manager of the waterworks contributed 2000 Kennet perch to the stock.[15] It is a comment on the quality of the water in the bathing place that its annual netting, along with ditches and the reservoir in Bath Road, regularly restored quantities of fish to the river and in 1892 the haul had been 12 trout, 3 dozen dace, 24 bronze carp, 10 sizable perch and thousands of small perch, roach and chubb.[16]

Henry Taunt also said that the largest trout ever taken from the river was captured in the pool of County Lock on the Kennet by a Reading fisherman and presented to the Queen. It weighed nearly 17lb. 'A capital cast was taken of the fish and it is preserved in the smoking room of the Great Western Hotel'.[17] Mr Barnett, fishing at the lower end of Fry's Island landed a pike of 18½lb.[18] Bill Moss' s record pike of 28lb was beaten in 1916 by one of 30lb caught at Caversham by his son-in-law, Peter Smith. In 1891 Edward Sheppard, a professional fisherman on the next reach, trapped two otters and was with a client while he caught a 12lb trout.[19] Further evidence of the popularity of fishing is shown by the *Berkshire Chronicle's* willingness, in a paper covering the whole county and including some national news, to give several column-inches each week to angling. Bill's presidency of the Reading Waltonian Club and his role as head water bailiff for the area are indica-

The army of bank anglers.

tions that he was personally concerned with the role adopted by the angling clubs to improve the river and to maintain angling standards during this phase of expansion and increasing popularity. By 1880 there were 30,000 Londoners who came annually as members of angling clubs to the Thames from Paddington to take advantage of cheap day tickets offered to their clubs. These were mainly bank fishers who came with rods, stool, bait and food and so contributed nothing to the local economy.

As head water bailiff Bill Moss would have been responsible to the Thames Conservators for seeing that all their requirements and fishing regulations were complied with. Night fishing and trailing lines from the sterns of boats became illegal, and by 1875 the practice of netting had been abolished. Water bailiffs looked out for 'snatching' of fish by poachers using multiple unbaited hooks which would catch in the flesh of the back or body of the fish. Convictions were brought against four notorious poachers illegally netting on the Kennet in 1882 and each was fined 40 shillings with 17s 5d costs but all suffered instead the alternative of one month's imprisonment and hard labour. In 1888 a case was brought to the Caversham bench under a byelaw, which stated that all coarse fish taken in the close season must be returned to the river forthwith. The son-in-law of the proprietor of the Griffin public house, who also rented the eel bucks, had been told by Moss to put back the fish he had caught but he did not do so quickly enough to prevent the death of several roach and perch. He was fined 6s 6d to impress on him the meaning of 'forthwith'.[20] At the AGM of Reading and District Angling Association in 1889 it was said that poaching had now nearly died out, thanks to the efforts of the officials.

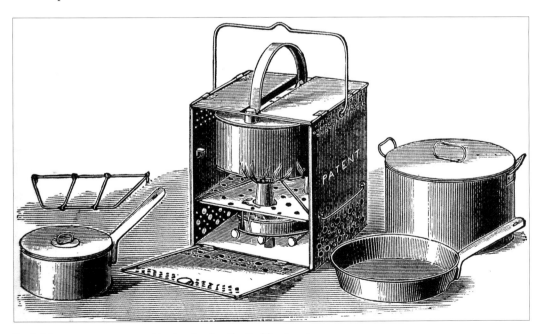

Bank fishermen came prepared to stay the day: the Boddington stove.

By 1875 steam launches were common enough to be a nuisance, their wash upsetting fishing punts, displacing spawn to be eaten by other fish and stranding spawn and small fry on the bank. Otters too represented a danger to fish and rewards of £1 were offered for their capture. A river keeper to the Reading and District Angling Association captured his nineteenth specimen in 1896. Twenty years later they were rare. Water bailiffs continued to check for poaching and the taking of undersized fish. The Thames was regularly restocked with salmon and trout. Bailiffs for the Reading and District Angling Association in 1891 had successfully used old wicker hampers given to them by Messrs Suttons and Sons, seedsmen, to protect perch spawn during hatching, the river stock having been reduced by an epidemic three years before.[21] Riparian owners claimed fishing rights to establish theoretical ownership, not to prevent public fishing if permission was sought. However Mr Blount, owner of Mapledurham House near Caversham, claimed quite correctly that riparian rights included ownership of the bed of the river to the centre line and on the strength of this claim he denied the right of public fishery.[22] Blount must have continued to claim his rights because Chalmers in 1932 said that Whitchurch and Mapledurham Weirs were the only two private fisheries still on the Thames.[23]

Endnotes

1   BRO, D/EX 1192/1, Minute book of Regatta Committee 1877–91.

2   P Burstall *The Golden Age of the Thames* (David and Charles, 1981), p 135.

3   *Berkshire Chronicle* Reports on the findings and the inquests, evidence against Mrs Dyer, 4 April and 11 April 1896 p 5; *Reading Mercury* 11 and 18 April and 2 May 1896 p 2; RM, REDMG 1987/21/1, the two boatmen who found the babies.

4   The headquarters moved to the Duke of Edinburgh public house at the town end of Caversham Road during 1893 while the Moderation was being renovated.

5   Burstall, p 188–191.

6   *Berkshire Chronicle* 4 April 1891, p 5 col 6, Report of Waltonian Angling Club annual dinner, President W Moss, Vice President A C Butler, Hon Secs Mr Howes and Mr Brown. The Treasurer was W Sergeant.

7   Fred Taylor 'Thames Angling' *The Thames Book: Navigator Directory Guide* (George Godwin Ltd, 1963), p 113.

8   D C Wilson *The making of the middle Thames* (Bourne End, 1977), p 49.

9   J Englefield *The delightful life of pleasure on the Thames and an angler's perfect sport: Before and since the fence months were legalised in 1869* (London, 1912), p 40.

10 This information came from a BBC Radio 4 programme, broadcast on 5 October 2003 and introduced by Matthew Parris, called 'Moving on: part 1, the eel'.

11 S Read (ed) *The Thames of Henry Taunt* (Allan Sutton, 1989), p 99, 103.

12 RLSL, R/QK Annual reports Reading and District Angling Association 1878–83.

13 *Lock to Lock Times* [*LTLT*] no 38 vol II, 23 Feb 1889, p 91. [Note that the journal uses this style, not the modern usage of volume number followed by issue number. In volume I each issue has its own page numbering system but in volume II both the issue and the page numbering continues without a break from volume I].

14 Charles Dickens *Dictionary of the Thames* (1890), *LTLT* no 82 vol III, 21 Dec 1889 p 336.

15 *LTLT* no 92, vol IV, p 131.

16 *Berkshire Chronicle* 27 Feb 1892 'AGM of Reading and District Angling Association'.

17 Read, p 99, 103.

18 *LTLT* no 4 vol I, 30 June 1888, p 5.

19 *Berkshire Chronicle* 30 May 1891, p 5, col 5.

20 *LTLT* no 2 vol I, 9 June 1888, p 8.

21 *Berkshire Chronicle* 27 February 1892 AGM of Reading and District Angling Association.

22 *LTLT* 'A new history of the Thames, part XVI' no 31 vol II, 3 Jan 1889, p 6.

23 Patrick R Chalmers *At the tail of the weir* (London 1932, reprinted 1984), p 32.

9 Expansion of the pleasure boat businesses: 1880–1890

Time off from work

There were in Reading and Caversham unprecedented numbers of people with regular wages and secure jobs on the railway, in factories, retail, banks and in service areas with money to spend and time in which to spend it. Many local people chose to spend their leisure on or by the river and increasingly they formed groups or joined clubs to develop a particular interest, sometimes clubs attached to their place of work, such as Suttons' Angling Club or Huntley & Palmer's football teams. The value placed on leisure time by workers brought about the introduction of Bank Holiday Monday in 1871 and the adoption in 1888 by Reading traders of the practice of early closing (4pm, later changed to 2pm) on Wednesdays, and it was reported that the boat proprietors were pleased by the increase in their trade as a result of this change.[1] Londoners were offered cheap railway tickets to get to riverside towns like Reading to swim, fish, walk or to hire a boat. Steam power had enabled large passenger boats to be built for their river trips. People could travel alone, with friends or family or in larger groups from the factory, workplace or club to take advantage of the combined rail and river tickets. Others became boat owners and of course some of their boats too were steam powered. This demand brought about not only an expansion of businesses to build and houseboats and provide craft for hire but alongside this a need to manage the river and banks and to regulate the increased traffic and use.

Competition

There was sufficient diversity offered by the businesses between the bridge and the lock to ensure that they were not all competing for the same sector of the market and the smaller companies, where competition was tightest, benefited

Antonio Bona, hotelier and boat proprietor.[2]

READING
(ON-THAMES).

CAVERSHAM HOTEL,

Beautifully situated on the Thames.
VERY COMFORTABLE.   FAMED FOR CUISINE & WINES.
Also Luncheons, Picnic Parties, &c.
CUSTOMERS WILL FIND EVERY FACILITY for BOATING.
LARGEST STEAM LAUNCHES AND OTHERS.
With Boats of every description for Hire and built to order.

A. G. BONA, Proprietor.

indirectly from the publicity and interest in the river generated by the market leaders, East (of whom more later) and Bona, and by Salters' fleet of steamers.

Mr Bona at Caversham Bridge had the White Hart Hotel, a coffee room, and a boatbuilding and hiring business. He added a large dining room seating 160, so fitted that it could be used for storing boats when not in use. His steam launch, the *Fashion*, was captained by J Keel, a Caversham angler with his own boathouse at Tilehurst. The boat trips were often combined with a meal and, if people came from a distance, the outward trip could be by river and the return journey made from one of the upstream railway stations. A group of 120 on a Masonic outing in 1888 started from the White Hart in four boats, including the *Fashion*, stopped for a meal in a marquee on the lawn at the Roebuck at Tilehurst, and continued to Streatley, from where some went home by train, the others going back to Caversham in the boats.[3] The *Fashion* was booked for the 1891 university boat race and was used for private and group hire by the day or half day but Bona reduced his prices in September to extend the season as far as possible. Among his customers around that time were: the Reading Police, the Girls Friendly Society, the staff of Jacksons store, Reading Sauce

A family outing in a steam launch.

Thomas and Mary Ann (née Bryant) Freebody who came to Caversham from Newbury.[9]

Manufactory, Messrs Lewis, builders, of Reading, the Church of England Temperance Society, the young ladies from Miss Knighton's school in Caversham (the boys went separately with Mr Frank Knighton in the *Lady Brassey*.[4]), and Bona's own workforce whom he entertained with his mesmeric and magnetic performances.

Bona also owned *La Mode* and *Chic* which were used for the same mix of private and group hire: officials checking the navigable state of the Kennet, the Cambridge crew for its coaches, Reading Ironmongers and the Reading Codgers Social Club. *La Mode* was captained by H Bulfer, the firm's longest serving employee. Bona launched the *Caversham* in 1890, a steam launch built by his own staff (foreman J Taylor), fitted with machinery by Clarke & Co of Stroud; it was between *La Mode* and *Chic* in size, but with coloured glass and movable seats in the 'omnibus pattern'.[5]

Ernest Cawston, also at Caversham Bridge, with two more sons added to the ten children he had already, was a boat and steam launch builder. His daughter Ada was his clerk. He was a boatbuilder by training who also hired out launches and in this one sector he was competing with

Bona. So direct was the competition that there are stories of the two companies patrolling the area, each with a board advertising their services and directing potential customers to their own landing stage. Cawston began using the *Starlight* in 1890 for trips but gave it up because the demand for more profitable private hire work was greater. The following year he launched the *Mystery* which, like Bona's *Fashion*, was fitted out by Clarke's of Stroud. Cawston built specialist boats to order, for example a cutter called *Water Queen* for Messrs Botly, and he also had his own fleet of small boats for hire with which he was in competition with Moss and Freebody. Cawston's aviary of prize-winning canaries and linnets were an attraction for his customers.

At census date in 1891 Bill Moss, now 42, was still living at the foot of Caversham Bridge and described as a boat proprietor. His stepchildren, Minnie and Frank Piper, had left home but his own children Rose and Frederick were there. The Moss and Freebody businesses were in the narrow backwater behind Piper's Island and these two were probably in closer competition than any of the others. Kate Freebody had died in 1888, a sin-

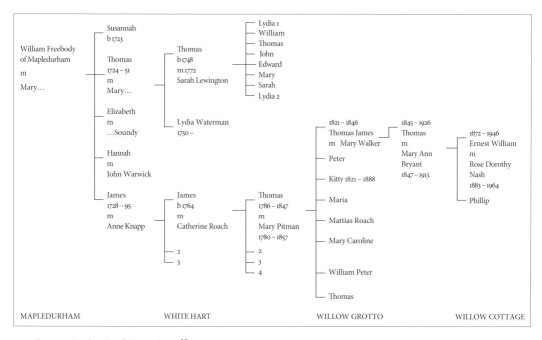

Family tree: Freebody of Caversham.[10]

gle woman aged 69.[6] The business at Caversham then passed to her nephew Thomas, son of an older brother who died young. Thomas was at the time running a boat-letting business, hiring out punts and skiffs at West Mills Wharf just above Newbury Lock on the Kennet and Avon. From this point local people could go upstream on the canal or on the old River Kennet to Benham Park.[7] Thomas had been in the Newbury area for some time: his son Philip was born at Aldermaston in 1869, less than 10 miles away. In 1881 Thomas and his wife Mary Ann (née Bryant) were at Newtown, Newbury, but by 1891 the couple were at Willow Cottage near Caversham Bridge with their sons Philip and Ernest.[8] The business moved ahead quickly and it was reported in 1891 that Tom Freebody had his first steam launch, the *Progress*, and he planned a second the following year.

Few people at this date had had the opportunity to learn to swim yet this did not stop them going on the river in small boats. When accidents happened it was the professional watermen and boatmen who, almost as part of their job, came to the rescue. Here it is one of the Freebody family who saved a life.

An accident which might have had a fatal termination happened at Caversham Bridge on Sunday last, caused entirely by the carelessness of some river 'Arrys. A small boat containing two ladies and two gentlemen was just putting out from Freebody's landing stage on the Oxfordshire side of the river when it was run into by a four-oar coming down stream. The river at this spot is narrow, deep and winding and always thickly studded with boats leaving or returning to the landing stages of Moss or Freebody and is strictly speaking not a usual course for traffic, except to the two pontoons mentioned. The four-oar containing six people was propelled at almost

A camping scene in the 1890s from *Lock to Lock Times*.

racing speed … the occupants of the small boat, none of whom could swim, were thrown into the water. Three managed to cling to the four-oar but the last was sinking for the last time when he was rescued by young Freebody and brought in a prostrate state to land. The crew who did the damage made no effort to render assistance although called upon by those on shore … they went on their way in the same reckless manner as before.[11]

Mr Talbot, bargebuilder and coal merchant, offered an island below Caversham Bridge as a camping ground.[12] Bill Moss too offered camping facilities although this might just mean moorings and landing rights for those in camping boats. G W Kimble at The Crown Hotel was offering the best accommodation for tourists and anglers. Mr White hired out his steam launch the *Lady Brassey* for group outings, one of which was for

The term 'Arry' was coined by the editor of *Lock to Lock Times* to represent a young man out to impress, who would later be conspicuous in the bar.

the assistants at Wellsteeds. The houseboat the *Queen of the Thames* that had belonged to John Fry was moored just above Caversham Bridge and was used as a meeting place for the Thames and Kennet Sailing Club, which was using the stretch above the bridge for its races rather than the Sonning reach.[13] Frank Attwells, the lessee of the Royal County Theatre in Reading, had just built a boathouse with living rooms and a veranda and with accommodation for his steam launch the *Coryphane* on the island (View Island) just

Winter fashion on the river.

East built dressing rooms so that ladies and gentlemen could change into their boating clothes before they took to the water.

above Caversham Lock and opposite the town swimming baths.[14]

The boats the local firms hired out were built in-house and both Moss and Freebody would have taken commissions to keep staff employed and to generate income during the winter months. 'Mr E W Tabor, auctioneer of Reading and Caversham is honorary secretary [of the new Minima Sailing Club at Reading]. He has recently had built a new sailer on the latest principles by Moss of Caversham.'[15] Freebody allowed use of his landing stage during a freeze in 1891 when hundreds of skaters and sledges were on the ice till late, illuminated by torches and lanterns, and this event too may have brought in some money. There are many reports in the *Lock to Lock Times* of Moss's fishing catches in winter months both as a Waltonian and when he took his private patrons out on the water, and this too generated winter income for him.[16] He worked as far upstream as the Whitchurch to Mapledurham reach and occasionally went up as far as Oxford.

Arthur East's new boathouse at Caversham Lock.

Decorated boats increasing the pleasure of an evening on the water.

Samuel Whiting Gyngell.[17]

Mr Spooner of Acton was taken by Bill to private water on the Kennet and he landed a 16lb jack. He took another client to the Loddon at Arborfield in January 1892 and again they were successful in catching a jack.

A H East had been an oarsman and a member of Isleworth Rowing Club. His nephew W G East was a champion sculler. Arthur East already had a boathouse at Kennet Mouth. The business he established above the lock on the Reading side was in a different league to those at Caversham Bridge. He was an enterprising boatbuilder and a good businessman who put Bona, the other real entrepreneur, into second place. East had exported two four-oars to the Demerara Rowing Club in 1883 and completed another two for the same customer in 1889.[18] He had orders for 19 double scullers for the Corporation of Southport and four for Liège Rowing Club, for a mahogany skiff for the Marquis of Downshire and small boats for the ornamental lake in Chislehurst of the Empress Eugenie. In 1892 he built a large horse-ferry for Captain Hargreaves of Wraysbury to take his hunters across the Thames.

Arthur East's new premises were in a prime position to capture the custom of those coming from the town centre and, most importantly, from the station. Everything recorded about his new business suggests that he targeted the well-to-do customer and that he realised that they would pay for extra facilities if he created the right atmosphere. He housed, repaired and varnished 'gentlemen's boats'. He had steam launches for hire and provided both regular and casual customers

with waiting and dressing rooms so that they could change from travelling to boating clothes before they went on the water. There were tennis courts so that patrons, among whom were a party of officers from Aldershot, could amuse themselves while they waited for their boat or could round off the day with a game. He had plans to apply for a refreshment licence, to add a bowling green and to rent out villas near the boathouse. His new boathouse, opened in 1890, (architect J H Goodman, Town Hall Chambers, builder F Hawley of Reading) was a very substantial three-storey brick building with a balcony at the front and a viewing area on the roof. He created a club atmosphere and Reading Swimming Club had its headquarters there, as did the GWR Paddington Clerks Boating and Angling Club. In the picture on the previous page a party of customers is arriving by carriage, there are more than twenty boats on the front ready to be launched and a steam launch is just coming alongside to pick up a group from the Society of Librarians to take them to Dorchester for the day.

Among East's best-remembered schemes were his evening riverside concerts. These were ambitious events of which the first was a Venetian Fête. The boathouse grounds were illuminated with lanterns, so extending business into a part of the day which would normally have been quiet. There were crowds of people on the balconies and seats in front of East's and the nearby Adams & Gyngell's boathouses, and on the river banks, to listen to the concert and to watch the procession of illuminated and decorated skiffs, punts and sailing boats set out from the boathouse. They went up one side of Fry's Island and back on the other, and were then judged by the mayor, Mr Dodd. In 1891 the band of the Sandhurst Military College played, and this was followed by an entertainment of races and water polo by Reading Swimming Club and a display of fireworks by Pains.[19] That year East (seeing a business opportunity) decided, for the comfort of his patrons, to enclose the area of his boathouse and to charge for entry. Adams & Gyngell and Moss had their boathouses illuminated too and must have benefited from the interest generated by the event. Of course these companies, like all boat businesses, were heavily dependent on the weather and the poor conditions in September that year caused Adam's and East's to cut short their concert programmes. However East made the best of the situation by offering moonlight trips on the *Countess* with music on board.[20]

Adams & Gyngell set up in business in about 1891 but their site is not marked on any map or defined by any photograph. Entries in directories are not helpful. The name 'Clappers Boat-house' indicates that it was near the weir. The house on View Island, built by Frank Attwells in 1889, was available during the period 1891–1896 when Adams & Gyngell were trading and its style was in keeping with contemporary descriptions of their boathouse. In the absence of any other property in the area that fits the bill, it is now suggested that the partnership traded from the building on View Island.[21]

One of the partners was Samuel Whiting Gyngell of Watlington Street, formerly a seedsman's assistant at Suttons Seeds, but described as a boatbuilder at his marriage in 1894 to Flora or Florence Adams. Flora's father, Benjamin, of de Beauvoir Road, Reading, was in 1891 a boatbuilder and water and gas fitter. Thus it appears that between them Samuel and Benjamin had building and engine installation skills. Flora took an active interest in the business and improved the look of the hire boats by embroidering cushions for them. The boathouse was built in a similar balconied style to that of East's and the business

The Clappers and the Adams and Gyngell's boathouse on View Island.[24]

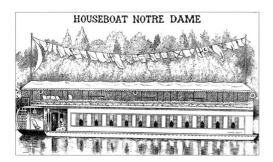

HOUSEBOAT NOTRE DAME

A houseboat was a place for the fashionable to be seen and to entertain.

CHARLES J. TALBOT

ALGOA WHARF READING

Bargebuilder

Houseboats, punts, landing stages,
pontoons, rafts, etc.

ESTABLISHED 1870

was in a position to pick up local customers and any overspill of business from its neighbour. Among Gyngell's boatbuilding orders were three boats for the Duke of Connaught.[22] They ran a steam launch called *La Mode* which may previously have been Bona's boat of that name. The partners apparently aimed at a similar market to East, although perhaps not quite the same 'officer class' of patron. Their riverside concert had only the Reading Professional Town Band. The *Lock to Lock Times* said in 1891, rather dismissively, that these premises, like East's, were patronised by the lady novelette reader, the lover, the lounger, the sightseer and the nursemaid and her charges.[23] Both companies issued illustrated calendars or almanacs to keep their names in front of their customers.

One of the people in business at Caversham Bridge was Charles Talbot at Algoa Wharf, Caversham Road, a boatbuilder, primarily a bargebuilder, who also offered houseboats, punts, landing stages, pontoons and rafts and was therefore not in direct competition with any of the other companies nearby. The buyers for houseboats would have been the fashionable people who gathered in the summer at Henley, Maidenhead or further downstream at Windsor or Richmond. The boats were places in which to be seen and to entertain, particularly at Henley Regatta where there was strong competition for mooring spaces on the course. Talbot may have been building for Reading people (he launched two hulls in 1891 for houseboat construction) but the riverside terrain was not stylish enough for

them to use their boats on that reach. His brother, George, was at Tudor Wharf in 1895 and making plans and having specifications drawn up for new offices there.[25]

Caversham Bridge

The arrival of gas in Caversham was indirectly responsible for an improvement in the bridge which had been built in 1869. It was

> … by no means a thing of beauty at its best but latterly the broken-backed structure has worn a most neglected appearance. The Reading Gas Company have recently hung a huge main on the upside of the bridge and this appears to have aroused the custodians as a contract is out for giving the ironwork a good coat of paint, to which it has been a stranger for the last 10 years.

The reporter also asked 'Why is it that the hoarding abominations flourish in this locality more than anywhere else on the river? … to place them on small islands and on the banks of the river is an absolute desecration which excites the indignation of all who love the Thames'.[26] Some of the hoardings may have carried advertisements for theatre productions. Frank Attwells and his successor as proprietor of the Reading County Theatre, Henry Dundas, were both boating men, Bona's niece Miss Custance appeared there and Dundas was said to have been 'roused to indignation' when some riverside residents objected to theatre posters. Some of the bill boards, the biggest being Cawston's, and the gas main can be seen in the photograph opposite. The small boats here

Caversham Bridge from Bona's boathouse on the upstream side showing some of the offending bill boards below it and the gas main hanging from it.

are part of Bona's fleet and among them is a treble skiff or randan with three sets of oars, an arrangement which took its name from an earlier style of boat with three oarsmen and four oars.[27]

Floods in Caversham

The river flooded badly in October 1891. The Caversham reach fared better than most because of the new weir and because of the good management of the lock-keeper, Mr Knight. As in previous years the low-lying land between the bridge and the mill was inundated, the higher bank on the Berkshire side coming off better. Upstream the towpath and meadow land were under water. The kitchens in the hotel had 18 inches of water and the road between Caversham and Lower Caversham had 12 inches. Foot passengers were charged 2d for a cart ride through the flooding. Bona, riding along the towpath one day, saw the steam launch *Jack-in-the-Box*, owned by Henry Dundas, adrift in the heavy current and he was able to let the lock-keeper know in time for him to drop the sluices and slow the stream enough to save the boat. At this time the GWR were widening the railway tracks above and below Caversham and, because of the high water levels, were not able to use the towpath to get supplies of materials to the sites. Bona hired out *Fashion* to the company as a carrier and as a tug for the ballast boats on the Sonning reach from October into January so that work could continue. In about March 1892 Bona was injured when he collided with a trap while he was out with the Royal Buckhounds. In June he had another accident and once again there was a steam launch in the story. He was driving his dog-cart to Norcot Scours and he stopped to cool the horse's feet in what he thought was about a foot of water. Unfortunately, dredging had deepened the shallows to fifteen feet and one wheel went over the edge, to be followed by the cart, horse and driver. Bona and the horse got themselves out and the cart was pulled out by the steam launch *Gnome*.[28]

While the problems at Caversham may not have been as bad as in some places, The Caversham Local Board received a deputation representing 485 residents on the subject of these floods because there were now more houses in Lower Caversham than before and properties had been damaged. The deputation made the point that five years earlier work at the weir had increased the flow of the river but corresponding work at

Floods in Caversham Road in November 1882.

Sonning had not taken place so that water backed up and was at a higher level between Caversham and Sonning than before. The residents believed that the Thames Conservators could do something at Sonning and requested that the Board would bring pressure to bear. The deputation further said that the greater part of the damage to Caversham was caused by the raising of the land on the Reading side at Mr Lewis's works.[29] The Board wrote to the Conservators and their letter was acknowledged and read at a later meeting. The Conservators then brought a complaint about the flooding to the Board and the matter was reported in the local press in May 1892. The extent of flooding in Caversham Road had attracted the attention of the national press in 1882 and a dramatic picture had appeared in the *Illustrated London News* in November.

Caversham had substantial drainage problems and the principal method of drainage at that time was to cesspools. The attention of the Thames Conservancy had been brought to the issue of pollution of the Thames from these cesspools when they were covered with water during periods of flooding. The Board replied that it was unaware of the problem.

The ferry and the ferryman's cottage as drawn by the artist from *Lock to Lock Times* in 1889 for an article about Reading and Caversham.

The Kennet ferry

In 1889 there was a ferry and a ferryman's house at Kennet Mouth as the contemporary drawing shows, and the ferry took people and goods across the Kennet or across the Thames to Lower Caversham.[30] The ferryman in 1888 was Richard Humphreys. Since there was no other way of crossing the Kennet, other than Brunel's brick bridge carrying the railway, the ferry must have taken the barge horses across so that they could continue along the towpath up or down the Thames. When the brick bridge was widened in 1891 to take two more railway tracks into Reading, a footbridge was built alongside. Its curved shape gave it the name Horseshoe Bridge.

The plaque on the brick bridge says that both structures are now listed and that the smaller was built to allow horses towing barges along the Thames to cross the tributary and to continue to follow the towpath on the other side. However there can have been very few, if any, horse-drawn barges in 1891 and certainly not enough to justify building a bridge for them, except only to maintain an established right-of-way across the river mouth for a towed vessel coming along the Thames. In practice the bridge was for cyclists and pedestrians.

Endnotes

1 *Lock to Lock Times* [*LTLT*] no 4 vol I, 30 June 1888, p 9.

2 *LTLT* 3 June 1899, p 10.

3 *Reading Observer*, 21 July 1888.

4 The *Lady Brassey* was owned by Mr J H White of Queens Road Caversham who objected in *Lock to Lock Times* no 2 vol I, October 1888, p 10 to comments in the journal on complaints about the speed of his steam launch.

5 *LTLT* no 153 vol V, 25 April 1891, p 741.

6 BRO, R/JQ/6/31/6 Coroner's inquisition 3/1/88. Kate's age at the previous census had been given as 62 and this was consistent with other census returns. However the coroner's report on her death says she died of natural causes aged 77.

7 The site was the subject of a planning application in about 1998 for redevelopment and provoked local comment on the loss of the old corrugated iron shed, Freebody's old boathouse. The Freebody family was not on this site at the time of the 1881 census.

8 The birth place of Ernest varies with the census and is either Greenham or Alderbridge Berks.

9 Photographs of Thomas and Mary Freebody provided by Mrs Jenny Freebody.

10 Tree compiled from parish registers and from information provided by Mrs Jenny Freebody and her family, to whom thanks are given.

11 *LTLT* no 187 vol V, 12 December 1891, p 3; no 6 vol I, 14 July 1888, p 9.

12 *LTLT* no 3 vol I, 23 June 1888, p 10.

13 This boat is not to be confused with the later steamer of the same name. This one was built by Mr Vokins and was sold the following year, when the sailing club ceased to exist, to Mr Woodhouse of Maidenhead. The later boat was built in the twentieth century by Maynards of Reading and Windsor. LTLT no 52 vol II, 1 June 1889 p 311.

14 *LTLT* no 49 vol II, 11 May 1889, p 264.

15 *LTLT* no 149 vol V, 28 March 1891, p 680.

16 In Nov 1891 he took two jacks of 5 and 6lb one day, three good ones another, in December two jacks of 4lb and a chubb of over 3lb, in January 1892 12lb of roach and a small jack. Mr Dolton of the Waltonians took 34lb of roach in a day in November. Mr Hyde, also of the Waltonians, and Mr Kersey were particularly successful and Mr Fisher was 'daily to be seen muffled in a huge ulster seated in his punt just above Fry's island'. The spelling of 'chubb' was current at the time although it later became 'chub'.

17 This photograph was supplied by Roy Gyngell.

18 *LTLT* no 31 vol II, 5 January 1889, p 4. There is a quotation from the *Demerara Daily Chronicle* in the item which said the first two boats were 'creditable specimens of workmanship and half as light again as any boat ever rowed in over there. They were much admired by a large and fashionable company who witnessed the launching of them'.

19 *LTLT* no 124 vol V, 4 October 1890, p 251–2. One of Mr East's best known launches was the *Countess*, 'a commodious steam launch to let for large or small parties'. Another of his boats was the *Derelict*, which he sold to Mr Bright of Elgar Road and which was subsequently renamed *Titbits*. This may have been the boat which Harry Isaacs later owned.

20 *Berkshire Chronicle* 1 August 1891, p 5 col 4.

21 Frank Attwells died in 1892 during his year as Mayor of Reading.

22 Thanks are due to Mr Roy Gyngell, grandson of Samuel and Flora, for this information about Flora and about the building orders.

23 P Burstall *The Golden Age of the Thames* (David and Charles, 1981), p 135, quoting *Lock to Lock Times*.

24 Oxfordshire County Council Photographic Archive, (ref ht 1881) 'The Clappers'.

25 BRO, D/EX 1468/1 Papers of William Wing architect and surveyor: accounts 1882–99.

26 *LTLT* no 177 vol V new series, 3 October 1891, p 2. The repainting was complete by July 1892 at which time the bridge was decorated with chinese lanterns for the Reading Amateur Regatta.

27 Oxfordshire County Council Photographic Archive, (ref d 2301 70a) 'Caversham Bridge from Bona's boathouse'.

28 *LTLT* no 183, vol V new series, 14 November 1891, p 3; no 194 vol V, 30 January 1892, p 3; no 195 vol V, 3 April 1982, p 2; no 214 vol V, 18 June 1892, p 2.

29 *Berkshire Chronicle* 9 January 1892, p 7.

30 *LTLT* 12 Jan 1889, p 19.

10 Rowing and regattas: 1870–1890

Time for sport

When people had regular time off from work in the late 1800s they turned to club and group activities as ways of spending their leisure time. There was a rise in the popularity of team games and competitive sport. Many of the clubs were formed by employees of the town's factories and businesses and may have been subsidised by their employers, and all of them had a social element that brought in families and friends. Swimming, water polo, sculling, horse racing, cycling, cricket and football all took place on or from the river banks between Caversham Bridge and the weir and at King's Meadow. The majority of club and team members were men but the 'New Woman' had arrived and she was not left out of the activities.

Reading Rowing Club

Reading Rowing Club was established in 1867. It was initially based at the Griffin public house near St Peter's Church, and A Berry, A Hurley and G Westall were prominent and active members. The Reading and Caversham Regatta in 1870 was run by the club and Mrs H J Simonds presented cups and goblets on the lawn of her house just along the road from the Griffin, and these were full of champagne from Mr Simonds's cellars. In the evening the bells of St Peter's were heard as the Reading Society of Change Ringers rang changes conducted by M W Newell. In 1880 the club moved to a piece of open meadow land on the Berkshire bank opposite Fry's Island and built a boathouse and dressing room on it. The plot, which later became George Lewis's timber yard, adjoined the land that was later to become Bill Moss's boathouse. 'It is difficult for strangers to realise that the spot was then quite in the middle of the open meadows, but building operations (on that bank) were carried on with such rapidity that in 1893 the club was practically compelled to make fresh arrangements'.[1] That year the rowing club moved across the river to

A single sculler on the Thames photographed for *Lock to Lock Times.*

a plot running the full width of Fry's Island, so giving it two river frontages. Of course the club members had to start again to build a club house and boathouse and it was reported in April 1894 that it had been

> ... quite a sight at Reading Rowing club boathouse last Saturday when some eight or ten members, stripped out in true navvy-style with pick and shovel and the veritable weed, were busily employed in removing ballast and a mound from the water's edge for the purpose of making a foundation for some grass slopes. The Hon Secretary Mr Lovegrove was the ganger-in-charge with F A East as deputy.[2]

The club had a landing stage built on the Oxfordshire side of the island in 1895 by 'Mr Fred Talbot the well-known river contractor of Caversham'.[3] Fred was one of the sons of Richard Talbot of the wharf at Caversham Bridge. The same year the club had two boats made for them by Adams & Gyngell.

The members competed against one another in sculls, double sculls, pairs and fours in an annual competition and in 1895 these events were rowed as a club regatta. It was a measure of the level of achievement of the club that the *Lock to Lock Times* ran an article in its editions of 1 and 8 August 1896 about the club, reviewing its achievements over the previous twenty years. One of these was in 1871 when the Reading crew of A Hurley, E Lyne, F Wilkins, G Westall (stroke) and C Lucas (cox) won both the Town Cups at Henley and Marlow Regattas. (Oarsmen were, by the 1870s, learning new techniques as fixed seats were replaced with sliding ones, making for faster times in competitions.[4]) The next high points were in 1881 and 82 when the club was strong enough to be able to enter two fours and an eight at Henley Regatta, winning the Town Cup the first year (another source says they won it three years running[5]) and coming second in the Thames Challenge Cup the following year. The four that rowed in the Wyfold was said to be the best the crew that the club had ever had: H G Lovegrove (bow), L Castle, E E Cottrell, W H B Lawes (stroke). The coach was S Biggs but on

Reading Rowing Club building on Fry's Island, from a photograph taken in 1896 for *Lock to Lock Times*. This is probably the earliest surviving picture of the club house.

occasions assisted by W Blandy, an Oxford Blue in 1894. At the time of the article the captain was F A East and the club had fours and an eight in training for Reading Regatta the following week.

The New Woman

An interesting point about the day's racing at the club regatta in 1895 was that the coxes in the double sculls were women: Miss Cundell, Miss Shakel, Miss Watson, Mrs Hart, Miss Archer and Miss G Williams. Although they were named in the results of the heats, their names were left out of the list of the names of finalists and winners.[6] By 1898 women were rowing and coxing in mixed pairs and taking part in the dongola races. (Dongolas are large canoes in which a crew kneel to paddle the boat.) Earlier in the year women elsewhere on the river had formed their own club and were planning to race. One of them said that she was often greeted with the remark 'Here's a New Woman!' but the interviewer for the *Lock to Lock Times* was very clear that this 'dainty young lady' was quite unlike the recognised type (or stereotype) of New Woman. She was invited to describe her club costume and in reply she held

Oarsmen going past St Peter's Church and the Simonds's house at Caversham. This is one of a group of pictures taken for the *Lock to Lock Times* in 1896 and they are perhaps the earliest images of a Reading Regatta still extant.

Two of the New Women in rowing costume, each with her own variations in hat, sleeve and collar shape and trimming and in bodice style.

Another early photograph, part of the regatta course on the Caversham side, showing a viewing point for officials alongside a wet boat-house belonging to one of the houses in the Warren, taken for the *Lock to Lock Times* in 1896.

up 'a Navy blue serge skirt prettily trimmed with cream-coloured braid, a full sailor blouse with a large cream-coloured collar, ornamented with a blue anchor; a white sailor hat with a band of Navy ribbon and cream-coloured letters.' The New Woman admitted to being self-taught and to being a non-swimmer.

Another attempt at a town regatta

The committee that organised a series of regattas at Reading between 1877 and 1891 had faced a disheartening lack of support and in 1892 it had stood down and returned the challenge cups to their donors. It appealed to Reading Rowing Club for help. A new committee was formed with A H Cane as Hon Secretary. Some changes were made to the kind of races on the programme and from 1894 August Bank Holiday was selected as a regular regatta date. The course was a mile long. There was a grandstand and an enclosure on the Reading bank. H J Simonds, the owner of Caversham House (formerly the Old Rectory), put the grounds at the disposal of the committee. The trophies consisted of: the Reading Grand Challenge Cup for Eights; the Sandeman Challenge Cup for eights; the Reading Challenge Vase for fours; The Maiden Erlegh Challenge Cup; and the Reading Challenge Bowl. A new addition in 1896 was The Vulcan Challenge Shield for junior scullers and that year a good entry for all the classes was promised. On the day the Band of the Second Battalion, the South Wales Borderers, played in the subscribers' enclosure but a hurdy-gurdy attached to a steam roundabout near the grandstand 'displayed staying powers of the most aggravating description'. The programme of 24 heats and 9 row-overs ran from 11.30 am to 7.20 pm and the successful day ended with Mrs W W Ridley, wife of the President of the Regatta

Committee presenting the prizes.[7] There had been some concerns that the overhanging tree at the top end of the Rectory garden might narrow the waterway and interfere with the course but it was not this that caused the accident, already described, that spoilt the day but an unsafe boat that overturned during the evening.[8]

The University Extension College

The College opened in Reading in 1892 and a boat club was soon up and running and in 1895 it was based at Adams & Gyngell's boathouse at the Clappers.[9] There was a women's sculling club established in 1904. The presence of the university on the Caversham reach was a strong influence on amateur rowing over the following decades.

Reading Working Men's Regatta

No manual workers, including those who worked on the river as boatmen or lock-keepers, could row as amateurs and any club for which they rowed was barred from entry to the Reading Amateur Regatta. This was open only to clubs whose members were in professional or clerical occupations. Some contemporary comments suggested that the amateurs would be disadvantaged by the muscle and fitness of the boatmen but since many of the amateurs had rowed at school and at university this was not a valid argument. The distinction was social and it had been introduced in the 1880s and established in the 1890s. An alternative regatta grew out of the efforts of J Apsey and Charles Brown of Huntley and Palmers. Mr Brown put up a cup for a pair-oared race in 1876 and the entry fees generated enough for another goblet for a sculling race. These formed the basis of a competition which became the Reading Working Men's Regatta. It was rowed on the Dreadnought reach below the Kennet because it was in east Reading that many of the Huntley & Palmers' employees lived and where the interest in rowing had been generated. In 1888 Caversham RC and Henley United RC competed, Mr Lovejoy umpired and

W T Simmons, Hon. Sec., Reading Rowing club.

A A Jones, the new Hon. Sec., Reading Regatta Committee, the right man in the right place.

James Simonds presented the prizes.[10] It grew quickly to a two-day event, well supported and well patronised, with an enclosure and a military band in attendance. In 1894 for example the Mayor and Mayoress attended with G W Palmer MP and Mrs Palmer. W Blandy of OUBC umpired from the saddle. One of the races was a four-oar competition for employees of Huntley & Palmers only and in this a team from the Sugar Wafers could row against one from Cakes and Rusks or the Packing Dept. Arthur East loaned some of the fours for racing in the early days and when he disposed of the boats, it left the regatta organisers with a problem. They approached George Palmer

A H Cane, Chairman of Reading Regatta Committee.

W W Ridley President of Reading Regatta Committee.

for a loan of £100 but he started a subscription list with a gift of £5 and, when the total was raised, three boats were ordered from Sims, the specialist boatbuilder at Putney. The umpire's horse was replaced by a launch (in 1895 the steam boat *Cigarette*) and the regatta became a three-day event. John (Jack) Eighteen gave an annual prize for a sculling handicap. The next objective was a boathouse and Mr Palmer gave £50 in 1900 to the committee towards building it.[11] Charles Brown was honorary secretary and was responsible with the committee for the regular regatta and for special events for the Golden and Diamond Jubilees and the Coronations of Edward VII and George V.

Reading Tradesmen's Rowing Club and Regatta

A start date has not yet been found for the club but it was well-established in 1894 with more than a hundred members, of whom 30 were honorary and 60 ordinary members, the balance being presidents.

By 1903 Reading Tradesmen's Club was taking part in the Working Men's regatta and by 1905 the Tradesmen had their own club regatta on the Dreadnought reach. In 1913 John Eighteen was its treasurer and A H Bull its President and it was then described as an excellent club with an increasing membership.

Endnotes

1   *Lock to Lock Times* no 428, 1 August 1896, p 7.

2   *LTLT* no 306, 28 April 1894, p 7.

3   *LTLT* no 404, 27 April 1895, p 2. Fred was one of the sons of Richard Talbot of the wharf at Caversham Bridge.

4   C Dodd *Henley Royal Regatta* (London, 1981), p 64.

5   Dodd p 227.

6   *LTLT* no 452, 19 September 1895, p 5.

7   *LTLT* no 452, 19 September 1895, p 5.

8   *LTLT* nos 428 and 429, 1 and 8 August 1896. The issues contain accounts of the history of the regatta and of the rowing club and full details of that year's results are included in the second of the two issues. It was on 1 August that the accident, referred to in Chapter 7, occurred and which resulted in several deaths.

9   *LTLT* no 404, 27 April 1895. The records of the club were lost in a fire in the University boat-house in 1989.

10 *LTLT* 18 August 1888.

11 *LTLT* no 531, 28 April 1900; *Berkshire Chronicle*, 20 July 1905, p 3.

11 Leisure time along the riverside: 1870–1890

Swimming

River swimming, or as the local paper described it, 'public bathing nuisance', was popular at Caversham. In June 1888 'Disgusted of Wargrave' wrote to the *Lock to Lock Times* to complain about 'indecent bathing especially at Reading and Caversham where a dozen or more men and boys lark about the banks in a state of nudity'.[1] A few weeks later the *Reading Observer* objected to the 'spectacle of persons in a state of nudity within a mile or so either side of Caversham Bridge' in broad daylight but added that the bathing accommodation that the authorities provided was defective and deficient and that one answer to the nuisance might be to restrict 'open bathing' to the early morning. In fact the offences against decency were so frequent that the Thames Conservancy had produced a byelaw in 1887 stating that 'no person shall bathe without proper bathing dress or drawers, bathe or prepare to bathe between the hours of eight in the morning and nine in the evening during the months of June, July and August or during the remaining months between the hours of eight in the morning and eight in the evening, except at bathing places authorised by the Conservators'. In 1889 they re-issued the byelaw and amended the first requirement to read 'no person shall bathe without proper dress or drawers unless properly screened from view'. At Caversham it was the bathing place on the back-water side of Fry's Island that may well have been one of the offending places because the swimming club and the winter bathers moved up to the island from April onward for their summer swimming and swam nude before the regulations came in.[2] A story handed down was that Jack Eighteen, a member of the winter bathers, went in the water wearing his drawers on his head. 'Well' he said, 'they said we had to wear them, but they didn't say where!'

Reading Swimming Club used the area near Caversham Bridge for its polo matches and attracted large crowds of spectators. However, its members looked forward to being able to use the swimming bath alongside the lock on the Reading side as their headquarters when 'the defective and deficient accommodation provided by the

No person shall bathe without proper bathing dress or drawers – unless properly screened from view.

authorities' had been renovated. (There had been a bathing place at King's Meadow, not much more than an inlet from the river, since at least 1834 open from 6am to dusk with single, monthly or season tickets available.[3]) They had been invited to give their views on the matter. The *Lock to Lock Times* in 1888 and 1889 carried a number of small items about the council's decision to undertake the work and said it was intended to increase the dimensions to 120yd by 20yd, to surround the pool by a platform 3yd wide and to have boxes along one end and a lavatory. The sides were to be concrete and the bottom specially surfaced. The editor (or one of his contributors with a vested interest) then pointed out that, because of the way in which the pool was constructed, the river water in it could not be emptied out below the level of the shallow end (3ft) without being pumped. He pointed out that while the council were making changes they should address this fundamental problem so that the river water in the pool would be clear and running and not stagnant.[4] It may have been partly in connection with the improvements to the pool that the Conservators gave notice to the Urban Sanitary Authority that it 'required the diversion of sewage or any other offensive or injurious matter alleged to flow into the Thames from a ditch, which runs under workshops and premises in the occupation of the Great Western Railway Company situate in Caversham Road, and communicates with a stream which flows into the Thames below Caversham Lock'.[5] However the president of the swimming club was still in 1892 having to make the point to the annual meeting that the membership numbers were only limited by the lack of a proper pool in the town so the project had not moved very far by that time.[6]

One side-effect of the increased use of the river by local people was an awareness of the importance of learning life-saving skills and the Lifesaving Society gave demonstrations on these and on resuscitation at local swimming clubs. There was scarcely an issue of the local paper in the summer months that did not carry a story of a drowning on the Kennet, or in the backwater of

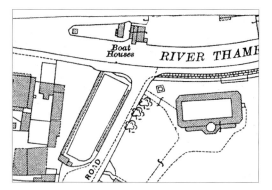

Plan based on OS Map 1934 showing the two bathing places opposite the lock, the long rectangle to the left of the trees being the men's and the semi-covered structure with the octagonal entrance being the later women's pool.

Caversham Mill where the local children played, so the clubs were giving a valuable service.

Skating

The river froze hard enough to support skating in 1891 and 1895. From the reports in these years, and from the number of people who were ready, with a pair of skates, to get out on the ice, it seems that these were not the only years it froze. Mr Cawston's skates are now museum pieces and Harry Isaacs' were still in the Moss Boathouse dressing room in the 1950s. Both sets had wooden bases with metal blades set into them and were held in place with leather toe-straps. The boots have not survived for either set but they must have been fixed by the heel into the wooden sole. Drawings from the time show two designs for the toe of the blade; a flat tip and a curved one. The *Berkshire Chronicle* reported in January 1891 that severe weather provided splendid skating on the Oxfordshire side between Caversham Bridge and Adams & Gyngell's boathouse. A couple went through the ice near the island by East's boathouse but were rescued. The following year in the days before Christmas there was skating right up to Norcot Scours although it was rather foggy. One photograph taken from Caversham Bridge at about this date shows about 50 people on the ice above the island. The 'great skating winter' was 1895 when local temperatures

Well dressed for skating on the Thames in 1891, a drawing from *Lock to Lock Times*.

dropped to -2°F in February and there were water shortages and unemployment.[7]

Horse racing

The arrival of the railway in Reading gave a new start in 1842 to horse racing in the town. The land at King's Meadow, the level field between the railway line and the lock, made a good site and it was intended that Reading Races should equal in popularity those held at Bulmershe Heath. No local map shows any permanent structure on the site but in August 1843 there was an enclosure and grandstand ready for the two-day Reading Races. Thousands of people came by rail or on foot to see the heats of Innkeepers' Plate, the Berkshire Stakes and a Hurdle Sweepstake, although their enjoyment of this race may have been spoiled when one horse refused a fence and jumped into the enclosure instead. Twenty years later the two-day meeting was still a success and was clearly a major event. There were more than a dozen races by this time, some attracting about twenty runners, and they included the Easthampstead Park Stakes, the Borough Plate, and the Abbey, the

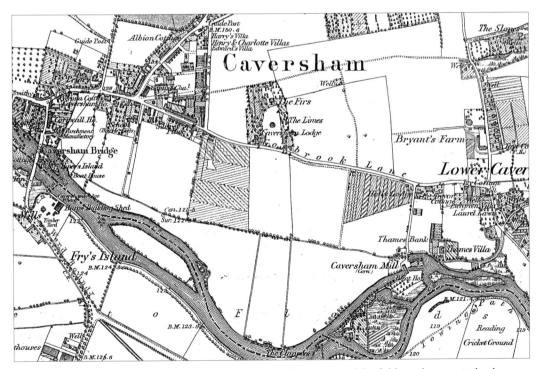

Map to show the cricket ground on King's Meadow (lower right corner) and the fields on the opposite bank near Gosbrook Lane where cricket and football were played. Adams & Gyngell operated a ferry between the two banks to get supporters to matches.

King's Meadow, the Caversham and the Whitley Stakes and a Selling Plate. The account in the local paper ran to two columns and gave full details of prize money, odds, runners and riders.[8]

Cricket

Reading Cricket Club played on a pitch at King's Meadow in the 1870s and later transferred to a ground on the other bank below Gosbrook Lane (Gosbrook Road). It was still on the King's Meadow site when the 1882 OS map was produced. In 1889 arrangements were being proposed for Reading Amateur Athletic Club to use a grass track within the grounds and cycle events were to be encouraged on the oval track by offering a Ladies' Challenge Cup. In 1889 the thatched pavilion belonging to the cricket club had stood out like Noah's Ark in a flooded landscape but in 1891 it was burnt down as a result of four small boys, the oldest only eight, lighting rubbish.

Football

Reading Football Club played its first game on 21 February 1872, a friendly match against Reading School on a pitch at King's Meadow, and continued to play there until 1878. Its teams played on the Cricket Club pitch at King's Meadow from 1878 to 1882 and then moved to Coley Park. Stanley Hayward, shown here, joined Reading FC in 1874, playing half back, and in 1876 became goal keeper for all Reading club matches. He kept goal in 1879, the year that Reading won the Berks and Bucks Challenge Cup. In 1883 he became secretary for the club. By 1889 the team was back on the riverside, this time renting and using the Cricket Club's new ground on the Oxfordshire bank beside Gosbrook Lane and they continued, already wearing the blue and white colours, to use these grounds.[9] They were not the only team to play there. The *Lock to Lock Times* reported on riverside games in which Reading, Reading Abbey, Reading Albion, Reading South, Reading Minster, Caversham, Earley, Maidenhead and Marlow teams played and in which the Berks and

Bucks league featured regularly. The GWR offered cheap tickets on match days. A key figure at this time was James Simonds who was president of the football and cricket clubs and of the Reading Angling Association as well.

When Reading Football Club had their ground on the Oxfordshire bank many of their supporters came from the town or Berkshire side. To get to the match they had a choice: they could go down Caversham Road, cross Caversham Bridge and go along the other bank to the ground or go down to the lock and cross on the footbridge to Mill Green. Samuel Gyngell, a member of the RFC committee in 1895, came up with an alternative.[10] The following extract comes from an on-line history of Reading Football Club (the spelling of the company name in the notice was as given):

> The oldest surviving Reading programme, from an FA Amateur Cup tie against Old Carthusians in 1894, includes an advert with the following words:

> *NOTICE.*

> *The MOST DIRECT WAY*

> *to the Ground is to ferry the Thames from*

> *ADAMS & GINGELL'S BOAT-HOUSE.*

> *Fare – 1d. Return.*

Many people did use this route and after Reading had played at the ground for a while, they started selling combined match and ferry tickets on the south side of the river to ease congestion. The ferry operators invested in a bigger boat after a couple of seasons and the local newspaper estimated that over a thousand people were making the boat trip in the half-hour before bigger games.[11]

The *Lock to Lock Times*, reporting in March 1894 on Reading's success by a good margin in three friendly games played on their home ground at Caversham, fronting Adams & Gyngell's boat-house, also mentioned the ferry and said that as many as 12 men were employed to work 3 large horse ferries and that the patrons numbered over 5000. The club played its last two games on the

Stanley Hayward: Reading Football Club player and secretary 1874 – 1883.

The town had responded to his gift by having a statue of him placed in the town centre and by offering him the Freedom of the Borough. The statue, exceptional in showing its subject with an umbrella, was unveiled and there was a procession from the town to the park.[12] Just about every organisation in the town that had a band was there to play and all the others had floats or marched: a mounted troop of the Berkshire Yeomanry, Berkshire Volunteers, the police band, the fire brigade, Albion Football Club. The riverside was represented by Reading Rowing Club and the Committee of Reading Working Men's Regatta but 'cheers all along the line greeted the Reading Waltonian Angling Society with their president Mr W Moss, better know as Bill Moss, in the get-up of Simple Simon fishing in his mother's pail. Numerous fine stuffed specimens of Thames trout and other fish adorned the two vehicles chartered by the Society which were prettily decorated with rushes and sedges.' Lastly came the mayor and the Recorder and George Palmer himself. The day finished with fireworks.[13]

cricket pitch at Caversham in April 1896, one against a touring Everton side in front of 3000 spectators which it lost 2 – 0 and another against Aldershot which it won 5 – 0. The football club decided in 1895 to turn professional and transferred from the riverside to Elm Park in 1896. A breakaway group of players who wished to remain amateur moved to Palmer Park at the same time.

Opening of Palmer Park

The focus of sporting activity had begun to shift from the riverside from 1891 when Palmer Park opened. The 49 acres of land for the park had been given in 1889 to the town by George Palmer in recognition of the demand for open spaces for leisure time activity by those who lived in the east of Reading in what is now the Newtown area. Much of this development was to house Mr Palmer's employees. He had already given 14 acres at King's Meadow to the Council.

Jubilee Celebrations

King's Meadow was the site of some of Reading's celebrations for Queen Victoria's Diamond Jubilee in 1897. There were outdoor sports all day long and the swimming club's comic events, such as canoe races with mop sticks, were very popular as was the water polo match and the tug of war. Church bells pealed and a procession headed by the Royal Berkshire Yeomanry made its way through the town. Behind them were representatives of local groups.

The amalgamated angling clubs were there with 'vans with real water and fish' and there were exhibits by departments of the Corporation, including Manor Farm (sewage works) and the Waterworks. The 60-gun salute from Forbury Hill was somewhat spoiled by the irregular intervals between the shots. Across the town the aged poor had a good dinner and the children had tea in their schools. The day finished with illuminations and a torchlight procession.[14]

View from Bill Moss's new site towards Caversham Bridge.[16]

Entertainments on Bill Moss's island site

In 1890 a formal agreement was drawn up between Bill Moss and Thomas Ayres of Elm Avenue, Caversham Road, Reading that Moss would rent from Ayres a piece of land near Caversham Road with a river frontage of 125 feet, at a rent of 6s 6d per foot per year for the remainder of 99 years from 1889. As a result of this leasehold agreement Bill moved his business from the Oxfordshire bank to the Berkshire one, on land known as Brigham's Mead, opposite Fry's Island. The land adjoined the Reading Rowing Club's premises. There were some objections to the building:

> Another new boat-house is in the course of erection at Reading adjacent to the headquarters of Reading Rowing Club. Like its neighbour the newcomer does not promise to become a thing of beauty but at the same time it will be in harmony with its immediate surroundings, where the demon of ugliness seems to reign supreme. Reading as viewed from the river is becoming more and more a bye-word and it is a pity that the good works of Adams & Gyngell and East near the lock are not more generally emulated.[15]

Bill Moss opened his new boathouse at Whitsun in time for the new season and there was a huge 'smoker' given by the Waltonians to celebrate the event.[17] It was a wooden building about 60 by 100ft, fronting the towpath, lit by skylights and opened by sliding doors at the side. In 1892 Bill Moss became the lessee of the upstream part of Fry's Island as well as the land on the Berkshire bank and this had important consequences for the way in which he conducted his business. The island was a potential source of income independent of boat-hire. It is likely that he used the island in the summer for safe moorings of his fleet of small hire boats and there is anecdotal evidence of his taking cows across to it in a punt. In the photograph looking from the new site upstream to the iron bridge the man in the boat crossing towards the island is pulling on a rolling line attached to the bank and to the boat to move it. This would have the advantage of making it immediately available for crossing in either direction without waiting for the previous user to come back across. A ferry was important in the plans he had for developing the island as a place of entertainment.

A map of Fry's Island was prepared and dated 2 December 1892 for George Lewis, by J H Clark of Caversham Road, Reading, to show the position of a proposed wet boathouse in the centre. It defined the part (250ft by 185ft) that Moss was taking and showed that Arthur East was leasing the downstream end.[18] The map shows one difference between the island then and now: what is now the downstream tip was then a separate islet about 100ft by 90ft. There are two other undated maps prepared by the same hand. They show the 320ft in the centre owned by George Lewis marked out into five plots, the downstream one of the five (50ft wide) being labelled as 'Reading Rowing Club', this being the site it occupied from 1883 onwards. The adjoining one of these was where Lewis would later build his barge sheds and the other three were used by the Lewis family as a garden. On both later maps the gap has been bridged and the island is now enlarged by the amount of the previous small islet.

The island became a place for leisure activity quite quickly. The *Lock to Lock Times* reported in May 1892 that a new covered wet dock was in the course of construction at the north-west corner of Fry's Island to house the steam launch *Jack-in-the-Box* for Mr Henry Dundas of the Royal County Theatre. This wet boathouse, which survived until the 1950s, faced the Oxfordshire bank. A wooden bungalow called Templecombe was built alongside it, probably at about the same date and for the same customer. A well-known houseboat, the *Golden Grasshopper*, was moored on the island in 1894 and another, the *Kelpie*, over-wintered on the backwater in 1895.

The Reading United Quoits Club had its headquarters on the island (The Reading Quoits Club was based at East's) and in June 1894 there was a tennis tournament. These activities brought in money to the business and attracted interest in the riverside. Bill Moss's big attractions on the island were his Riverside Concerts and Venetian Fêtes (these and Baden Baden concerts were outdoor entertainments), the first taking place on 25 August 1893 and the second in September, with another series to come in the following spring. The island did not have the facilities of East's boathouse but Bill was aiming at a less

> MOSS'S ISLAND.
>
> GRAND FANCY DRESS CARNIVAL
>
> will take place
> ON WEDNESDAY, AUGUST 21, 1895,
> commencing at Six o'clock.
>
> SPLENDID ILLUMINATIONS!
> GRAND COSTUME PROCESSION
> AT NINE O'CLOCK.
> DANCING to the strains of MOSS'S ISLAND BAND, under the direction of Mr. R. S. COATS.
> M.C s : Messrs. W. Payne and Jones.
>
> PRIZES for the best FANCY DRESSES and most ORIGINAL and COMIC CHARACTER have been contributed by the following gentlemen:—Messrs. A. H. Bull, W. Archer, Farrer and Sons, Kirby, Awmack, Cutbill, and Sudul. — Judges: H. B. O. TRENCH and JONES, Esqrs.
>
> ADMISSION, ONE SHILLING.
> TICKETS obtainable at Messrs. Attwell's, Farrer's, Phillips' (Kings Road), and Moss's Boat House.
> N.B.—Should the weather prove unfavourable the Carnival will take place on Thursday, the 22nd. See bills.

sophisticated audience and required very little capital outlay for his events. He was a professional in the entertainment field and knew what people enjoyed. Crossing the river by ferry was an attraction in itself and provided a sense of exclusiveness to an event and it seems from the descriptions that people came ready to enjoy themselves and willing to play an active part:

> On Monday evening Mr W Moss gave another riverside and Baden Baden Concert on the island just below Caversham Bridge. The island being profusely decorated and illuminated with Chinese lanterns and myriads of coloured lamps, the effect was of the prettiest as viewed from the bridge. A large number of dancers disported themselves on the greensward, to the music of Mr Moss's Island Band. Mr C Wing opened the vocal part of the entertainment with a laughing song, which was followed by a graceful exhibition with the Indian clubs by Mr J F Lightfoot. Mr J King Heslop, eccentric comedian, was well received, while the evergreen W Moss was, as usual, heartily greeted for his comic songs.[19]

In 1895 he was planning Sunday evening sacred concerts. Another evening there was a Baden Baden concert with the Mississippi Minstrels and dancing to Moss's Island Band. In August he arranged a fancy dress carnival and river fête:

Illumination lamps for fetes and regattas: 2 shillings a dozen complete with candles, from W G Smith, soap and candle maker, Kingston and Staines.

The island is exceptionally well-adapted for an entertainment of this nature and the whole of the surroundings were tastefully illustrated by coloured and fairy lamps. The Island Band, under their conductor Mr R S Coates, supplied good music and dancing was kept up till a late hour. At nine o'clock there was a long procession of competitors for the best fancy dress costumes, for some useful prizes offered by the leading local tradesmen. The chief prize-takers were Mrs Dee as the Countess of Argyll; Miss Dee – shepherdess; Mr George May of London – *à la chevalier*, who was well received; Mr H B Jones of the Reading Swimming Club – Monkey Brand; Master Warren – Lord Fauntleroy; Miss Hawkins – May Queen and Mr Taylor – the New Woman. Mr Ormsby French, proprietor of the Reading Theatre, and Mr R Jones of Oxford acted as judges and Messrs J A Meads, H Bruce Jones and W Pryne were the stewards. Taken altogether Mr Moss is to be complimented upon his enterprise. He is now preparing for another one on similar lines.[20]

While outdoor events could be lit by oil lamps, the fairy lamps and Chinese lanterns held candles. The illumination lamp in the advertisement was about 4 inches high and made of coloured glass with a faceted surface to increase the effect of the night-light inside it. The lamps could be hung on strings or placed along ledges on buildings.

It was just after this event that Bill's employees did the then fashionable thing; they went on a works outing. His son Fred took them to London for a day's sightseeing. They had a good day out and the weather stayed fine.[21] Moss's band was part of the entertainment when 1200 members of the Reading Primrose League went on an outing to Purley Park. They were taken there on the *Bonafide* and the *Fashion* and other private steamers and electric boats, including Frank Attwells's *Coryphine*.[21] Another business outing that year was the wayzgoose for the employees of the *Reading Mercury*, which took the form of an outing on Cawston's launch *Mystery*.

Endnotes

1 *Lock to Lock Times* [*LTLT*] no 1 vol I, 9 June 1888, p 9.

2 *LTLT* no 431, 25 April, 1896. The journal stopped using volume numbers in 1894. Issue numbers continued in sequence.

3 OS map 1879 and *Stevens's Directory of Reading*.

4 *LTLT* nos 36 and 37 vol I Feb 1889, p 62, 74.

5 *LTLT* no 103 vol IV, 17 May 1890, p 307.

6 *Berkshire Chronicle* 7 May 1892. Report of AGM of Reading Swimming Club.

7 Ian Currie *Frost, Freezes and Fairs* (Coulsdon, 1996), p 71–72.

8 *Berkshire Chronicle* 24 August 1843 p 3 col 1 and 16 August 1862 p 5 col 1–3, Reading Races.

9 Information from the website of Reading Football Club in 2003 and acknowledgement is made to the compiler. (http://www.readingfc.premiumtv.co.uk/page/History/0,,10306~122791,00.html).

10 Thanks are given to Mr Roy Gyngell for this information. Other RFC committee members in 1895 were the river and rowing men A Cane and H Isaacs.

11 Reading Football Club website.

12 The statue has since been relocated to Palmer Park.

13 *LTLT* no 182 vol V new series 7 November 1891, p 13.

14 *LTLT* 26 June 1897, p 2–3.

15 *LTLT* no 150 vol V, 4 April 1891, p 695.

16 RM, REDMG 1975/153, view from Moss's boathouse towards Caversham Bridge.

17 Patricia Burstall *The Golden Age of the Thames* (David and Charles, 1981), p 135. A 'smoker' was an informal concert at which those attending were often the entertainers. The information about Bill's willingness to perform is supported by a report on a smoking concert held by Reading Albion Football Club at the Foresters Hall at which professional, and some of the best local, performers in the town had appeared. 'Bill Moss, A Bonner, K Tenser and A Lewis all made big hits with their humorous songs'. *Berkshire Chronicle* 14 February 1891, p 5 col 4.

18 Privately owned.

19 *LTLT* no 323, 25 August 1894.

20 *LTLT* no 422, 31 August 1895, p 4.

21 Bill's son Fred died in 1896.

22 *LTLT* no 418, 3 August 1895.

12 The peak years for pleasure boating: 1890–1896

The electric launch

The expansion of the various companies with new buildings and expensive stock during the late 1880s and early 1890s was very costly, with a long period between outlay and return of capital. Income from the new stock had to be generated over a short summer season and was dependent on weather conditions. Technical changes were still coming thick and fast. The arrival of the electric launch, quieter and cleaner than the steam launch, and without the fire risk, must have caused some concern. Sam Saunders of Goring built his first electric boat in 1885 and was instrumental in reducing hull weight by a process of layering wood and canvas and stitching them together with copper wire.[1]

A local owner of an electric launch was William Thompson Crawshay, Welsh iron master of Caversham Park. This was the *Florenti* which he kept at Adams & Gyngell's boathouse. Bona was quick off the mark. He built two electric launches and installed an electric charging station at his premises. East also set up a station in 1892 and used it to light up his building as well. There were also floating charging stations, such as the *Ampere No 3*, which apparently charged launches as they towed them along. Another station, the *Watt 4,* having brought a launch up from Henley in August 1889, stayed at Caversham Bridge for the rest of the season. (There was also an *Ohm* somewhere on the river.) The Immisch Electric Launch Company was an innovator in the business of combining the presence of charging stations, one of which was moored at Reading, and hiring or selling electric boats.

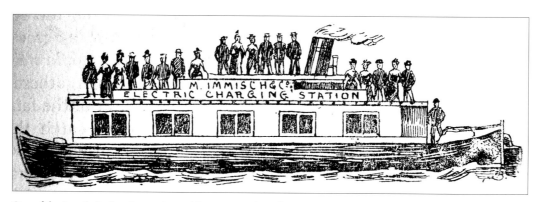

One of the Immisch charging stations with a party on board.

John, one of the three Salter brothers.

The electric canoe came on the scene in 1893. Then the arrival of the portable electric battery, which worked on the principle of the modern car battery and which was suitable for lighting and propulsion, enabled the owner of the launch to by-pass the charging stations. About this time there was a vogue for naphtha launches which had

the advantage of not needing charging but which left a smelly residue behind them.

Salters' Steamers

The main Salter base was at Oxford where the three brothers, John, James and George had a staff of 80. They had 12 boathouses and their original business, established in 1858, was that of supplying racing boats to university and other crews. They established the regular Oxford to Kingston runs, which of course came through Reading, in 1888, and by 1891 they were using large boats built specifically for the purpose by Edwin Clarke and Co of Brimscombe, Stroud. The first of these was the *Oxford* taking up to 140 passengers, the next was the *Kingston*, followed in 1892 by the *Windsor* and the *Cliveden*, both these boats coming during May, via the Kennet and Avon Canal, up through Reading on their journeys from their makers to Oxford. The steel-hulled boats were fitted with engines which used the best Welsh smokeless fuel. Passengers could board a steamer at any joining point during a scheduled run and stay on board for as long as they wished. The steamer timetables linked with train services so that passengers could make their return journey by train. Thus Salters were not in direct competition with any of the Reading companies although they may have drawn some custom from East and Bona. Their

One of first steamers built by Salters, the *Oxford*, as it appeared in one of the company's advertisements in the 1890s. There are eel bucks and a mill in the background.

simple timetabled journeys and the large, stable boats, both factors having something in common with the familiar train and tram, may have persuaded new people on to the river who may have returned later to try a different kind of boat.

Prosperous times in the town

Even if Salters drew some trade from the local businesses, they were all forward-looking and the feeling among them was buoyant. East, Adams & Gyngell, and Moss were subscribers to the Reading Telephone, numbers 44, 151 and 197 respectively, and all three paid eight shillings a year to have their numbers advertised in the *Reading Observer*. The Reading Electric Supply Company was rolling out the supply of electricity to consumers by area and Caversham and Vastern Roads were scheduled for the spring of 1895.[2] Bill Moss appeared to be working from his premises on both the Caversham and the Reading banks at this time.[3] Freebody improved his landing stage and frontage for the summer of 1895 and he let his boat *Thirlmere* to Mr Shepherd of Henley for the season. He was enlarging his boatbuilding

department at the end of the summer. Adams & Gyngell were running *La Mode*, perhaps Bona's earlier boat.[4] Edward Cawston was confident enough in continuing popularity of this side of the business to start building two more steamers while Antonio Bona planned to begin his sixth steamer in October 1894 and to launch it the following April. The launching of the *Bonafide* attracted nearly a thousand spectators to the bridge and the riverside and they saw the hull leave its dock without any problem. The boat was described as the largest on the Upper Thames, half-decked, of a very light build, single screw and shallow draught. Many of Bona's customers combined a river trip with a meal in the hotel and the feature of the *Bonafide*, its under-cover dining accommodation for 50 people, was an extension, and probably a profitable one, of the hotel side of the business. Clubs, teams and employers wanting to use the *Bonafide* for their annual outing would certainly pre-book the event and in this boat would be independent of the weather, important factors for both proprietor and customer in the boat-hiring business. To celebrate the launching Mr Bona arranged a meal in the hotel for all the

Telegraph poles along Thames Side and on Piper's Island mark the expansion of the telephone service. The tip of Fry's Island is on the right of the image and the Temperance Hotel behind it on the far bank.[5]

35 employees who had worked on the boat.[6]

About three years later Mr Bona used the *Fashion* to tow the men and vessels of the Pontoon Detachment of the Royal Engineers from Tilehurst, where they had been encamped for river practice, down to Wargrave. Here they stopped to put a bridge across the river before moving on to Marlow.[7] Bona had another connection with the military. When the Royal Berkshire Yeomanry assembled at Reading on 16 May 1895 for their annual training, the local boatmen were pleased because they knew that the officers and men would spend leisure time on the river and the event would be good for business. The Yeomanry was a volunteer force that had first come into being in 1793 during hostilities with France but in the following century it saw action only in dealing with civil disturbances. Its units were based on the main towns of the county and its members were farmers, tradesmen or gentlemen who had the free time to take part and to attend the annual training week. Amongst the non-commissioned officers at the training that year was Sergeant A G Bona, one of the oldest members of the troop, and the event concluded on 1 June with a smoker at Bona's when over 200 sat down in the hotel where the lawn and trees were decorated with lights. The Regimental Band was in attendance.[8]

Sometimes training exercises would involve building pontoon crossings or getting horses across the river and then there would be work to be picked up by the local boatmen. In August 1888 a troop of 200 men and officers of the Royal Engineers marched from Aldershot to Reading for their summer camp at Norcot Scours. While they were there they built a swing bridge of pontoons and barrels borrowed from H and G Simonds's Brewery. When they finished they moved off to Henley, sending the pontoons down by river.

The huge interest in boats and in the river

generated business elsewhere in the town. Messrs Haslam & Son, agents to the Knollys estate, offered in their Friar Street Chambers furnished riverside houses to rent anywhere in the Upper Thames from Iffley to Maidenhead, and both they and Messrs C G Cleaver & Co held boat sales. When private and commercial owners of launches needed fittings, warning lamps, night lighting and cooking stoves, there were ironmongers to supply them. Itinerant photographers offered to 'take you in the boat, Sir; take you all afloat, Sir'.[9] Flags and bunting were available from T H Blake in King's Road. Hill & Co of the High Street and the Market Place (5 minutes' walk from Caversham Lock) sold waterproof gear, a new restaurant opened in Caversham Road specialising in picnic and boating hampers, D J Cook of Reading offered a fine array of picnic hampers, wicker chairs and tables and reminded his patrons that he was the sole agent for Thetford Patent Pulp or Floating Ware. Cutbill of Cross Street advertised a range of basket chairs and tables. Andrew Potter of Reading advertised 5000 army bell tents (scarcely used, bag, pegs, lines and mallet included) whose white canvas would look attractive on a riverside lawn. Stransom and Son of Market Place, athletic outfitters, could supply flannels and boating outfits in club colours, ready to wear or specially made. Villas in Caversham were advertised by their owners for holiday lets. Hickies and Attwells included among their range of musical instru-

The Reading Vastern Hotel.

ments a small piano which was a popular item among houseboat owners.[10] Phippen, a florist in Friar Street, advertised that he could supply plants and flowers for decorating houseboats and that he would have his usual stand at Henley. The Reading Vastern Hotel, facing the new Clappers boathouse, was one minute from the river and trains and could offer its customers hot and cold baths; and in 1892 Yaxley, a builder in Mundesley Street, Reading, was offering for sale or to let the Temperance Hotel (13 beds and 120ft landing stage) at Caversham Bridge. The town was economically buoyant enough in 1893 to stage the first Reading Annual Industrial Exhibition at the large town hall and in 1894, a year when G W Palmer performed the opening ceremony, Arthur East was an exhibitor, displaying Canadian canoes and double sculling skiffs. The river traffic was a good enough source of income for the Friendly and Trade Societies of Caversham to station collectors at the lock and at Caversham and Sonning Bridges for the annual Hospital Sunday parades.[11]

The riverside activity also generated new fashion and the *Lock to Lock Times* ran feature articles on it. In August 1896 the subject was the outfit worn by a girl passenger in a boat and its description is very detailed because any reader, or any dressmaker, wanting something similar would need to understand the design well enough to translate the text into a paper pattern and a set of sewing instructions to make the outfit for themselves:

Fashion for the river: a dove grey jacket worn with a bodice of moss green satin.

The skirt and jacket were of a soft dove grey, the former quite plain and not so full as usual. Inside the jacket was a perfectly plain bodice of moss green satin cloth high up to the neck, and fastened so cleverly that it was almost invisible at the side. The bolero or jacket was allowed to be only just short enough to display the bodice at the back like a waist band. The green sleeves were slightly fulled or wrinkled up the arm, and finished off with ruffles of lace. The young lady's neck arrangement struck us both as very unique. There was first the band of green; and apparently by two brilliant steel clasps the collar of narrow organ pipe flutings made of the grey cloth was fastened to the green one underneath. Two large enamel and steel edged buttons finished off the sides of the bolero and completed one of the smartest little costumes I have ever seen. Of course the colour of the cloths can be varied according to the fancy of the wearer and the suit would look well in black. This especial young woman had a mixture of cut green silk and white and orange shot gauze in her hat, and a black and green shot sunshade.

There is no difficulty in finding drawings and photographs of girls poling punts but very few

Fashion for the river: a masculine boater, high collar, tie and belt worn with a plain dress but enlivened with full sleeves to create a very feminine outfit.

of them in other kinds of boats. Since punt poles are quite heavy and the art of punting not so easy, these images were perhaps staged for fashion purposes or simply for the attractive picture made by a girl with a small waist reaching for the top of the pole. Frederick Hines, a landscape painter of the late 1800s, produced an oil painting called 'Punting at Caversham', showing just such a girl poling at the top of Lock Island, with View Island and Adams & Gyngell's boathouse recognisable in the weir stream.

The lock-keepers

Throughout this period of economic activity there was one group of people, the lock-keepers, whose work load was increased but whose wages remained low, £40 or £50 per year. The old stereotype of a man with a free house and garden and opportunities for earning money from the passers-by was still current. A full-page article in the *Lock to Lock Times* in 1899 put a solid case for the man dealing with hugely-increased traffic, on his feet all day in the summer, no day of rest and

regularly responsible for the safety of a lockful of boats of all sizes and types. As many as 500 to 1000 boats could go through a busy lock on a summer Sunday and each had to have its paperwork completed. Then in the final paragraph the writer changed tack completely and concluded that the men at the busiest locks deserved a rise but that there was no such case to be made for those at the quieter ones. All the old arguments were brought out about the right to free fishing and the free time in the winter for making baskets and fishing tackle, with some new ones about the market for selling bulrushes and water lilies, providing hot water for tea and lending out cups for picnics. The job of the lock-keeper was once again presented as a sinecure.[12]

The end of the golden days of the riverside

Despite all this economic activity, the peak of the popularity of the river for pleasure boating, other than steamer trips, had passed. The fashionable rich had moved on somewhere else and boating, like angling before it, had moved down the social scale. There were alternative leisure activities for all. By mid 1895 and 1896 changes were taking place. The landscape along the riverside, particularly on the Reading bank, had altered as a result of the expansion of the railway, the level of economic activity and prosperity in the town, the increase in the population of Caversham and Reading and the consequent flourishing leisure sector. The recently-formed Berkshire Cricket Club had its own ground in Reading, and fixtures with adjoining counties, and the Reading Football Club's new site was very close to it. The Reading Cricket Club left its ground at King's Meadow to join the Berkshire Club at Elm Park in 1897. The partnership between Adams & Gyngell was dissolved in 1896.[13] Although East was still building boats to special orders and showed skiffs and Canadian canoes at the Royal Counties Show in 1897, he also had a motor car on display. There was a demonstration of 'road skating' in Reading in 1898.

The houses in Thames Side taken by P O Collier on a snowy day in about 1920. There is a commercial steam vessel coming under the bridge.[14]

The *Lock to Lock Times* recognised the changes in its issue of 26 September 1896:

> The boating season of 1896 has, so far as the Reading district is concerned, closed, and the boat proprietors will soon be busy storing away their craft for the winter. On the whole it must be admitted that pleasure craft have not been so freely used as heretofore, a fact accounted for by the popularity of the bicycle and the increase of steam launch trips.[15]

The beginning of development

The meadows on the Berkshire bank were rapidly becoming developed and urbanised. Bill Moss, fisherman, had become Mr W Moss, boat proprietor, with a boathouse on this stretch. George Lewis had extended from his earlier base in Caversham Road and opened a saw mill and timber yard with river frontage at one end and road frontage onto Caversham Road at the other. Reading Electric Supply Association built a new depot and stores in Vastern Road, backing on to the river opposite the lower end of Fry's Island. This had the incidental advantage to boat owners that electric launches could be recharged there.[16]

The Thames Bank Iron Works opened on the downstream side of the Electric Works, towards East's site. One huge change was the extension of the GWR lines to form a coal yard on the south side of Vastern Road, effectively removing the need for coal wharfs on the river front. In 1893 the *Lock to Lock Times* reported that a strong effort was being made to save the Berkshire bank from the lock to Caversham Bridge from the ravages of speculative builders and 'a scheme for an esplanade or boulevard was submitted to Reading Corporation, which body however threw out the bill. The consequence is that the stretch of bank alluded to bids fair to equal in ugliness any other between the source of the Thames and the sea.'[17] It was however housing development that had taken up most of the meadow land between Caversham Road and Vastern Road and the river. There was terraced housing on both sides of Caversham Road and on the north side of Vastern Road and four side roads of smaller terraced housing, Thames Avenue, Brigham, De Montfort and Lynmouth Roads running down towards the river. Brigham Road also had some industrial sites on the town side. Along the river frontage a terrace of five three-storey houses, with balconies on two

Browne and Lilly, a local firm which later moved to Thames Side, take an opportunity to advertise bungalows and boathouses while there was so much riverside land coming onto the market for development.

levels, had been built in 1895 and sold as having extensive views over the river and the Oxfordshire hills. Another four houses were built on the other side of Thames Avenue.

Fry's Island had the wet boathouse and bungalow first occupied by Henry Dundas, the Reading Rowing Club premises and a substantial semi-bungalow on the downstream end on the part leased by Mr East. At some point George Lewis built a large wooden shed for bargebuilding or repair (present day Bridge Boats) next to the Rowing Club with a slipway on the Caversham side because he was still using water transport for his timber business. Stephen Ivens of Emmer Green, born 1878, learnt his carpentry skills as a bargebuilder with George Lewis and was followed there by his 14-year-old son Maurice in 1919, information which both confirms the use of the shed for bargebuilding and gives some dates when it was in use.[18]

On the Oxfordshire side the increase in housing was causing the Caversham Local Board to consider sewage disposal. It proposed in 1894 to buy nine acres of riverside land from Mr Crawshay across which the effluent would flow through a drain and discharge into the Thames at an outfall site below the lock. Mr Crawshay would not agree to one of the Board's routes for the drain because he said that the amount of fall was not sufficient and the outflow was sometimes below flood level. He objected to another possible route because the drain emptied into ditches for part of its way to the river. He wanted a direct outfall to be

constructed but not so near to Deane's Farm that the letting value of it would be reduced. (Typhoid was still a fatal disease and there had been a case in Caversham that year.) When all his conditions were met, he agreed to sell the land.

The area upstream from Caversham Bridge was altering. The Borough of Reading offered in a public notice a lease of 80 years from Lady Day 1897 on the property at the bridge known as the White Hart Hotel, and now occupied with other property by Antonio Bona, and of the meadow adjacent to it on the south side of the White Hart Hotel and on the west side of Caversham Road, for the erection of a new first class hotel and connected buildings. Bona's 53ft teak steam launch *Buoyancy* was put up for sale in April 1898. There was a proposal that the meadow land above the bridge on this side of the river and alongside the regatta course should become a public park but it came to nothing for financial reasons. Simmons and Son of Reading offered to sell 85 building sites by auction on 10 October 1896, comprising 110 acres in all, above and below the Warren, with Thames frontage and river scenery but within easy reach of Reading Railway Stations. The account books of William Wing, architect and surveyor, and a man well-known in the swimming club and on the waterside, describe the work he did for the estate agent in preparing plans of the roads and building plots and pegging out the site. He also drew up plans for the portions of the estate that were proposed to be sold to Messrs Nicholas and to C Fidler.[19] Further upstream Mr Blount had offered for sale The Fishery, 335 acres of riverside property, by auction at Reading on 22 September 1896 in 45 lots. When the Warren Estates Sale took place in 1900 it was arranged that a steam launch would be available at East's to take prospective buyers to the site, entirely free of charge.[20]

Still in business

Although the peak of the small pleasure boat business had passed there was still plenty of activity with the larger boats and in specialist markets. Cawston's *River Queen* was at the boat race in 1897 with the staff of the *Sunday Times* on board. Bona was building an electric launch, the *Regina* and a second *Bonavista*, the original having been sold. His *Bonafide* was registered for 250 passengers, *Fashion* for 120, *Caversham* 110, *Bonasera* 45 and *Bonaventure* for 12. Freebody had been concentrating on building punts for sale and was finding a ready market. His 35ft steam launch, *Thirlmere*, with engines by Baron, was for sale. Neither he nor Moss had competed for the market for steam launch outings. Arthur East had a stand at the Yachting Exhibition where he showed a pair-oar skiff with gold plush cushions and silk canopies, a picnic punt with tables and a luncheon and tea basket, and a canoe to seat three with a steam engine whose size made it the smallest launch ever constructed. He had two special orders on hand, one for a teak steam launch and the other for an American skip boat. He had many titled patrons and much foreign trade. East had four boathouses by 1897, at Shiplake, Kennet Mouth, The Clappers and the Roebuck at Tilehurst. He also maintained a fleet of small boats on the lake at the Royal Military Academy at Sandhurst. By 1898 East had two of the tiny powered canoes, the *Filiola* and the *Swift*. He formed a limited company in this same year. Moss in 1898 built two mahogany skiffs for Mr Ayres and Mr Lewis and a mahogany fishing punt for Mrs Baker of Brighton. Bona's *Regina* was launched and registered for 28 passengers and he was working on a 20ft open launch of teak for a private customer in France. The motor was supplied by the Reading Installation Company

and was concealed in a model swan attached to the bows of the boat.

Mr Bona was still a hotel and launch proprietor at Caversham Bridge in 1901 but he was in new premises. The old White Hart had been pulled down and had been replaced by the new Caversham Bridge Hotel, set slightly further from the road and with gardens running down to the riverside. Thomas Freebody was at Willow Grotto and had recently rebuilt his premises to suit modern requirements.[21] His son Ernest William was with him as a boatbuilder. Edward Cawston was living in the Waterman's Cottage on Piper's Island but his twin sons were working elsewhere. Bill Moss was living at 1 Thames Bank View with his second wife. From the property sequence in the census enumerator's notebook it seems that this was what later became 19 Thames Side, one of the block of five villas built in 1895.

Mill Green

The Clappers footpath at Mill Green was the responsibility of the Caversham Local Board to maintain. It was a very well-used short cut into town from Caversham and its very popularity caused 'A Pedestrian' to write bitterly to the local paper in 1894 of the inconvenience caused by people actually using the footpath, especially those with bicycles or perambulators. The force of the water across the weir put pressure on all the structures around it and there was always repair work to be done. New deal campshedding (supporting timber) was put in place along the banks in 1894 and a tumbling bay installed at the weir in 1896. The deal was replaced by oak and pitch pine after the bank had suffered flood damage and needed repair in March 1900. By this time it was estimated that the tumbling bay needed to be three times bigger than it was and the Caversham District Council was going to talk to the Thames Conservancy about it. The Conservancy did have plans for a new weir to take more water and to help to prevent flooding.[22]

Mill Green housed a small community of its own during the 1890s. Thames Bank, a large villa

Caversham House on View Island, formerly Adams & Gyngell's boathouse and later occupied by a stockbroker from London.[23]

where Joshua Champion had lived in retirement, was occupied by Mrs Barton in 1896, owner of the launch *Kingfisher*, and by Sarah Stent, of independent means, in 1901. A terrace of smaller villas faced the river and the mill foreman, miller's clerk, mill workers and carters occupied the Mill Office and Mill Cottages in 1891 and 1901, with Stephen Maton and John Backburne there at both dates. The presence of a machine minder at the mill in 1901 suggests that technology was catching up with the trade. Henry Knight, basket-maker, was at the Clappers with five children in 1891, the year

Caversham Mill.

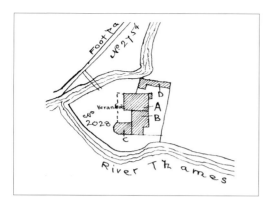

A plan of the house on View Island made by the Inland Revenue when they carried out a survey in 1910 of every building in the country.

of his bankruptcy. The willow trade still had some hold in 1901 because Helen Hedges was keeping osier beds and John Maton, son of the miller, was a basket worker. When the mill and mill cottages were sold in 1905 to E J Jesse and the mill occupied by A Clarke, the Hedges continued to rent a 3-roomed cottage, a vegetable garden and the osier beds from the owner. In 1901 a house on View Island, called Caversham House, formerly the Adams & Gyngell boathouse, was occupied by James Watts, a member of the London Stock Exchange. He was still in occupation in 1910. The mill was valued at nearly £7,000 and the house on View Island at £1,800 in 1910.[24]

Endnotes

1   E Hawthorne *Electric boats on the Thames 1889–1914* (Alan Sutton, 1995), ch 7.

2   *Reading Observer* 2 March 1895 p 1.

3   Bill was trading on the Reading side from 1891 but a new advert for the Crown on Caversham Bridge in 1895 (new because it announced a change of management) still described its position as along side Moss's landing stage.

4   *Lock to Lock Times* (*LTLT*) no 194, 6 February 1892. A boat of this name had been sold to Freeman, a boatbuilder in Wargrave.

5   Oxfordshire County Council Photographic Archive, ref 2004/8/1, 'Thames Side looking towards Caversham Bridge'.

6   *LTLT* no 404, 27 April 1895 p 3.

7   *LTLT* no 322, 18 Aug 1894.

8   A Verey, S Sampson, A French and S Frost *The Berkshire Yeomanry: 200 years of yeoman service* (Alan Sutton, 1994). This volume describes the training at Reading in 1895 (p 24) and has photographs of the regimental band and the Reading Troop, both in 1898 (p 21–22); *LTLT* 25 May 1895 no 408.

9   *LTLT* no 174 vol v, 12 September 1891, p 5.

10 *LTLT* no 414 6 July 1895, p 1. *The Shop Girl*, 52ft x 15ft, contained a salon, a dining room to seat 14, 2 bedrooms and a room for the servants. 'As is the case with most well-equipped boats, the saloon contains that indispensable aid to harmony, a piano'.

11 *LTLT* no 301 and 302, 24 and 31 March 1894.

12 *LTLT* 22 July 1899 p 4–5.

13 Information from Roy Gyngell, grandson of Samuel and Flora Gyngell née Adams, to whom thanks are given. A statement in *The Times* on 9 May 1896 about the dissolution refers to S W Gyngell and R Adams. This may be an error for Benjamin or there may have been a third person involved.

14 MERL, P DX 323, PH1 E4S/29, Thames Side.

15 *LTLT* no 451, 26 September 1896.

16 *LTLT* no 404, 27 April 1895.

17 *LTLT* no 233, vol v, 8 April 1893, p 3.

18 Emmer Green Residents Association *Emmer Green Past and Present* (Map Reading, 2003), p 76–77. Further detail about Stephen Ivens was supplied by Margaret Ormonde of Map Reading from the research for that book and thanks are given to her for this information. Frank Pearce who later bought the sheds referred to them in family papers as barge sheds.

19 BRO, D/EX 1468/1, papers of William Wing, account book 1882–99 p 15 & 19. In 1900 Messrs Nicholas were offering building plots for sale in Caversham and Mapledurham, many with frontage to the Thames.

20 *LTLT* no 584, 10 May 1902 p 6.

21 *LTLT* 13 May 1897 p 13 and 2 July 1898 p 13.

22 *Berkshire Chronicle* 10 March 1900.

23 RLSL, photographic collection, house on View Island; Caversham Mill.

24 *LTLT* no 446, 22 Aug 1896 p 3; TNA, IR 58/68946 entry 2056 and /68938, entries 2028, 2029 and 2036.

13 The old riverside pattern begins to break up: 1896–1910

A new century begins

The Coronation of Edward VII was the big event of 1902. The town celebrated it in great style, as it had the Jubilee five years earlier. There were aquatic sports at King's Meadow and a water carnival between Caversham Bridge and the lock, this area being illuminated splendidly. The lighting at the bridge was by gas and the Reading Electric Light Company lit the riverside from East's boathouse to the bridge with arc lamps and ran a cable across to the Oxfordshire side. The illuminations on the island were arranged by Reading Rowing Club and the Codgers, a social and philanthropic club that was the forerunner of the Island Bohemian Club, or at least had members in common with it.[1] After the illuminated boats had been judged – Mr A H Cane of Reading Rowing Club won the first prize of £5 – they formed up in procession and were towed by a steam launch. The mayor was in a barge lent by Arthur East, there was a troupe of pierrots and the band of the Royal Berkshire Regiment played.

By 1903 the pattern of riverside business that appeared during the boom years was still discernible but it was beginning to break up. The firms were competing now for people's leisure time, not just with one another, but also against other interests and activities. People were joining sports clubs or going cycling or just enjoying their homes. Caversham was a pleasant suburb;

the houses were lit by gas or electricity and they had gardens. There were allotments too. The boat companies would have been pleased by any novelty that brought people out of their homes to the riverside and in June 1904 they welcomed Tom Barton, the champion log-roller of the world. He came to give a performance of Canadian log-rolling on a log made of Bovril tins. He left Caversham Bridge at 7pm and went downstream and through the lock to the Recreation Ground at King's Meadow.

Adams & Gyngell had gone, although John Tims was operating from the Clappers site. East was still building. Bona and Cawston with their big steam launches and steamers were still there, (although Bona had tried unsuccessfully to sell the *Bonafide*, licensed for 215 passengers, by auction with Simmons & Son), and Freebody and Moss with their small boats, were also still there.[2] All these four had been in business for over 30 years and two, Cawston and Freebody, had sons to follow them. (Bill's son had died in 1896.) Salters continued to run steamers through their area. It was still on foot or by public transport that people came to go on the river; Moss advertised that he was 5 minutes walk from the stations and on the tram route from the town.

The 1903 season was disturbed by unseasonable floods in June. Winter floods were not too much of a problem to the small boat firms but summer floods were a different matter. Both Bona and

Cawston had to suspend services, river traffic was at a standstill and there was serious damage.

Antonio Bona died in 1905 and the Caversham Bridge Hotel was offered for sale by auction shortly afterwards but it did not sell. His boats also went into the auction: the *England* sold for £700, *Bonafide* £750, *Fashion* £440 and the *Caversham*, bought by Mr East, made £350. In 1909 a company called Country Hotels Ltd was formed to take over Bona's hotel and to run it as 'a catering establishment for persons using the river and for residents in Reading'. Catering would be its primary object and the sale of drinks a mere subsidiary.

In 1908 there was some extreme weather in the Thames Valley. There were three days of snow at the end of April, which settled to a depth of 8in, followed by a hard frost. The body of a swan that was nesting above the bridge was completely covered by the snow so that only her head and neck were showing. When the snow melted further up the river, the water level rose 15in in eight hours at the bridge, the meadows on the Berkshire side were flooded, and the flow caused a great deal of work for the boatmen who had all their boats out ready for the season. The swan's nest was swamped by the floods but the eggs were saved and taken away to be hatched. Reading Rowing Club had to cancel a regatta because of the flood but held an evening smoking concert at the Thames Valley Hotel instead.[3]

The site of Bona's boat business was occupied by East in 1910 but was later in the hands of a branch of Maynards of Windsor, under the management of E J Maynard of 225 Caversham Road. In about 1914 they were running the *Britannia* which took 200 passengers and the *Princess Christian*. They also ran the *Lady Emily*, originally part of the Windsor fleet and in use since the 1890s, a typical steamer in design, with covered and outside seating, but smaller than most and advertised for the use of family parties.[4]

All passenger boats capable of carrying 200 passengers had to be registered with the Board of Trade and every Thames boat registered with a unique name. Although the name *Britannia* had been used at least three times before (William Freebody's barge in 1815, a barge auctioned at Maidenhead in 1832 and a Mr Southwart's steam launch in 1895), only one boat could hold the name at any one time. The others were either no longer afloat or had been renamed by the time that Maynard's much larger steamer was registered.

Two steamers moored above Caversham Bridge, the outer one Maynard's *Britannia*.

There were fashions in boat names, as in house or street names, and national events like the Boer War could bring about a spate of changes, introducing names like *Pretoria* or *Mafeking*.

The petrol engine

As early as 1886, before the peak years of steam and electric boats had even been reached, the engineer Daimler had fitted a launch with an internal combustion engine. By 1891 a boat with a petrol engine was running regularly between Richmond and Wandsworth and in 1895 Lanchester had designed a boat as a motor vessel and two years later had extended the design to include a reversible propeller. The spark in these early engines was produced by an explosive charge of petroleum spirit and air, ignited by compression in a heated platinum tube. A British engineer, Priestman, created a marine engine with a timed electrical spark in 1901 and this development marked the beginning of popular, and safer, motor boating. The first motor boat owners were primarily interested in racing and so they stayed in the estuaries and on the coast. Then on the river the motor boat did exactly what the steam launch had done fifty years earlier. It pushed boat ownership back up the social scale, speed and effluent caused new problems on the water and new controls were brought in to regulate use.

A motor punt appeared at Caversham in 1903 but local people were doubtful that the idea would catch on. The same year East launched and offered for sale a 35ft carvel launch with a 12 horse-power petrol motor. There were enough privately owned petrol-driven boats on the Thames by 1904 to generate interest in a weekly item called 'River Motor News' in the *Lock to Lock Times* and in the first issue of the magazine *The Motor Boat*. That same year Huntley and Palmers had a fireboat driven by a petrol engine built by Merryweathers, the fire appliance builders at Greenwich, and this was kept on the canal close to the factory. The engine was 60hp with pumps which delivered 600 gallons of water a minute in 6 jets.[5] There was a sufficient number of motor boats in 1905

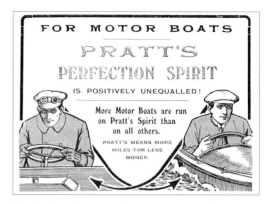

FOR MOTOR BOATS

PRATT'S

PERFECTION SPIRIT

IS POSITIVELY UNEQUALLED!

More Motor Boats are run on Pratt's Spirit than on all others.

PRATT'S MEANS MORE MILES FOR LESS MONEY.

Pratt's advertisement projects a sporting and racy image for the boat owner on the previously quiet waters of the Thames.[6]

to require the Thames Conservancy to produce new regulations.[7] Each motor boat had to carry sand to soak up any oil spilled in the boat (and this was to be enforced at Henley Regatta) and bins of sand were to be placed at each lock below Oxford. The most noticeable change was that, because of the risk of fire, no motor boat was permitted to go through a lock at the same time as any non-motor boat. On a busy day when there were queues of boats waiting their turn, the inevitable queue-jumping caused some friction.

There were enough privately-owned boats on the upper reaches to justify Pratt's Motor Spirit setting up local agencies to supply the fuel. Moss's was the first boat company in the area to appear on their lists. Other local agents included: Mr F Gale, Prospect Street; Brooks and Woollan, Caversham Road; Allen & Simmonds, De Montfort Road; Messrs Smith and Co, Vastern Road.

The riverside in public ownership

A change in land ownership on the north side of the river took place in 1902 and this made possible the present-day public access to the waterside downstream from Caversham Bridge to where Reading Bridge now stands. The Dean and Chapter of the Cathedral Church of Christ Church, Oxford, had acquired cottages, farm buildings and land, about 25 acres in all, under the will of Robert South who had died in 1716. In 1902 the Dean and Chapter sold this land to the trustees of the late Joseph Charles Fidler, potato merchant of Friar Street. The land was bounded 'on the north by other land of the vendor and by Elliotts, on the south by the river, and on the rear thereof by land reputed to belong to St Vincent's Convent, on the east by land recently purchased by the Corporation of Reading from William Dalziel Mackenzie and on the west by land reputed to belong to Frances William Knighton'.[8] It included the two small eyots alongside the tail of Fry's Island which had once been let by Crawshay of Caversham Park to Thomas Freebody for osier growing. The trustees of Mr Fidler then conveyed the land they had bought to the Corporation of Reading. In this ownership it later became accessible to the public as Christchurch Meadows with riverside paths, paddling pool, putting green, tennis courts and football pitch. The pool was built in 1924 and opened as a yachting and paddling pool, a place where model boats could be sailed and where children could play.

As well as buying Christchurch Meadows in 1902, the Corporation also bought a strip of land in 1903 which followed the river alongside the regatta course from the Caversham Bridge Hotel almost to Tilehurst. It had begun negotiations with Mrs Saunders and her trustees in 1900, under the powers of the Public Health Act 1875, to rent it at £100 a year.

The negotiations for the sale of the land were of concern to the regatta committee because it was the site on which they put their enclosure and, if it became unavailable to them, it would be a major set-back at a time when they were already going through a bad patch. The background to the situation was that in 1892 the Committee of Reading and Caversham Regatta had asked and been given the support of Reading Rowing Club to help put on a financially successful event. August Bank Holiday was selected as a regular date for the regatta so that clashes with other events could be avoided and to ensure a good turnout of local people. All kinds of entertainments were put on to attract them, displays, concerts, dancing, military

bands and illuminations. Attendance was high, up to 17,000 spectators, and the one penny entrance fee that was charged for entry into the enclosure brought in a useful sum. Despite all this support and goodwill, a meeting of the regatta committee in May 1900, chaired by James Simonds, was told that the previous year had finished with a deficit and that the outlook was gloomy. The regatta meadow was for sale; it was available for just one more year, and that only because a sale had fallen through. Conditions had been imposed which would stop the building of an enclosure and the presence of sideshows on regatta day and so prevent the event being financially sound.[9] The long list of names of committee members, including well-known river men such as Ayres, Bona, Cane, and East, suggested that support had been widely canvassed in the effort to make the event secure. James Simonds was the treasurer and A Hill the president.

However, because it was the local authority that bought the land in 1903, the outcome was much less gloomy than the members feared. The Committee of the Reading Amateur Regatta was pleased to be able to announce at the AGM at the Caversham Bridge Hotel in 1903 that the meadows along the riverside would be available to them in future.

The Promenade opened in 1906. The land along the riverside was made into an informal public park, separated by an iron fence from the meadows, with well-kept grassland, flower beds, shrubs and evergreens and a line of seats beside a tarmac path. The park became an extremely popular place. It was close to the terminus of the trams and it had tea rooms. On Sundays the Promenade was the site of a church parade and band concerts were arranged. In 1912 the Friendly Societies' Hospital Parade was held there with the Town Council walking in procession. Horses and ponies were raced and driven on the Promenade on August Bank Holiday in 1918. This event was in aid of the Royal Berkshire Hospital. There was the added bonus of a newly-built public lavatory at the bridge, open daily from 6am to midnight. This was a square building made of decorated iron

The public lavatories for men and women at Caversham Bridge.

Elementary Schools Swimming Association's medal awarded to Frank Pearce in 1920 in a lifesaving competition.

panels, and painted green. The white roof was topped with a green turret and decorated at the peak with some ironwork. The panels were cast at Walter MacFarlane's foundry in Glasgow.[10]

The opening of the new Ladies' Swimming Bath at King's Meadow on 27 May 1903 was the result of another piece of forward thinking by the Corporation of Reading about the use of the riverside. It was a brick and tile building surrounding an open-air pool 120ft by 40ft, 6ft at the deep end and 3ft at the shallow end. The walls continued into an arch held up by wrought iron pillars that formed a roof to the surround and the changing rooms. The pool was lined with a white ceramic surface and it was filled from the river through a filter that prevented fish getting into the pool. The opening ceremony was performed by the Mayoress, Mrs A H Bull, and there was a special exhibition of swimming and life-saving. The pool was opened to bathers the day after the ceremony. Such a facility for women was welcomed. The ladies' section of Reading Swimming Club was founded in 1904 and the whole club met at the Ladies' Swimming Bath in 1905 for its coming-of-age events. The Parks and Pleasure Grounds Committee announced that arrangements were made for free instruction in swimming and life-saving to be offered to children at the local public elementary schools at both bathing places.[11] This was particularly important since the local authority had made so much of the river bank available to the public for leisure activities and since there were so many deaths from drowning each year.

One of the speakers at the Winter Bathers' meeting on New Year's Day in 1906 said that Reading Swimming Club had worked with the Elementary Schools Swimming Association to award for the first time life-saving certificates to 21 boys and 14 girls in local schools. The elementary schools continued their support for swimming and an annual gala was held at the Ladies' Bath. Badges in sterling silver with green lettering were awarded to winners of individual and team events. Reading Swimming Club changed its meeting place in 1912 from the Corporation's open-air pool at King's Meadow to the indoor pool at the Arthur Hill Memorial Baths. By 1914 there was a Ladies' Swimming Club whose president, Edith Sutton, organised monthly races at the baths.

There was another purchase of land by the local authority in 1911. The three small islands above Caversham Bridge and the eel bucks on them were purchased jointly by the Corporation of Reading and the Thames Conservancy. At the time the islands were let on an annual tenancy to M[ary] A[nn] Freebody with Crawshay of Caversham Park as the freeholder. The bucks and buck hedges were removed later the same year and the islands some time after, the purpose being to prevent a back-up of water behind them and so to lessen the effects of floods in the area.[12] In 1912 the Conservancy dredged Buck Stream to make it more navigable to small boats.

Rowing

Reading Rowing Club had a particularly good season in 1901, winning the Vulcan Challenge Shield and the Reading Challenge Vase. Members had competed at Henley for the first time for many years but heavy expenditure had put their finances out by £60. The club rowed its trial fours in May. It had contributed to the Coronation events along the riverside and had entertained family and friends on the island. Like the regatta committee when faced with difficult times, it had turned to local men to support it, this time as vice presidents: J H Benyon, H B Blandy, W F Blandy, A H Bull, H Burr, A S Cooper, J H Cooper, H Creed, W C Eppstein, S B Joel and six members of the Palmer family, to name only part of the list. The president was James Simonds. The committee urged members to help the club by bringing in new people.[13] All was going well in 1910 when the regatta scheduled races for sculls, pairs and fours, Mr Dryland Haslam lent his garden for an enclosure, Mr Wiltshire lent his launch for the umpires and there was a supper at the Temperance Hotel afterwards.[14]

Property values

There have been remarkably few national listings of land and property since the survey ordered by William the Conqueror. The nineteenth-century tithe records are among the few sets which hold information about ownership of land and its state of cultivation or development. The 1910 Inland Revenue valuations (sometimes called the modern Domesday) go much further, giving names of occupants, lessees and owners; rental, building and land values; descriptions of the building materials of every house and business premises, sometimes with sketches of the ground plans. The

valuations in each town were organised by parish and each one has a number which corresponds to a plot number on a plan and a page in a ledger.[15] An unprecedented picture of properties and their comparative values along the riverside comes out of this survey. It shows too how rare it was for businesses and houses to be owner-occupied and how often there was a chain of owner, leaseholder, sublease holder and occupier.

The Thames Valley Hotel at 2 Bridge Street, Caversham was owned by Annie May, occupied by G Bone on a 7-year tenancy from 1905 and valued by the survey at £2,500. It had on three floors: two kitchens, scullery, three cellars, store room, pantry, WC, coffee room, smoking room, lounge, another pantry and WC, six bedrooms and another WC. There was a billiard room in the yard. The Griffin, facing on to Church Road and with a 77ft river frontage, had similar facilities although there were only five bedrooms. It had a clubroom and outside it had stabling for three horses and a coach house and was valued at £2,000.

The Old Rectory, a detached house in its own grounds, was valued at £5,000 by the Inland Revenue, but at the time it was unoccupied. It had been put on the market the previous year. This was the house that had replaced the Striped House where the Alexanders had lived, a house on one of the most desirable sites in the town and owned by H C Simonds, who was the town's leading brewer. It was bigger than the two hotels put together, with 16 bedrooms on two floors and all the usual offices, butler's pantry and servants' room, wine cellar, billiard room and three reception rooms (A, B, C on the plan overleaf). In the centre of the back of the house there was a brick and glass fernery (D). Outside, to the right as one entered the gates, were two coach houses, stabling for seven horses and dog kennels (E, F, G, H, Q). Within the pleasure grounds there was a kitchen garden, a summerhouse (J) and boathouse (K). Along the boundary were 4 glasshouses (L), a palmery (M), and a potting shed (N) close to the river. There was a staff cottage and a coachman's house close to the main house and a fishery linked

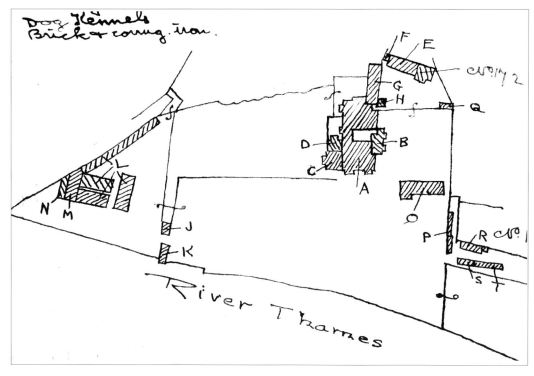

Plan of grounds of the Old Rectory from the Inland Revenue survey.

to the property was valued at £15.[16]

Mary Ann Freebody, widow of Thomas, who had come from Newbury to Caversham about 1890, was running the family business with her son Ernest. Her property was quite extensive. She owned and occupied land, a shed and boathouse in Bridge Street with a small lawn and a landing stage. Alongside was an old flint cottage used as a store and various corrugated iron sheds. The total value was £2,800. Valued separately and owned by Mrs Freebody were Willow View, a detached dwelling and boathouse combined, occupied by Ernest Freebody, and Willow Grotto, a detached house with 8 rooms and a garden, occupied by M A Freebody.[17]

The Inland Revenue entries for E H Cawston's island site immediately raise some questions about where their bigger boats were actually built. The site was rented at £60 pa from Vanderstegen, a local landowner, valued at £1,250 with the structures at £300.[18] There were two small boathouses on the island, one under the bridge and the other on the downstream side of Waterman's Cottage.

Neither of these was big enough to have housed the steamer *Majestic* while it was under construction two years earlier, nor was there a slipway on site. This boat was the flagship of the Cawston fleet. It had a wooden hull with a bowsprit, and its varnished woodwork distinguished it from the other steamers and continued to do so even when it was running as part of the Salter fleet 50 years later. Cawston had built the *Starlight* and the *Mystery*, both full-sized steamers, some years before and was advertising his new steam launch *Eclipse* throughout 1900 for hire by small or large parties. He must therefore have had access to larger premises for the construction work. Some press comment in 1895 from two sources when the *River Queen* was being built takes on a new significance in considering where these big boats might have been built. The press in April 1895 had said that extra men from London had been brought in to try to complete the work to schedule.[19] It was reported in August that the machinery had been made for that boat by the late E Clarke of Stroud and that Mr E Marsh, a well known down-river expert, was the designer and builder and could be congratulated on his skilful workmanship.[20] Local directories place E L G Marsh at Caversham Bridge so there may have been co-operation between the two boatbuilders on large projects, with perhaps the Talbot bargebuilding shed as a possible site.[21] Edward Cawston died in 1912 and was succeeded by his twin sons, Edward William and William Edward.[22]

Bill Moss retires and Harry Isaacs takes over

When Bill Moss retired in about 1909 his business was taken over by Harry John Isaacs. The first time the two names are linked is in 1892 when both were at the AGM of the Reading Swimming Club, Harry attending as a member and Bill as an entertainer.[24] Harry was born in London in 1867, son of Isaac Isaacs, a stockbroker, and was in Reading by 1881.

He was a keen sportsman, a founder and life member of the swimming club, a sprinter and a supporter of Reading Athletic Club, a player

The steamer *Majestic*.[23]

and committee member of the amateur Reading Football Club, a member of the Amateur Boxing Board of Control and an honorary member of Reading Rowing Club. In 1886, when he was 24, he was awarded the bronze medal of the Royal Humane Society for rescuing at great personal risk William Godsell, an engineer's clerk, from drowning in the Thames at Reading. Godsell, who was also awarded a bronze medal, had gone into the water to try to save Robert Jackson but had failed and got into difficulties himself and had to be

The winter bathers, 1912. Harry Isaacs is behind and to the right of the tall white-haired man who is in the front row. He appears in all the photos up until 1913. Numbers are much reduced in 1914.

ENTRIES for CHRISTMAS MORNING HANDICAPS

VETERANS

Dr Stansfield	Mr Mosdell
Mr Clemetson	" Rawlings
" Cusden	" Sawtell
" Eighteen	" Watson
" Holloway	" Wyatt

OPEN HANDICAP

Mr Bosher	Mr Kent
" Butler	" Makeham
" Childs	" Mason
" Clemetson (Jun)	" Mitchell
" Cooper	" Newton
" Cusden (jun)	" Pearce
" Daniels	" Pounds
" Davis	" Skowronel
" Ellis	" Spyer
" Emslie	" Pudge
" Freeman	" Thorne
" Gardener	" Tucker
" Goodson	" Wills
" Griffin	" Wood
" Hewitt	" Wright (Sen)
" Isaacs	" Wright (Jun)
" Jones	

Reading Winter Bathers

THE ANNUAL
BREAKFAST
WILL TAKE PLACE AT
Phillips' Restaurant
DUKE STREET

ON

Christmas Morning 1908
AT 8.45 PROMPT

Chairman	Mr A. WATSON
Vice Chairman	Mr J. EIGHTEEN

saved. Harry Isaacs was an active swimming club member, playing in its water polo team in 1888, acting as a steward for the club's seventh costume entertainments at South Street baths and winning one of the heats for the one-length handicap race in 1891. That same year he was awarded a bronze clasp in recognition of rescuing someone from the sea at great personal risk when on holiday in Great Yarmouth.[25] He was a member of the Reading Codgers and its debating society and a committee member of Reading Philanthropic Institution.

Harry Isaacs turned out regularly with the Winter Bathers, a group of local business people and members of Reading Swimming Club who swam regularly in the river and who followed their swim at Christmas with a breakfast. The group was swimming in 1908, when there were 10 veterans entered for a handicap race and 33 others for an open handicap. Their breakfast that year was at 8.45 am at Phillips Restaurant in Duke Street, and they were photographed at the Abbey Ruins. These events are well documented by a series of photos taken at Christmas between 1908 and 1914 at the Old Shire Hall in the Forbury, in the Abbey Ruins and near the present Reading Bridge. In the 1911 photo there are two ladies among the group, one of whom is well wrapped in furs. One of the youngest in the photo that year, the group mascot, James Sargeant, recalled when he was in his 70s, that it was cold enough for ice to be broken on more than one occasion.[26] He said that one of the women in the photo was Miss Cusden, daughter of J Cusden, a local printer, and sister of Albert Cusden, both of

ON GUARD

A mop tournament, a popular event at riverside parties like those held on Moss's Island.

Island Bohemian Club members photographed by P O Collier in or before 1917. This was one of three Island Bohemian Club group photos rescued from a rubbish heap, but not before it had suffered some damage.

BACK ROW: H S Awmack, G Gray, F C Rivers, F Holt, J F Booth, P S Clemetson, A Hope, A H Goodey;
FRONT ROW: C J Stockwell, G L C Rivers, W G Barton (Hon Sec), W Moss (President), S H Newport (Hon Sec), E Shuttle, H J Isaacs (Hon Treasurer).

whom were keen Winter Bathers and swimming club members.[27] James remembered also the fish, ham, eggs, bacon and tea that were served for breakast afterwards.

With Harry Isaacs' interest in swimming he must have come to know Bill Moss quite well. Reading Swimming Club's outdoor section had been using a bathing place on the Caversham side of Fry's Island since the 1890s and at a meeting of the committee in 1905 chaired by Isaacs, it was suggested that members should use Moss's bathing place as the swimming headquarters in the morning and evening but that the monthly races be held in the baths and that Mr Moss should be approached for a reduction in his 2s 6d season ticket. So it was from this sporting and social connection that Harry saw the opportunity to change his job and left Huntley and Palmers in 1909 to take over the boatbuilding and boat-letting business from Bill.

Bill Moss moved across to Mill Green after he retired. He continued to fish and to be active in the preservation of fish stocks. He was a member of the Island Bohemian Club, which had opened in 1908, and was president in 1917, a year when Harry was treasurer. Both are in the photograph taken by P O Collier: Bill is in the centre of the front row and is easily picked out as the only one wearing a hat.[28] Island Bohemian Club members played tennis or bowls, swam with the Reading Swimming Club members from the bathing place or simply enjoyed the riverside environment. The overlap in membership of these two clubs and the Codgers and the Winter Bathers group suggests

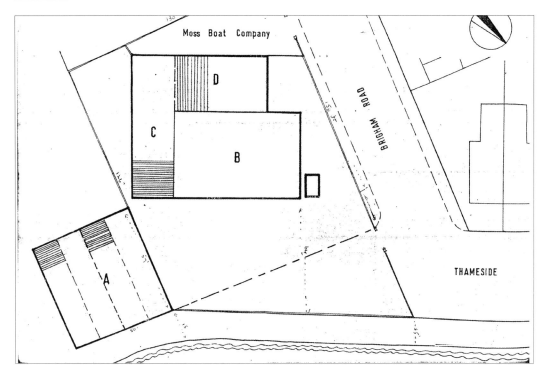

A plan of Moss's Boat House buildings.

that very much the same social group belonged to all four. In 1909 the swimming club joined with the Island Bohemian Club to hold a gala on Moss's island, followed by a concert and dancing. On that occasion the club planned a one-mile open race, comic costume competition, fancy diving, a mop tournament, 44yd handicap, duck hunt, greasy pole, water polo and an elementary schools race. Prizes would be given by Mr Awmack and Harry Isaacs, both of whom are in the Island Bohemian Club photo.[29]

This event is a very good illustration of how membership of a single-interest club at this time could extend into social events for friends and family. In about 1910 the IBC sent members to take part in the Tilehurst Water Carnival with teams entering the mop tournament, the tug-of-war in punts and the mixed dongola races and in 1912 the club combined with Reading Athletic Club to hold a carnival on the island for members and their families. There was a whist drive, a concert and dance and sports in the afternoon.[30]

Moss's Boat House

When Harry Isaacs took over from Bill Moss, the main boathouse consisted of one big wooden shed with a mainly earth floor and heavy sliding doors. This was the building on the right in the photograph opposite and marked B, C and D on the plan.[31] It had a high, domed corrugated-iron roof under which were suspended slatted wooden lofts. These were where the horse-hair cushions and the canvas camping covers were stored. For working purposes the shed was divided into three bays: B was fitted with storage racks for all boats except punts and for oars, poles and paddles and the others, C and D on the map, with concrete floors, were the working areas for boat repair and boatbuilding and for the storage of paint, varnish, linseed oil, putty and all the tools of the trade. There were some small rooms, originally dressing rooms, built within the shed but the main part was completely open and unheated. On the left, A on the plan, was the punt shed, so named for the boats stored in it in the winter, stacked upside down and

The buildings as they appeared in a magazine article on the boathouse in the 1920s. Punts ready for camping lets are on the water and the skiffs are pulled up on the front.

supported on racks or trestles. This shed fronting the towpath was Bill's original building.

A small wooden office was at the side, with two wooden steps leading up to a 'stable' door. There were wooden shelves on two sides and two items left by Bill Moss: a stuffed pike in a glass case and the clock from his original building at Caversham Bridge. On one wall there was a series of framed cartoons of local sportsmen, originals from a series that appeared each week in the local paper. The telephone mouthpiece was fixed to the wall below the pike and the bell-shaped earpiece hung alongside it. There was an extension to the house at Thames Side, brought into use by a turning a small handle attached to a box. The main bell was outside the big shed. The ledgers, bought from Knills in Minster Street, in which were recorded the hiring details (boat number, time out, deposit paid) were on a desk near the door. Just in front of the office were a flagpole and a well-established black poplar tree (which in some years attracted large moths). There was enclosed land to the side and the rear. The boathouse was set back some 50ft from the river edge. There was a wooden landing stage with metal mooring rings along the entire river frontage. Punts were traditionally moored between lets on the left, skiffs on the right, looking

from the river, as in the photograph above.[32]

The Moss's team is shown overleaf photographed outside the boathouse and the date is about 1920. Harry John Isaacs is sitting on the right and his stepson Frank Pearce is in the boat. The others are (from the left) Dick Parker, an unknown, Alfred Cook and Ernest Simmonds. Ernie had been in a mustard gas attack during the First World War and suffered from the effects of this for the rest of his life. He and Alf stayed with the firm for many years. It was Ernie who said 'All our boats have been "christened"', a commentary on the use of the privacy provided to couples by a punt moored under the willow trees! Behind the group of Moss employees in the photograph are some skiffs pulled out of the water with the rudders taken out of their seating on the stern of the boat and stowed in-board. There is also a canoe with the bow section just visible between the second and third figures from the left. The metal bars set into the ground parallel to the water, over which boats could be slid from the shed to the water or back again, can also be seen. The boat in the front is a clinker-built dinghy pulled up, also with its rudder in-board. It has metal rowlocks and the length of the oars is in keeping with that of the boat.

Moss Boat Company work team.

Boats for letting were mostly single and double Thames skiffs and punts, an occasional treble skiff or randan, with some Canadian and other canoes, dinghies and fishing punts.[33] They were all handmade, varnished inside and above the waterline outside to show the wood grain and tarred outside below the waterline. Oars and paddles were also handmade with each oar having a band of leather round it where it made contact with the rowlock. Layers of leather were built up on the end of the band to make a stop to prevent the oar slipping out of the rowlock when in use. The punts were sent out with two pairs of paddles and a punt pole but not many custom-ers used the poles because the depth of the river on this reach was too great to make it easy, and it was also very weedy in places. Most preferred instead to sit as a pair in the stern of the boat and to send it along with one pair of paddles. Hire boats were not normally given names. Each boat carried a numbered licence plate to show that the Thames Conservancy fees had been paid for the current year and some private boats also carried

a lock pass which allowed them to go through the lock without further payment. The company was a member of The Thames Boating Trades Association Ltd which was established in 1838 and the sign to this effect was attached to the corner post of the punt shed just below roof level.

The Moss premises appear twice in the Inland Revenue documents with different valuations: £900 and £1,250. The first said that Harry Isaacs was owner and occupier with a leasehold interest from G E Cooke to Miss Bull for 99 years. The second said that Harry was the owner, W Moss had a leasehold interest and a superior interest was held by G Lewis and Cooke's Estate.[34] Family records suggest that neither of these was accurate. Some notes in a pocket diary for 1910, the year of the Inland Revenue survey, belonging to Harry and made in his own handwriting, add some more variations to the dataset.

The information in the Inland Revenue sur-vey about those with interests in Fry's Island, here called De Montfort Island, again threw up some new names and some surprising omissions

P. O. COLLIER

Press and Commercial

PHOTOGRAPHER

13, THAMES BANK, Reading

PHONE : 1482

Boathouse: Parish of St Lawrence;
Occupier: H J I;
Repairs: made by H J I;
Leasehold: 99 years from 10 Feb 1890;
Lessor: T Ayres from the late J C Fidler;
Description: boathouse and shed;
Value: only valuable as boathouse;
Repairs & insurance: occupier.

Information from Harry's notebook about his premises.

although the description of the area used by the Island Bohemian Club does generally match with further information in Harry's notebook.[35] There are also some inaccuracies in the information given about some of the small islands. One reason for the discrepancies is perhaps that Fry's Island and the small islets are exceptional kinds of landholdings and allowance should be made for this. These inaccuracies are not significant in

the story of the river and do not detract from the value of the survey as an addition to the sources available to local historians, but they do add a note of caution in using it.

The three-bedroomed house at the down-stream end of the island, valued at £1,200, was occupied by Mrs C Hutchinson but no other information was given about ownership. Its identity can be confirmed by some references in the Inland Revenue ledger to the nearness of the ice factory and the electric light works. The rowing club premises are described but not the adjoining barge sheds. The small wooden bungalow and wet boathouse built in the 1890s by Henry Dundas, the manager of Reading Theatre, was described as a leasehold property worth £150, owned and occupied by Mrs Dundas.

The houses in Thames Side (originally Thames Bank) including the block of five with balconies and frontage to the towpath (nos 15–19), were individually occupied but collectively owned by T Chapman who leased them for 99 years from Cooke's Trustees, major landowners in the area. The surveyor added a note to say that 'these houses are very unlettable' but despite this they were valued at £465 and £470 each. Chapman lived at no 18, next door to Harry Isaacs, and P O Collier was at no 13 with a lease from A H Bull.[36] At about this time the premises of E B Badcock, timber and slate merchant, on the upstream side of the houses were a new development and an engineering company had replaced the Talbot timber mill at Caversham Bridge.

Endnotes

1 *Berkshire Chronicle* 'A Reading convivial society' 23 Sept 1938 p 6. The Codgers Club (1890s) offered a social evening free from political argument and rancour at the Sun in Castle Street and later at the Bell in Broad Street. Members contributed musical or other items or put money into a charity box. River men among the early members were T J Waldron, Bill Moss and Will Hives.

2 *Kelly's Directory* 1903 John Tims and Sons, The Clappers, Reading; East's Boat Building Co Ltd, Caversham Lock and Kennet Mouth; W Moss, 19 Thames Bank Reading; Freebody, Caversham Bridge; Cawston, Caversham Bridge.

3 *Lock to Lock Times* [*LTLT*] no 723, 2 May 1908 p 10.

4 Reading Local Studies Library photograph collection (reference R/IM) has pictures of these three boats mounted on Maynard's trade cards and dated by the library as about 1914.

5 *LTLT* no 628, 30 April 1904, p 12.

6 *LTLT* 10 June 1910, p 1.

7 Thames Conservancy Act 1905.

8 BRO, D EX 1279/2/3 Will of Joseph Charles Fidler.

9 *Berkshire Chronicle* 5 May 1900.

10 In 1985 the building was donated by the Council to the Chiltern Open Air Museum at Chalfont St Giles.

11 *LTLT* no 612, 13 June 1903, also no 608, 16 May 1903 and no 610, 30 May 1903.

12 Thames Conservancy report, Minutes of Berkshire County Council, 1912 p 160.

13 *LTLT* no 609, 23 May 1903.

14 It seems that the Temperance Hotel changed its name to the Thames Valley Hotel but local use of the new name may have lagged behind.

15 Unfortunately the map for Caversham has not been deposited at TNA and so the notebooks are the only source for this parish. The approach to Caversham Bridge on the Reading side comes within St Mary's parish and the riverside into St Laurence.

16 TNA, IR 58/68919 Inland Revenue survey, Caversham.

17 TNA, IR 58/68932 Inland Revenue survey, Caversham.

18 TNA, IR 58/68932 Inland Revenue survey, Caversham.

19 *LTLT* no 404, 27 April 1895 p 2, .

20 *Berkshire Chronicle* 3 August 1895 and *LTLT* 3 August 1895 both carried this information;. *LTLT* no 427, 25 April 1896 provided construction details of *River Queen*: 72ft by 12ft 10in by 4ft 8in, double skinned, 1½in thick, and copper fastened and bolted throughout. Board of Trade trials were in April 1896.

21 There is a reference to a Mr E G L Marsh as a local boatbuilder in the *Victoria County History of Berkshire* vol 1 p 386.

22 Two younger sons, Percy Frederick and Arthur Reuben were also boatbuilders. Percy died in Reading in 1919. Arthur ran the business on Pipers Island while Edward had the mainland site opposite.

23 Salter Brothers River Thames Passenger Boats, www.simplonpc.co.uk/SalterBros.html, *Majestic*

24 *Berkshire Chronicle* 7 May 1892 col 2. AGM of the swimming club.

25 Royal Humane Society case numbers 23090 and 23091 and case number 25635 jointly with George Ceily.

26 The series of photos and the original of the 1908 breakfast invitation are the property of Mr R Butler. The recollections of James Sergeant are from the *Evening Post* 16 December 1971. A copy of the 1912 photo is at the BRO and Mr Butler senior, Mr Cottrell and Mr Wood and others have been identified in it.

27 A Stout *A bigness of heart: Phoebe Cusden of Reading* (Reading, 1997), p 19–20.

28 P O Collier (1881–1979) was an electrical engineer in 1901 and a commercial photographer and postcard publisher working in Reading from around 1905. 'Os' Collier was a neigh-

bour of the Pearce family in Thames Side, formerly Thames Bank.

29 BRO, D Ex 1502/1 Reading Swimming Club committee minutes 1903–1911.

30 BRO, D Ex 1502/1 Press cutting with Reading Swimming Club committee minutes 1903–1911.

31 Map by Eric Hives and Sons, chartered architects (1966), for H Markham Ltd. The basic structure had not changed between 1920 and 1966.

32 Photo taken from an article 'Boat Building on the Thames' from *The Country Illustrated* about 1922. The caption is 'Some of our Camping Craft, Moss's Speciality'.

33 J Cox and M Edwards *Glossary of Thames Boat and Punt Terms* (Thames Traditional Boat Society, 2004). This book is illustrated with drawings and plans of boats and has explanations of rowing terms back to the 1860s.

34 TNA, IR 58/69228 plot 936 and 69232 plot 1383, Inland Revenue survey Reading St Laurence. The boathouse has two entries each with a different value.

35 TNA, IR 58/69221 Inland Revenue survey Reading St Laurence.

36 TNA, IR 58/69228 Inland Revenue survey Reading St Laurence.

14 Two difficult decades: 1900–1920

A new management board

In 1908 the Port of London Bill transferred responsibility for the Thames below Teddington to the Port of London Authority while leaving the Upper Thames with the Thames Conservancy. The representation of local interests on the proposed new Conservancy board caused much discussion and dissatisfaction. Reading Corporation and Berkshire and Oxfordshire County Councils would each nominate one member to represent them. Caversham, which had a long river frontage and an Urban District Council, would have no right to nominate a member to the board, either individually or collectively with the other UDCs. Special interest groups thought that the boatbuilding trades, barge owners, fisheries, preservation societies, riparian owners, boat owners and sporting clubs should all have a say in how the river was run. They could see however that their representatives would have to be elected rather than nominated and that the constitution of the board would have to be changed to accommodate this. Even the London Metropolitan Water Board was reported to be unhappy with its single representative on the new board because this would give it just one vote on behalf of consumers wanting pure water to set against the votes of representatives of areas from which the water was drawn, and where there was no such agenda. The key to the argument was that only

the bigger authorities were contributing directly to the cost of river management and they were the only ones with a real need to be represented. A conference was held at Reading by invitation of Berkshire County Council and was attended by representatives of interested County Councils and of Reading Corporation. This meeting endorsed the proposals of the Bill but agreed that a deputation should go to the minister in charge to discuss including a provision in the legislation for borrowing or raising further revenue, since capital expenditure of £70,000 would be required for work on locks, weirs and the towpath, and up to £4000 a year for dredging. In this decade revenue for the Conservancy came from the London Water Companies (£30,000), pleasure traffic (£9000) and barge traffic (£1000).

Fishery protection

Angling remained a very popular sport and regulation of fishing and preservation of fish stocks continued to be the concern of the Thames Conservancy and the fishing clubs. The Reading and District Angling Association reported in 1905 that a lack of funds was preventing restocking and that visiting anglers must be encouraged to contribute to the care of the river. The time would come when voluntary societies would have to give up their efforts and press for a Fishery Board with power to impose a rod tax. Bailiffs and river-keepers had been active, after floods went down, in restoring fish left stranded in meadows to safe homes. In March the Caversham and District anglers held a peg-down competition but the results were very poor, with only one member catching anything. They finished the day with dinner at the Prince of Wales in Prospect Street.[1] The Reading and Thames Angling Association netted part of the Kennet in April 1905 and as a result 1500 fish (grayling, perch, dace, roach and chub) were transferred to the Thames.

In the same year the Conservators expressed their concerns about the considerable traffic that existed on the river in undersized fish for use as live bait. In a letter to the Upper River Committee attention was drawn to the byelaws which stated that casting or bait nets should only be used by an assistant river-keeper to obtain bait for those angling in the Thames, and that no person should have in their possession more than 50 fish for use as bait in any one day, except for use in baiting eel baskets. However there was nothing to prevent trading in fish caught by rod and line as long as no more than 50 undersized fish were taken. So not only were the approved river-keepers netting bait for club members, and individual anglers taking undersized fish for their own needs, but some were making money from selling bait caught illegally. This was a major problem because weekend anglers arrived on the riverbank by the train-load, and the potential market for the illegal bait was great. Anglers were reminded in 1906 by the Thames Angling Preservation Society that it was permissible to fish for trout in the way of live baiting, fly fishing or spinning but in no other way. Worms were *not* permissible under the byelaws. Fish stocks were further damaged in the hot summer of 1911.[2]

It was decided that one way to stop the illegal netting was to authorise a limited number only of assistant river-keepers or water bailiffs to be entitled to use, or to have the power to use, cast nets. The granting of this right or 'deputation' was at the discretion of the Conservators and it had to be renewed each year. The holder had to understand that any contravention of the byelaws

relating to catching or possessing undersized fish to be used as bait would result in the immediate withdrawal of the deputation. A limited number of deputations was assigned to the recommendation of each of the leading angling societies, and only registered fishermen prepared to assist with enforcing fishery byelaws were eligible to be put forward. Thus both the provision of live bait by casting and the policing of the illegal use of nets were put into reliable hands within the framework of the angling associations. Bill Moss was one of about nine appointees in 1915 recommended by the Royal Counties Angling and Preservation Society. This body included the Reading and District Angling Association and the Reading Waltonian Angling Society. Bill's deputation was renewed in 1916 and continued until his death in 1918. His son-in-law, Peter Smith, was also a deputation holder over the same period.[3]

The 'King Alfred'

In 1909 a new vessel arrived on the Caversham bank just below Piper's Island. This was a two-masted brig, moored at the edge of Knighton's Meadow, which was to be fitted out as a training ship for boys of 14 to 17 years of age. The idea had originated with Herbert Grey of Bradfield College in 1902 as something which would form a permanent memento of the Coronation of Edward VII. It was estimated that the cost would be £250 and the running costs £60 a year.

Work began in June to fit it out under the supervision of Rear Admiral Fleet, Hon Secretary of the Brig Committee, using materials bought locally where possible. Mr J Rushton, late Chief Petty Officer RN, had done the rigging, helped by Walter Owen, a local boy and the first recruit, and assistance had come from, among others, Messrs Knighton, Talbot, Cawston, George Lewis, and Harry J Isaacs, and from the Navy League. Twenty boys had been enrolled and Martin J Sutton of Suttons Seeds had donated 20 jerseys and caps. On Trafalgar Day the ship was named *King Alfred* in the presence of a huge crowd on both banks. The event began with a procession which started from the Caversham Coffee House and consisted of the Caversham Brass Band, boys from the brig and from the Windsor sister ship, two troops of scouts, the Reading and the Caversham Fire Brigades and local veterans from the Crimea and the Indian Mutiny. All these, and the principal visitors, were taken across from the Berkshire bank on the steamer *Majestic*. Archdeacon Ducat conducted a service and Sir John Carrington spoke about the history of the project. Lady Rose of Hardwick performed the naming ceremony and she 'hoisted the flag with the assistance of Rear Admiral Fleet while the boys presented arms and the band played a verse of the National Anthem. A salute of 21 guns followed and the band struck up 'Rule Britannia''. One of the speakers said that:

> It was important that there should be an outlet for a certain class of boys who hitherto it had been hard to place. There was a chance for a boy whose parents felt he was a splendid boy but who could

not help being naughty sometimes and could not keep to a task or occupation under cover and this was just the boy to send to sea. The brig offered an opportunity to a boy to decide how he liked the life before going to sea. He would be serving His Majesty on board ship which every Englishman should be proud to do.[4]

Working conditions of lock-keepers

The men who looked after the locks and weirs had a difficult job and had previously put forward their case for changes without success. Many of them were retired naval men, with a pension in addition to their wages, and it was a popular view of their situation that they were well off, particularly living rent-free, with their opportunities to sell produce and refreshments and to make and sell fishing tackle, fishing flies and baskets. In 1910–11 a subcommittee of the Thames Conservators looked

The brig *King Alfred* lying at Knighton's Meadow just below Freebody's premises.

into the state of the lock-keepers and found that they were very poorly off, and that they could not exist on annual wages of £40 or £50 alone, sums which had not been changed for many years. The Caversham lock-keeper was said to be too poor to marry and too near to Reading to derive business from refreshments. The long hours of work, particularly in the summer, made it impossible for them to take a second job, or even a day off, and they were always on call, winter and summer, to regulate the water level by raising or lowering the sluice gates on the weir. The Sonning keeper had the added task of seeing barges through at night when they came down from the Kennet and Avon. Although there were no immediate changes after the review, a Lock Staff Special Committee was formed to keep the issues under consideration. Many of the keepers went back to active service in 1914 and their wives took over their roles, but it was to be another few years before their wages were adjusted and it was not until just before the second world war that their working conditions were improved.[5]

Accidents on the river

One of the points made to the Conservancy on behalf of the lock-keepers was that the potential for accidents in a crowded lock was great. There was a fire risk associated with the use of the petrol-engined boats that were now quite popular. When there was an accident – fire from a petrol engine or someone falling down the steep sides of the lock into the turbulent water among the boats – it was the lock-keeper who had to attempt a rescue or get the body out of the water if the rescue failed. Their own lives were at risk when they were drawing the sluices in the winter when the river level was high. All those who worked on the water knew that they would be called on to help when there were accidents and all had stories of the rescue of fishermen swept into the river from the weir, children falling from the bank or from a boat, swimmers and oarsmen in difficulty, and of suicides. Many of them had police or other commendations for their rescues. Bill Moss's

A lock-keeper at work on a summer day, winding open the sluices to alter the level of water in the lock.[6]

son-in-law, Peter Smith, went into deep water at Caversham with the lock-keeper, Ward Knight (son of Henry Knight, basket-maker), after dark one evening in May 1915 to rescue a woman and child who had fallen in, and both were awarded Royal Humane Society medals for this.[7]

If a rescue was not successful then the body would be swept down to the next lock or weir and it would be a lock-keeper or boatman who was responsible for its removal. There were particular places on the river where bodies returned to the surface and one of these was on the Reading bank at Norcot Scours, below Poplar Island and Appletree Eyot, where the river narrows and turns near Scours Lane. It is known locally as 'the Deadies' because of its history. The reason behind the phenomenon of the rising bodies appeared in an inquest into two brothers who had fallen into the water at the Scours in 1900. Both had sunk beyond reach and the Tilehurst boatman, Joseph Keel, called on to help, and knowing the spot, sent for a 19ft gudgeon rake but it was not long enough to reach them and they drowned. The inquest was told that there was a hole 22ft deep there called

Dead Man's Hole, which could not be filled in because the current would eventually scour it out again, and both boys had gone into it. Bodies drifting downstream on the river bed could also fall into this hole and when decomposition made them rise to the surface, then it was at the Deadies that they did so.[8]

The licensing system for motor boats

In 1913 the Conservators acknowledged that although new byelaws had helped to reduce the risks of petrol engines, there were still concerns, and an additional safeguard would be to regulate the carriage of petroleum in bulk.[9] They introduced a licence system for petrol boats under the Thames Motor Launch Byelaws 1914 to ensure that boat owners complied with the regulations. Before the licence plate was issued, the boat had to be available for inspection with the engine in fully-working order and the tank filled with petrol. The licence plate, which was valid for one year, had to be fixed to the boat and any accident, fire or explosion had to be reported to the Thames Conservancy within 48 hours. Inspection and licensing were free but registration cost from £2 a year for a boat under 20ft to £4 for one of over 55ft. Lock tolls for the same lengths were 1s and 3s 6d. The byelaws were very specific about the need to prevent petrol leakage from fuel pipes and carburettors and to ensure that any spillage of fuel or oil was kept in the engine tray and prevented from getting into the bilge. They were also clear on the need to avoid short-circuiting or sparking in the ignition system, and equally clear that no sanitary arrangement on the boat was to be connected to the river and no sewage was to be put into the river in the non-tidal reaches above Teddington. This subject was an issue because petrol engines gave boats a longer running time and distance and consequently there was a need to have on-board toilet facilities, especially in those boats that used the estuaries and coastal waters.

Proposals for a new bridge

Caversham became incorporated into Reading in 1911 and changed its county status from Oxfordshire to Berkshire. Like all political boundary changes, the move had its supporters and its detractors, one of the latter being William Crawshay. The opponents believed that Reading wanted a larger population base so that it could increase its ability to borrow. Caversham residents feared that their favourable rating valuations would be reassessed, but the reality of the scheme had been brought home to them in a preliminary enquiry in 1909. They found that Reading had plans to link the two places by a second bridge. It based its proposal for a proper crossing on the need identified in a census of traffic across the Clappers footbridge in 1905 when in one day there were 4836 pedestrians, 19 trucks, 130 bicycles and 70 prams going across. (A count in 1900 had logged only 3000 people crossing.)[10] To some Caversham residents this plan for a bridge spelled out extensions of the tram routes, road widening and depreciation of property values as a result.

In 1913 the Reading Corporation Bridge Bill sought powers to build two new bridges, one of which would replace the existing Caversham Bridge. Mouchels of Westminster submitted a plan to Reading Corporation for a 180ft single-span bridge to run from de Bohun Road to George Street, a bridge whose design would be far in advance of any in the country. The Conservators were worried that these new structures would cause problems with the flow of the river. They had, after a period of neglect caused by a shortage of money, previously drawn up a programme of work which included the installation of new lower gates for Caversham Lock and the removal of some nearby shoals by a steam dredger. At a meeting between the Corporation and the Conservators, it was agreed that Caversham weir should be enlarged, the tumbling bays beyond it increased and land below them cut away, both parties contributing to the costs. The outcome was the removal in 1914 of part of View Island and campshedding of the new frontage to improve the

THERE'S ROOM IN THE CREW FOR YOU.

ROYAL NAVAL DIVISION.

RECRUITS WANTED

IMMEDIATELY at the Royal Naval Depot, Crystal Palace.

For particulars apply to—

Commander the Hon. RUPERT GUINNESS, C.B., C.M.G., R.N.V.R.,

R.N. Division Recruiting Office, 112, Strand, London, W.C.

approach to the lock and to facilitate the flow of water from the weir.[11]

The beginning of the war

The years leading up to the war were not particularly good ones for the boat businesses on the Thames. The death of Edward VII in 1910 had caused cancellations. Heavy rain at the end of 1911 had continued into the following spring. The summer of 1912 was wet and cold with rain every day in August, more than 6 inches in total. The new King and Queen were at Henley Royal Regatta that year but, despite this stimulus to business, the bad weather brought the 1912 season to an early finish. By December every weir on the river was fully drawn and riverside land was flooded.

The 1914 season ended early because of the outbreak of war. Reading Regatta was brought to a halt because the order for mobilisation was given on the day that it was held. Many regattas, fêtes and galas which had been arranged for August and September were cancelled and those that were held suffered from poor entries and gate receipts. The racing programme collapsed, river traffic fell considerably and commercial plans were dropped. The strategic importance of bridges was recognised and there were orders to the public not to loiter under them. (Despite this, the Reading Temperance Society opened a coffee stall alongside Caversham Bridge to serve non-alcoholic drinks.) Anglers shared the riverside gloom as they complied with new regulations which increased the minimum size of fish

which could be taken during the season. In June a whirlwind drew the water to a height of forty feet by Caversham Bridge, rocking boats, scattering their cushions into the water and drenching their occupants. In the autumn there were nine weeks of heavy rain (12.36 inches against an average of 5.55 inches), and more wet weather in early 1915 (8.51 inches in the first two months and 5.06 inches in June, as measured in the Forbury Gardens). Customers going on the river in July were warned of the risks of going near the weir because of the flow. The year 1894 had been the last comparable one for rainfall but river management in 1915 was so much improved that there were not the floods of the earlier time, though there was much damage to banks, camping plots, bridges and towpaths.

Throughout 1915 it was apparent that the rowing clubs were going to be hit very hard by the war. Their members were of just the age and fitness to join the colours and the *Lock to Lock Times* produced weekly rolls of honour, lists of names of men who had enlisted in the services from various rowing clubs and from the British Motor Boat Club. It also carried recruiting advertisements for the Navy.[12] Before long it was also reporting the names of those oarsmen who had fallen, including in May the name of one member of Reading Rowing Club. In July it gave the names of 10 members of the committee of Reading Amateur Regatta who were serving with the forces. The regatta for 1915 was cancelled and the committee had liabilities it could not meet. The editor of the magazine was keen to promote the Thames as a

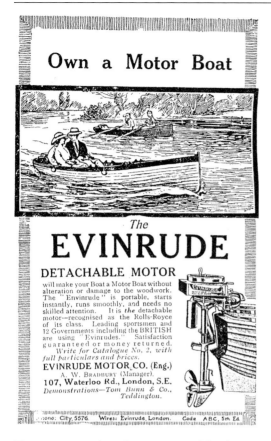

Own a Motor Boat

The
EVINRUDE
DETACHABLE MOTOR

will make your Boat a Motor Boat without
alteration or damage to the woodwork.
The "Evinrude" is portable, starts
instantly, runs smoothly, and needs no
skilled attention. It is *the* detachable
motor—recognised as the Rolls-Royce
of its class. Leading sportsmen and
12 Governments including the BRITISH
are using "Evinrudes." Satisfaction
guaranteed or money returned.
*Write for Catalogue No. 2, with
full particulars and prices.*
EVINRUDE MOTOR CO. (Eng.)
A. W. BRADBURY (Manager).
107, Waterloo Rd., London, S.E.
*Demonstrations—Tom Bunn & Co.,
Teddington.*

'Phone: City 5576. Wires: Evinrude, London. Code ABC, 5th Ed.

The oarsmen, watching the more successful male
in the boat with the outboard engine – and the girl
– show all the proper astonishment.[13]

place for recreation and holidays during hostilities and it also encouraged volunteer service in the Special Constables for river men who could not enlist. It reminded readers that their launches might at any time be required by the Government and that failure to have the engine ready to run satisfactorily could cost lives. It put forward the suggestion that coarse fish might be considered as a source of food if required. The Thames Red Cross organised collections at the locks and sold buttonholes and pennants. In Reading the War Hospitals Care and Comforts Committee was already set up and between six and seven hundred wounded were already in various hospitals in the town and in Caversham. Messrs Heelas arranged with Maynards for 40 of them to take a trip on Fry's old boat, the *Queen of the Thames*. Collections were made for the Royal Berkshire

Regiment's Tobacco, Pipe and Cigarette Fund. Weekly concerts for the wounded were held at the war hospitals and at Reading Barracks, and Bill Moss was a popular performer at them. Salters became a private company in 1915 and went over to military and naval work for the duration of the war.

All the boat companies were increasingly short of skilled labour as their men joined up. They were unable to build because wood was scarce and high in price and this was one factor which slowed down the progress of the motor boat on the river. The introduction of the portable outboard motor which could be attached to an existing small boat was a great success, even though its use upgraded the boat to a launch for the purpose of lock fees. Outboard engines were ideal for the river. Popularity brought down prices and the best-sellers were the 2 or 3hp models which by 1915 had reversible propellers. The great advantage of these engines were that there was no danger of petrol vapour being trapped in a closed space and they were not a great fire risk.

Problems in river management

By the beginning of 1915 the Thames Conservancy was facing a shortage of labour. Over one hundred of its workforce had been called up. Not only were they were short-handed for the routine management of the pleasure traffic through the locks, but repairs could not be carried out and some of the dredging and weed-cutting had to be halted.[14] For Caversham the delays to the work programmes that had been planned were significant. One of them was for major work on the weir, the cost of which was to be shared between the Conservators and Reading Corporation and the other was the construction of two new bridges between Reading and Caversham. The Treasury put a stop to the two projects because it would not permit the Corporation to make the capital expenditure.[15] By the beginning of 1916 the work force had been further reduced by active service and heavy rainfall during the year had once again caused problems. Only absolutely essential work was carried

The steam launch *Titbits* with Frank Pearce waiting to take her out.

out and then by men over age, or categorised by the services as medically unfit. There were heavy floods in March 1916 when the towpath from the bridge to the lock was under water and the Moss buildings were cut off. Registrations and lock tolls were down and so income was reduced.[16] This was the situation until the end of 1918.

A new problem was the military camps and other establishments that were set up in the catchment of the Thames and the arrangements for the disposal of the drainage from them which required the supervision of the Conservators. Where the outdoor staff found signs of pollution, representations had to be made to officers at the camp and work carried out to prevent public water supplies becoming contaminated. The populations in the camps were changing constantly and so the message had to be repeated and a watch kept.

Care and comforts for the wounded

During 1915 and 1916 there were schemes all along the river to give wounded soldiers opportunities to go on the water and medical officers from the hospitals said that the outings were of great benefit. The Conservators lent their launches for the scheme whenever they were free. The *Britannia*

was also used for outings for the wounded and this boat was big enough to take a piano and a team of musicians and entertainers. Moss's had a steam launch called *Titbits* which they also lent. Mr E B Awmack of the Care and Comforts Committee arranged a programme of outings in the *Titbits* in conjunction with riverside house owners at Sonning, Shiplake, Henley and Whitchurch, who would serve tea to the wounded before they returned to Reading.[17] Frank Pearce, who became Harry's stepson in 1916, spoke in later years about this boat being used for taking war-wounded soldiers from Battle Hospital for trips on the river because it was his job, at about 11 years of age, to drive the boat. He is standing by the *Titbits* which has steam up and is ready to go. Frank also remembered Bill Moss' involvement with Care and Comforts and the Reading Concert Party for the soldiers in the war hospitals and on the river, and of how Bill sang to them and entertained them and it is likely that Bill travelled with him on the *Titbits*.

Bill Moss was a great success with the troops and made a huge contribution to their welfare; he was an experienced performer and he had just the right manner and just the right songs, performing them 500 times in 1917 alone.

But somehow several of these sad, young, but very wizen, faces among the badly wounded have a very far-off look in their eyes as they sit, some minus legs, some minus arms, propped up with pillows, and tended by their comrades. The smile does not yet come on their drawn faces … But when Bill Moss is taken on board at Caversham Lock those among the wounded who have heard him before immediately call out 'Come on, Bill', and come on he does, not waiting for gangway or anything of that sort but clambers over the side of the launch like the good Thames boat-man he is. He is pressed to sing at once … The saddest-looking among the wounded brighten up …in a word, Bill Moss is the humorist the soldiers like and he succeeds in making them forget their past experiences awhile and tickles the fancies of even the sad, worn faces of those young fellows who have endured so much and are such helpless creatures now.[18]

His performance was suitable for any audience – the soldiers had their nurses with them – and one of the most popular items was called The Magistrate, a song acted out with nods and winks to the audience. The trips in the *Titbits* went on into 1918 but came to an end when a safety inspec-tor looked at the steam boiler and declared it to be too rusty to be used safely.

Bill died of peritonitis, aged almost 70, after only 6 days' illness in the first days of 1918.[19] He had been singing right up until he was taken ill. His funeral was organised by his old friend Mr C Lovegrove and attended by representatives of every philanthropic and riverside club and organisation, including the Thames Conservancy, in the area. His coffin was carried by four police constables: PCs Young, Pullen, Barlow and Bone. Harry Isaacs and George Talbot were among the mourners and John Eighteen, another old friend, was in the congregation. He was buried in Caversham Cemetery.

The local papers were so full of the contribu-tion of the local regiment to the war and of lists of names and photographs of the captured and fallen that there was no room, and certainly no appetite, for any light-hearted items. The only boating advertisements were one-line statements that Maynards were running the *Britannia* and Cawstons the *Majestic* on timetabled trips to

Bill Moss, 8 April 1848 – 4 January 1918.

Henley and Goring.

The press ran some regatta reports and angling notes, and the occasional story about a soldier involved in a boating accident while on leave does show that the small boat trade was surviv-ing. Fuel shortages and the national mood had finished most of the club and group outings of earlier years. The *Lock to Lock Times* ceased in 1915 because there was very little social or sporting activity on the riverside to report.

Allen & Simmonds, iron founders of Thames Side, were supplying materials to the war effort and to do this they had taken on women workers for the first time. When the firm went on an out-ing in 1916 on the *Majestic* Mr Allen told the staff that he had viewed with misgivings the employ-ment of women to fill the gaps left by the men on service but that they were doing excellent work in quantity and quality.[20]

The scale of human loss can be measured in a small way by the number of men who in 1918 were on the roll of honour of just one local firm close to the river, Samuel Elliott and Son in Gosbrook

Road. There were 127 men on Elliott's list: seven had been killed, 16 wounded, six had been decorated and five staff had lost sons. The firm had sent 91 parcels to employees at the front and were raising funds to welcome the men home again.

Caversham Park, still in the ownership of William Crawshay, became a convalescent home for wounded soldiers throughout the war, with his wife Florence taking an active part as a Red Cross nurse, and in 1918 the Reading Philanthropic Institution arranged an outing to Caversham Court for servicemen, many of whom were wounded.

Endnotes

1 *Berkshire Chronicle* 25 February 1905 'Reading Anglers at dinner' and 18 March 1905 'Caversham and District Angling Association'.

2 Thames Conservancy report, Minutes of Berkshire County Council 1912 p161.

3 BRO, D/TC 194 River keepers' deputations 1894–1949. Other local representatives were J White of Caversham and G King and H Leaver of Reading.

4 *Berkshire Chronicle* 23 October 1909 p16 col 3–4; RM, REDMG 1997/197/47, The brig *King Alfred*.

5 J R L Anderson *The Upper Thames* (London, 1970), p49.

6 *Lock to Lock Times* [LTLT] no 657, 20 May 1905 p110.

7 Royal Humane Society Case 39066 Ward Knight and Peter A Smith.

8 *Berkshire Chronicle* 4 August 1900.

9 Report on the work of the Thames Conservancy presented by H W Russell to Berks County Council on 22 January 1913 and recorded in the Minutes of BCC 1913 pp164–9.

10 *LTLT* no 657, 20 May 1900 p11.

11 Minutes of Berkshire County Council February 1914 p187–9. Campshedding is the protection and retention of a riverbank by facing it with timber or other material.

12 *LTLT* no 870, 16 July 1915 p8.

13 *LTLT* no 861, 14 May 1915 p11.

14 Russell, Minutes of BCC 1915 p164–71.

15 Russell, Minutes of BCC 1916, p112–117.

16 Report on the work of the Thames Conservancy in 1916 presented by A E Preston to Berks County Council on 14 April 1917 and recorded in the Minutes of BCC 1917 pp170–2.

17 *Berkshire Chronicle* 12 July 1918.

18 *Berkshire Chronicle* 11 January 1918 'Death of Bill Moss', p8; *Reading Observer* 12 January 1918, 'The late 'Bill' Moss: a popular townsman' p5.

19 GRO registration of death entry March 1918 Reading 2c 510: Bill Moss died on 4 January 1918 of appendicitis and peritonitis at Florida Villa, Mill Green, Caversham, the home of his daughter Rose and his son-in-law Peter Smith where he had been living during his retirement.

20 *Berkshire Chronicle* 1 September 1916.

15 Building and rebuilding: 1918-1939

Post-war rowing

There was a slow start to post-war activity on the river. Reading Rowing Club held a regatta in 1919 but the committee of Reading Amateur Regatta did not meet until 1920 and then it decided that fund-raising would be difficult and so there would be no regatta that year. The committee held on through 1921, but disbanded in 1922 when the Mayor was made trustee of its trophies. Despite the problems a regatta was held in 1923. Quite apart from the shortage of money caused by the depression, the definition of occupational status under the Amateur Rowing Association rules was making it difficult to get entries for regattas. Amateur status was debated by Reading Rowing Club members at their AGM in 1924. The rule was that no person could be an amateur who: 1) had raced for a fee or a stake; 2) had competed against a professional for a prize; 3) had taught or pursued athletic exercise for profit; 4) had ever been employed in or about boats in manual labour; 5) had been in trade or employment for wages as a mechanic, artisan, or labourer or engaged in any menial duty; 6) was disqualified as an amateur in any other branch of sport. Those present thought that rules 4 and 5 were particularly ridiculous because many of them had done manual work in the war and it was proposed that the meeting should invite the ARA to review the rules.[1] However the amateur rules were not completely

removed until the 1950s.

A new club, the Kennet Alliance Rowing Club, was established in 1928 for those debarred from amateur status. It had its own regatta and also entered those of the Working Men and the Tradesmen.[2] The Mayor, Alderman John Rabson, was president of Reading Tradesmen's Rowing Club and a crew from Samuel Elliott's firm rowed in its regatta in 1925.

The presence of the University Extension College boat clubs at Caversham was a positive force for amateur rowing in the 1920s and was valuable to the Reading Amateur Regatta in helping it to maintain its position and to grow in strength. At least some of the college races were rowed on

The boathouse of the University Women's Rowing Club, built in 1939.

the Dreadnought reach in the early years. The college became the University College in 1906 and gained full university status in 1926. By the 1930s there was a club house on the Caversham bank below the bridge and crews based there used the upstream reach. The University introduced the Head of the River races in the mid 1930s and has continued them ever since, apart from the war years. Head races are time trials rowed over a fixed distance. Crews set off at regular intervals and timing begins as they cross the start line. By this point they are rowing at racing speed. There are various classes in which crews can compete and they can start two or even three abreast. As well as competing regularly in the Head of the River the crews rowed at Marlow and at Henley Royal Regattas. A boathouse was built for the women's club alongside the men's building on the Caversham site in 1939. Coaches at this time were Dr Logan Dahne, a GP at the Priory Avenue practice for many years, and James Bee, a lecturer at the University.

Reading Rowing Club had some of their best results in the 1930s when crews reached the final of the Thames Cup and won the Wyfold Fours at Henley Royal Regatta in 1934 and 1935. In 1938 Len

Habbitts, a member of the winning Wyfold Fours crew, reached the final of the Diamond Challenge Sculls. That year a Reading School crew took part in the Rowing Club regatta.

The Thames Conservancy: river management

When the representative of the Thames Conservancy presented his report to Berkshire County Council in February 1922 it was the first one for five years and covered a very difficult period in river management. The later years of the war had depleted staff and revenue and the board had been prevented in the post-war years from carrying out major projects or new schemes because it was kept short of money by rises in wages and cost of materials. Its income had fallen from £56,000 in 1914 to £48,000 in 1921. Maintenance and dredging were carried out as funds permitted and the Conservancy was concerned about its statutory duties which now included river purification and the prevention of pollution. The state of the river in London was so bad that no fish could survive for a distance of 30 miles between Gravesend and Kew, a complete barrier to the migratory eels. An

Reading University VIII in 1928 photographed on a snowy day outside the boathouse.

unprecedented drought in 1921 had added to the problems. At this time the revenues were still from the Metropolitan Water Board and other water companies, from tolls and charges from business and pleasure boats and various rents and sales of ballast. The Conservancy had approached the government to seek increases to its income from the water companies and a revision of the tolls and charges.[3] The hard facts were that the river was expensive to manage and, with falling income from traditional sources, the Conservators were looking for contributions from the councils whose areas bordered the river and who benefited from it as an amenity. The Thames Conservancy Bill of 1924 proposed in clause 31 that all riparian county councils, boroughs and urban district councils should pay a rate of one penny in the pound to the Conservators. This was opposed by Berkshire County Council, Reading Council and all the riparian councils in Berkshire, Buckinghamshire and Oxfordshire on the basis that it would be unfair for them to pay for advantages in other parts of the river.

The increase in the number of launches on the river, and the higher speeds the petrol engines gave them, re-created many of the problems of river management that the introduction of steam boats had done in the previous century. The weir was enlarged in 1922 with six deep cill sluices and a lowering of the tumbling bays. The Caversham lock house was rebuilt in 1930. Once again the lock-keepers made a case about the increased traffic, the tolls they had to handle and the long hours they worked on the locks and the weirs. In summer they had no meal breaks and a day off once a month only if they could get a replacement. In 1938 they were still, as they had been in 1910, available 24 hours a day, summer and winter, for boat traffic and toll collection and to control water flow. Although holidays were allowed by this time, they could take them only out of season. The benefits they had of rent-free houses, working clothing and cheap coal simply did not make up for their poor wages and long hours. This time their case was presented to the Lock Staff Special Committee with the Caversham keeper as their spokesman. They

wanted a 48-hour week. One particular grievance was the requirement to scrub the lock sides 4 or 5 times a year to remove the algae, and the need to do this at 4am so as not to interfere with traffic. It was agreed that they would have set hours of 7am to 11pm in summer and 6pm in winter, with a full day off once a week as well as annual leave. Their request for an increase of £2 per week was not met but a rise of 4 shillings was agreed.[4] When the war began the following year, lock-keepers were conscripted, as they had been in the first war, and river traffic was much reduced.

In 1923 Reading finally got its second bridge, delayed from before the war, a single span concrete structure which ran from de Bohun Road, Reading, to George Street, Caversham. It was a road bridge linking residential Caversham with commercial Reading rather than an access point to the river. At the time that it was built it was the longest single span of its kind and there were concerns about its strength. Before it was opened steamrollers, traction engines and loaded lorries were driven on to it so that they filled its width and length, and the bridge held firm. It was opened by the Prince of Wales. The next year work began to replace the iron bridge at Caversham with a double span concrete one of similar design to Reading Bridge. This change was long overdue and had been under discussion since 1900. The old bridge was closed to traffic in May 1924 and a footbridge was built which crossed Piper's Island below the ferryman's house (see overleaf). The old bridge was not demolished until the new one was completed but during the work an archway was uncovered which had carried the approach road to a former bridge.[5] This new bridge too was opened by the Prince of Wales but the event had to be postponed twice, the second time because of the general strike. The Mayor opened the bridge to traffic before the ceremony.

Hill's Meadow

Arthur Hill, alderman and mayor of Reading, was a member of a family known for its philanthropy and its contribution to municipal and educational

Looking upstream through the arch of Reading Bridge, in 1923 the longest single span of its kind, to Christchurch Meadows.

reform. He was responsible for sending thousands of emigrants to the colonies through a depot in Plymouth. His half-sister Octavia is remembered for her work in housing for the poor and as a co-founder of the National Trust whose aim was to make houses, parks and open spaces available to the public. Arthur bought and presented to Reading in 1895 the replica of the Bayeux Tapestry which now has its own gallery in the museum. He bought the land for Tilehurst Reservoir and other town centre plots. When he died in 1909 he gave land near Caversham Mill to the council. It was in the hands of his executors in 1910, described as a meadow with frontage to the River Thames, occupied by George Leach, liable to flooding and over 13 acres in extent. Part of it became a riverside walk, but it was not until 1928, after the new bridge gave more access to it, that the council formally agreed with the Parks Committee that is should be used as a recreation ground. It was already known as Hill's Meadow at this date.[6]

Day-to-day activity at Moss's boathouse

Harry Isaacs, lacking practical skills himself and needing them in the business that he had taken over from Bill Moss, apprenticed his stepson, Frank Pearce, to Sidney Turk, a boatbuilder at Kingston. Members of the Turk family were, and still are, well-known on the river as Queen's Watermen and Swan Masters with the duty of swan-upping, the process of marking and culling swans belonging to the Queen. Once Frank's apprenticeship was over he returned to Reading to work with his stepfather.

At Moss's (the old name was retained under new ownership), as at all boatyards, work in summer began with mopping or baling out all the hire boats if there had been overnight rain, getting enough of them equipped for any customers that might arrive, and repairing anything damaged the previous day. There were always building orders to be worked on and, very demanding of time, the needs of the private customer to attend to. A customer whose boat was stored by the company could come as often as he wished and have his boat lifted from over-head racks, launched and fitted out. He was offered every polite attention he required, helped into his boat and given the same service when he returned, whether it was one or ten hours later. This service cost 1s 6d a week.

Preparations for the new Caversham bridge: building a temporary foot bridge.[7]

This same attention to the needs of the customer was repeated all day long to those hiring boats although the boats were not lifted out of the water between lets. If it rained during the day all the cushions had to be taken out of the boats and put into the shed, and of course the boats dried out again when the rain stopped. If it rained when the boat was on hire, then all the wet cushions had to be dried before they could be used again. Boats were left on the water until the end of the day when the punts were towed across to the island and left there overnight. The skiffs and canoes were all put on racks in the shed, the men working in twos to lift the bow out of the water on to the landing stage, pulling the whole boat onto dry land and then running it across the iron bars set into the ground parallel to the river to the shed.

The working day was not over until the last boat was in, and that might easily be 10 or 11pm. If the hirer, still at Tilehurst, realised that his hire charge was going to be more than the 10s deposit he had left, or that he could more easily walk up Cow Lane and catch a tram home than row back to Caversham, then he might leave the boat tied to the bank, or even adrift, where he had finished with it. Sometimes boats were abandoned because they had been damaged or the oars had been lost, and then the first morning job for the boatman was to go out to look for the 'winger', as lost boats were called, upstream and down, round backwaters and islands, until it was found. The metal trade plate on each boat identified it as belonging to a particular company and all the boatyards co-operated by phoning the owner when an abandoned one turned up on their reach. Hire charges were 1s or 1s 6d per hour in the 1930s and 2s or 2s 6d in the 1940s.

Between the wars, when the Palace Variety Theatre was thriving in Reading, the artists used often to come down to the river to hire a boat before or between performances. Among Moss's regular customers was Gracie Fields who lodged in Greyfriars Road when she was working in Reading. A punt named *Violet*, which belonged to the family, was always reserved for her use. Margaret Rutherford and her husband Stringer Davis were also regulars.

Saturday was the peak day, busy with hourly lets and with camping boats coming in and going

'Get a Hornless Gramophone for river use. It is the ideal instrument for outdoors.'[8]

out again, clean and refitted. At the height of the season one of the men would stay overnight, sleeping in a camping punt, so that all the hire boats could be left on the water with safety. It also gave a very early start to a busy day. Moss's had a stock of about 120 boats at one time, which gives some idea of the amount of work which could be involved. Holidays in camping boats were very popular, some families returning year after year. Skiffs and punts were adapted by slotting a series of metal hoops into channels on the side of the boat, and covering these with a tent of green canvas. This could be rolled up and tied in place at the top of the hoops during the day. At no point could one stand up under canvas and at either end one could scarcely kneel. Each boat was equipped with blankets, primus stove, Tilley lamp, paraffin and methylated spirit, frying pan, kettle, saucepans, large stone water bottle, crockery and cutlery. There was no table, except for a board that rested across the width of the boat. Space also had to be made for the campers' personal gear and food as well as leaving room for four people to sleep. Beds were made up by removing all the footrests and backrests and putting all the cushions flat on the bottom of the boat. In a wet spell the canvas had to be down all the time to protect the gear and food and this precluded rowing or paddling so the boat remained moored until the rain stopped. Care had to be taken not to touch the canvas while it was

wet because this would start a leak.

During the winter all the small boats were taken off the water into storage and the long process of overhaul and repair began. The size, particularly the height, of the boathouse made effective heating impossible and in these cold conditions men repaired cushions, stitched and patched canvas, and scraped and rubbed down every boat ready for seam caulking and revarnishing. There were also willow trees to pollard, mooring piles to drive in and the landing stage and towing path to maintain.

Moss's busiest week

The busiest week in the whole river year, until the second world war, was at the beginning of July, the week of Henley Royal Regatta, when, as the firm's headed notepaper said, boats were available for hire there as well as in Reading. The earliest recorded date for this was in 1908 when an advertisement in the *Lock to Lock Times* said that Moss would be at plot number 5 for the Olympic Regatta and would give special terms to anyone mentioning the journal. At the beginning of Henley week dozens of craft were assembled, stacked on floating pontoons, or stacked on one another, and a whole cavalcade towed downstream from the boathouse, through the locks at Caversham, Sonning, Shiplake and Henley. On arrival, a small marquee was put up on the regular site at Mill Meadows near the railway station, rented from Henley council, and this was the working base for the week. This was a good site because many of the customers came to Henley by rail. All the cushions and equipment were unloaded and the boats moored and the staff made ready to stay day and night while the regatta lasted. Business was conducted as usual, with the addition of providing hampers for those spending the day on the water. Most of the hirings were for a full day, so once the boats were all out, there was time for pleasure for the work force and their families before all the customers returned after racing had finished.

On Saturday, Finals Day, the regatta ended, as now, with a display of fireworks at dusk, so

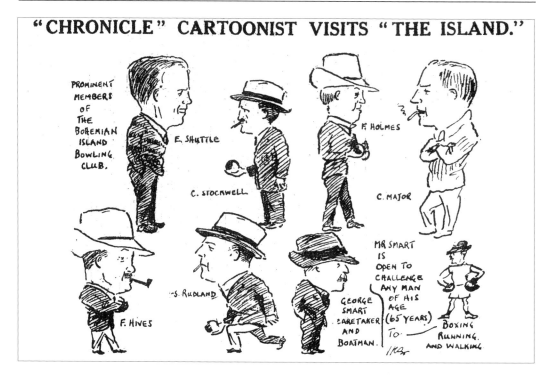

the working day was late in finishing. When all the boats were in, the whole cavalcade was reassembled, however late it was, and at daybreak the journey back to Reading began. The locks, then hand-operated, had to be filled and emptied, for the lock-keepers had finished work at sunset the night before and would not be on duty so early in the morning. Sometimes there were patches of low mist hanging over the water and surrounding meadows and this was not easy to negotiate with an awkward column of boats. If the mist was very thick the boats might have to moor and wait for it to lift before they could continue the journey. The whole task was a highly-skilled piece of watermanship which had to be completed without too much delay, in order to be ready to open for 'business as usual' in Reading the next day.

The Island Bohemian Club

The Island Bohemian Club continued, as it had since Bill Moss's time, to rent the upstream end of Fry's Island from the boat firm as a social and sports club. At the tip of the island there was a club house which had a bar and a snooker table,

and then there were two tennis courts and a bowling green. There were also bungalows or chalets on the island for camping or summer use by members. The club held off-site dinner dances and children's events during the winter. E Rudland was its president, its honorary secretary was W Hives and E Shuttle an active member. When John Osbourne Collier died in 1938 he had been its treasurer for 22 years. Moss's also still owned the bungalow called Templecombe on the Caversham side which it let and it retained a plot for its own use on the Reading side. There were no main services on the island at this time. The principal value of the island to the business was the safe mooring which it provided.

Boatbuilding at Caversham Bridge

Maynard's ran the *Britannia* and some smaller boats from Bona's old site, and built at least one steamer which was launched for them from Arthur East's slipway there in 1924. This was the *Queen of the Thames*, an attractive-looking white boat with a red trim that was the largest boat on

The launch of the *Queen of the Thames*.

the Upper Thames at the time. John Fry's old boat must have gone by then and so freed up the name to be used again. The first photograph shows the hull of the steamer, already bearing her name and carrying the Red Ensign, being launched from the slipway, and the second, the firm's employees who have been installing the wooden decking. Whether this new boat was steel- or wooden-hulled is not recorded. These two images, taken against the background of the building of the new Caversham Bridge, (together with another photo of the hull tied up outside the hotel), are of special value as the only remaining photographic record of building boats of this size at Caversham.[9] The presence of Harry Isaacs and his wife at a party

on the partially-decked *Grand Duchess*, built by Lance Summers of Windsor in the 1920s, with an engine by Plenty's of Newbury, and also part of the Maynard fleet, suggests that that it was usual to have a celebration when a new boat was launched.[10] However there is no longer any information on naming or launching ceremonies or the form of any events for workers or owners.

Change of ownership on both sides of the river

Browne and Lilly, a joinery company that made sectional buildings, moved from Greyfriars Road where they had been since the beginning of the

The team who built the *Queen of the Thames*.

century to Thames Side about opposite the top of the island. They had specialised in providing riverside bungalows and advertised them when the Warren was under development. They stayed at the riverside until after the war.

Caversham Park estate, originally owned by Knollys and more recently by Crawshay, was put up for sale in 1920 by Mrs Golding Palmer. The sale included the mansion itself and the home farm at Dunsden, the pond in Peppard Road, land between the mansion and Sonning and more land between Henley Road and the river (Donkin Hill, Star Road, Lower Henley Road). Four lots in the sale, over 30 acres in total, were plots under osier cultivation. The estate included Deane's Farm near the mill, small islands near the bridge, and Pipers Island and islet. The first set of islets were valued at £7 pa and occupied by the representatives of Mrs A Freebody (£1) and A T Cooper (£6) and the second, 'suitable for mooring purposes' were valued at £5 pa and occupied by the representatives of Mrs A Freebody. In this document the word 'eyot', so frequently found in earlier land transactions, was not used.

The building that had been Caversham Mill was taken over in 1934 by British Metal Powders Ltd and altered completely in 1941. The company produced aluminium and bronze metal powders and at the end of their shift the employees used to walk through Hill's Meadow with their clothes and skin covered in silver-coloured metal dust. There were 13 fires at the site in ten years. An enquiry was held in 1948 because local residents objected to the noise from the stamping sheds, 24 hours a day, and to the proposed extension of the unsightly buildings, already detracting from the use of View Island and the riverside.[11]

There was a very important sale of freehold ground rents on land and property on and behind the Berkshire bank in 1932. It was held at the Great Western Hotel on 14 April and the auctioneers were Messrs Haslam and Son, Friar Street, Reading. It was an important sale because of the size of the lots and because the reversion dates made them attractive investments. The land was part of the Knollys estate, for which Haslams

A launch party on *Grand Duchess* built at Windsor for Charles Maynard.

had been agents for nearly a century, and this was the first time it had been on the market since the family acquired it in 1552. The sale catalogue said that 'the lots form part of the estate which has been in the Knollys family since the dissolution of the Abbey and are now for sale consequent on the necessity of raising capital.'[12] (Part of lot 7 in this sale, including Moss's boathouse, with ground rents valued at £122, had been advertised, but perhaps not sold, by Haslams in 1906 as long leasehold investments.[13]) The sale by John Weldale Knollys of Lock Island in 1815 and information in the tithe records of ownership of Fry's Island, Brigham's Meads and the Vasterns had already shown how much land the family retained after the mansion and the main estate changed hands. This sale showed how far the original estate at Caversham Park extended across the river and into the town.

The sale catalogue said freehold ground rents formed the best and safest investment especially as they were, in this particular case, on lands in a prosperous and improving town and were secured by well-built properties occupied by substantial lessees and with a high reversion value. For so much land to come on to the market at one time made the sale a significant event, for the disclosure of the names of the lessees and the amount of rent they were receiving, if for no other. Even though most of the Knollys riverside land listed with Fry's Island in the tithe records was in this sale, the island was not included.

It was lots 6 to 11 which contained holdings alongside the river between the bridge and the lock on the Berkshire bank, and immediately behind it. Lot 6 comprised nos 106–120 Caversham Road (evens); 1–19 Brigham Road (odds); and 16, 17, 18 and 19 Thames Side (but not number 15 where Harry Isaacs now lived, although this property was leasehold); and a stable and coach house in Brigham Road. Lot 7 took in the whole of the other side of Brigham Road and yards behind it and 'a boat-house in the occupation of Messrs Moss Boat Building Co'.

Lot 8 was the odd numbered houses on De Montfort Road, Lot 9 was the even numbers, offices, the premises of Allen & Simmonds Ltd and houses in Vastern Road. Lot 10 took in more houses in Vastern Road, the odd numbers of Lynmouth Road and no 20 Thames Side. The final set, lot 11, comprised parts of Vastern Road, part of King's Meadow Road, the premises of Robert Cort & Sons and those of the Thames Conservancy. One of the conditions of sale was that rights over the towing path would remain with the vendor and another that each purchaser should covenant that he would not permit a theatre or music hall to be built on his land so long as a theatre or music hall was being carried on at the Palace Theatre on the west side of Cheapside.

The sale catalogue showed that, since the Inland Revenue survey of 1910, the leaseholder of the Moss site had become A H Holdstock. After the sale the site belonged to George Lewis, timber mer-

chant, and the Moss lease continued as before.

The later timing of residential and commercial developments of this side of the river can be seen to follow closely the reversion dates of these eleven lots. The private ownership and development of land on this side of the river forms a strong contrast to the open public access provided by Reading Borough Council on the Promenade, Hill's Meadow, Christchurch Meadows and King's Meadow.

Lot	Locality	Gross est. rental	Lessee	Reversion date
1	Oxford Road	£160	South Berks Brewery	2000
2	ditto	£260	A C Sheppard	1972
3	ditto	£268	E R Jackson	1972
4	ditto	£160	H Blach	1999
5	Cork Street	£72	Miss Watsham	2003
6	Caversham Road	£646	Mrs C Haslam	1988
7	ditto	£460	A H Holdstock	1988
8	De Montfort Road	£599	F T Husband	1991
9	ditto	£885	ditto	1991
10	Vastern Road	£645	Commercial Union	1991
11	ditto	£915 10s	Thames Conservancy	1988

Table to show land in Reading put up for sale by the Knollys estate in 1932.

VIEW FROM CAVERSHAM BRIDGE, READING.   221442.JV.

Arthur Reuben Cawston's island site offering boats and bathing, with Freebody's lido in the background.

War memorial

In 1928 a ceremony was held at a war memorial in Knighton's Meadow, just below Piper's Island, put up to commemorate the Caversham dead of the First World War. It was attended by representatives of local churches, the army, police, and civic leaders. Some 40 trees were to be planted around it.

Boat companies still in business

In the early 1930s there were only Maynard, Cawston, Freebody and Moss still in business between the bridge and the lock, the first two with steamers, some of which were built in the previous century, and the latter two now moving into offering for hire by the day or the hour petrol-driven open launches. All except Maynard still had traditional Thames skiffs and punts for hire. Steamers were still enormously popular for family trips and for group charter. Salters had an office just below Caversham Bridge on the Berkshire bank. The company was still running Oxford to

Kingston trips every day, picking up and setting down at stopping points throughout the journey as they always had. Passengers would still do one section of the trip, returning to their departure point by bus or train.

Arthur Cawston's island site offered mixed bathing at the lido and the photo shows his stock of canoes, skiffs and punts of different widths for letting, and gives a very clear picture of how labour-intensive their management must have been. The Cawston twins, Edward and William, were running *Starlight*, *Majestic* and *River Queen* but they were, according to their advertisements in 1925, at the slipway below Caversham Bridge and the steam launch and steamer on the right of the photograph of Piper's Island may have been their boats. They were advertising a tea room and garden close to the tram terminus where 'chars a bancs parties' could be catered for and motors parked.

Freebody also had a lido marked by the outline of a diving figure in the backwater behind Piper's Island. (This can be seen in the photograph of Cawston's premises above). The company had a

Freebody's fleet of small launches: the way boating was going.[14]

The *Redwing* with the Freebody family on board, Ernest William in the bow and Rose Dorothy in the stern.

The *Gull*, the Moss family boat, moored at Fry's Island in 1934.

fleet of small launches including *Loverbird*, *Sonny*, *White Wing*, *Hurley Bird* and *Lilibet*. They also had a 19ft boat called *Chic* which might have been a conversion of the boat that Bona had built earlier. Moss was slower to offer motor boats because Harry would not consider going into this side of the trade and it was left to Frank Pearce to

raise the capital to buy a boat. His first one was called the *Gull*. He bought it from a customer of the business, a Mr Higgs, owner of one of the Tilehurst brickworks and many terraced houses in Caversham, who seldom used the boat because his wife did not like the river. Frank ran the *Gull* independently of the main business. By 1934 he had bought two more boats and was doing well with them. The *Gull* was used for family outings and it is interesting that the Freebody family boat, the *Redwing*, was of very similar construction, a comment perhaps on the quality of the design chosen by the professionals for their own use.

The Old Rectory

The Old Rectory was purchased by Reading Borough Council in 1932 and demolished in preparation for a road development scheme that would have linked the Warren with the main road. The staircase with the newel post carved with the date 1638 and part of the ceiling with the Alexander shield and initials were saved from the house.[15] The road scheme did not go ahead, perhaps because of the war, but the gardens became Caversham Court, one of the council's parks and open to the public. The sheltered area of the garden below the churchyard was separated off and given over to allotments.

Endnotes

1 *Reading Standard* 15 March 1924.

2 *Berkshire Chronicle* 28 June 1929 'The Kennet Alliance RC held its second regatta'.

3 Report on the work of the Thames Conservancy 1917–21 to Berkshire County Council on Feb 1922 and recorded in the Minutes of BCC 1922 p 100 and in the BCC Finance committee report p 69.

4 J R L Anderson *The Upper Thames* (London, 1970) p 56–57.

5 *Reading Standard* 14 June 1924.

6 TNA, IR 68946 entry 2091. Thanks are due to David Cliffe of RLSL for the information supplied from minutes of the Parks Committee of Reading BC 1928.

7 Reading Museum Photographic Collection, preparations for the new Caversham Bridge.

8 *Lock to Lock Times* 24 June 1910 p 7.

9 RLSL photographic collection, three photographs of the *Queen of the Thames*.

10 P Chaplin *The Thames from Source to Tideway* (Whitter Books) p 100.

11 *Berkshire Chronicle* 30 January 1948, p 7.

12 BRO, D/EX 931/4 Sale catalogue for freehold ground rents to be auctioned on 14 April 1932.

13 *Berkshire Chronicle* 12 May 1906, advertisement for sale by auction at Queen's Hotel of long leasehold investments.

14 The photograph of the launches and of the *Redwing* are the copyright of Mrs Jenny Freebody.

16 World War II and after: 1937–1947

Sweet Thames

One of the classic books about the river, *Sweet Thames Run Softly* by Robert Gibbings, had its start in Reading. Gibbings says in the preface to the book that he wanted to explore the Thames, in whose valley he had lived for 15 years, and during the journey to float along at the river's own pace. He needed a flat-bottomed boat in which he could sleep and keep his equipment while he was travelling. He could find nothing to fit his requirements and so decided that a boat would have to be specially built.

> *The Willow* was therefore home-made, that is to say, she was built in the woodwork department of Reading University by Hubert Davis and Norman Howard, with my son and myself as unskilled assistants. None of us had done anything of the kind before but H.J. Izaacs [sic] and Frank Pearce of Moss's boatbuilding firm, near Caversham Bridge, gave us freely of their many years' experience.

> We launched her on the fourteenth day after beginning construction, and she did not take in as much as a bead of water.[1]

The boat was built at the University's London Road site, where Gibbings was a lecturer in typography, and was tested and launched on 26 July 1939 from Moss's landing stage (see overleaf).

Present on the day were Robert Gibbings, Hubert Davis, Anthony Betts, Patrick Gibbings, James Hudson (a student in the School of Art) and James Bee (lecturer and rowing coach at the University).[2] *The Willow* was taken to Lechlade and the journey downstream began on 1 August.

The book that Gibbings wrote was a commentary on the people he met, anecdotes from his own life and descriptions of the plants and animals he saw along the way and watched in the water through his microscope and glass-bottomed box. It was illustrated with his own drawings produced as woodcuts.

He wrote that 'After Mapledurham the face of the country is blemished by the marks of man and if one cannot navigate that stretch of water by night, the best alternative is a state of mild inebriation'. Since he could not do either, he thought himself fortunate to arrive in Reading at the same time as a steamer and to watch four small boys trotting along the Promenade, following its course and performing acrobatics to entertain the passengers: cartwheels, somersaults, walking on their hands, combining into a knockabout turn. He was at this point in his journey when war was declared, but he continued as far as Kew. The book was published in 1940.

His second book about the Thames, *Till I End My Song*, its title completing the quotation from Edmund Spenser's *Prothalamion* that the first one began, was published in 1957 and was written from his home near Clifton Hampden.

World War II

The declaration of war in 1939 brought back the problems for the boat trade and river navigation from which they had taken much of the last twenty years to recover. Staff were conscripted and at the same time demand for boats was increased. Harry Isaacs and Frank Pearce had joined the police as Special Constables before the war and as a result Frank was drafted immediately into the War Reserves in Reading. Harry had already retired from the business but now came back into the office, Ernie Simmons was still working and Frank's shift work allowed him to keep things going. Business was reduced to boat-hire and the essential repairs to the existing stock that the supply of materials permitted. Motor boats were laid up because petrol was rationed from 1939. Companies had their traditional Thames skiffs, punts and canoes to offer and there was a demand for hourly and daily hire and for camping boats, because people were taking their holidays and outings near home and there were soldiers on leave

or stationed in the area looking for something to do in their free time. The lock-keepers returned to active service. The Thames Conservancy, as in the first war, had to reduce its work to a minimum and carry out only urgent dredging and repairs to weirs, banks and locks.

Two brick overground air raid shelters were built in the yard behind the main shed at Moss's for the use of local people. A public overground shelter to take 50 people was built at the rear of Freebody's wharf, and underground shelters were built under the arches of Caversham Bridge for 50 people and under Reading Bridge for 80 people.[2] A map of Caversham Court dated 1932 shows an air raid shelter just inside the main gate and its outline can still be seen in the courtyard. If it was scheduled and built by 1932 it must be a very early example of planning for war. There are reports from Air Raid Precaution committees in the minutes of Berkshire County Council from 1934 to 1937 (presented in 1935–38) but no references to air raid shelters. Neither does this shelter appear in the official list issued at the beginning of the war as

Robert Gibbings' boat *The Willow* is launched from Moss's landing stage.[3]

Elliott's of Caversham launch a landing craft from the end of Wolsey Road in Christchurch Meadows.

public information.[4] There were suggestions that an underground shelter for 1000 people should be cut into the chalk quarry behind Caversham Court but there was uncertainty about whether it was necessary or desirable and also about the cost of digging and lining the tunnel and the availability of labour to carry out the work, and the idea came to nothing.[5]

In January 1940 the river froze sufficiently hard from below Caversham Bridge to the lock for people to get out on it but this time on foot, not on skates. This cold weather was not mentioned in broadcasts or newspapers until there was a thaw at end of the month because it was decided that no evidence should be given to the enemy of any difficulties on the home front.[6]

The early days of the evacuation of London children to Reading were difficult ones for those who lived and worked by the river. The children, free from parental control, made straight for the water and for the first three days after their arrival Harry and Frank did not leave the boat yard even for a meal break. At this time there were still timber barges moored at George Lewis's timber

yard, just next door to Moss's landing stage and these unattended, large flat-bottomed boats were a particular temptation to children. If a child went into the water alongside a barge, or between two of them, they could very easily get underneath and get trapped under the flat bottom. Rescues from these barges were fairly frequent and a two-man routine was worked out. Provided the rescuers could get there quickly enough, while the child was still buoyant, one would hang over the side while the other held his legs and kept a gap between the boats. In this way they had a reasonable chance of reaching under the barge for the child. Both Frank and Harry had police commendations for their rescues and Harry had a total of 13 life-saving rescues to his credit. One local child that Frank pulled out of the water just before the war was Ronald Allen, later to become a film and television actor, and a member for many years of the Crossroads cast, playing the part of David Hunter.

One corner of Moss's premises, the old dressing room, was used as the headquarters of one of the branches of the Upper Thames Patrol, a river-based civil defence force, and the walls of the room were decorated with propaganda posters and illustrations of enemy military uniforms and aircraft. The first members of the UTP were lock-keepers and ferrymen but they were later joined by civilians who had gained a qualification in watermanship. Their duties were to patrol the river at night to check the safety of locks, weirs, bridges and pumping stations.[7]

The Freebody business went over to building lifeboats and Salters to building landing and support craft; they had available the necessary resources and the skills. Many vessels in the Salter fleet were used as medical emergency vessels in London. All passenger services ceased. Owners of boats between 30 and 72ft length on the Thames were required to register them and some were requisitioned or taken by their owners to take part in the Dunkirk evacuation. Browne and Lilly, the joinery company at Thames Side, turned to war work. Vincents at Reading Station and Great Western Motors in Vastern Road on the Reading side of the river and Thorneycrofts, on the Oxfordshire bank behind the island, were also contributing to the war effort. Samuel Elliott's business, formerly carrying out carpentry and joinery for church and shop fitting, began producing boats and aircraft and fitting out military vehicles. They built LCAs (landing craft, assault), boats big enough at 41ft by 10ft to land a platoon from ship to shore.[8] They were taken downstream to Sonning Bridge and test-driven back at speed to the Dreadnought public house, a reach where there was little to be damaged by the wash. These landing craft were used during the D-Day landings in preparation for the invasion of occupied Europe and proved to be a very valuable part of the transport programme.

Any company or any individual not conscripted was liable to be directed to war work, and in the second half of the war Frank Pearce was required to leave the police and to use his skills at John Bushnell Ltd, boatbuilders at Wargrave, to work on installation and trials of engines in air-sea rescue boats. The boats were 25 and 36ft wooden launches capable of high speeds.

Frank's experience of the stages of construction and installation was extensive and he was able to contribute to them all. He said that there was one boat which, because of the way the pattern of work fell, he had built himself, installed the engine with the mechanical and the electrical components and taken it on its trial. At peak times two or even three of the boats were taken on their trials lashed together side by side. The completed boats went up to Reading and onto the Kennet from where they were taken to the coast.

All the former hire companies kept going through the hostilities. At the end of 1945 Reading held a thanksgiving week to mark the end of the war and it began with the Admiral of the Fleet, Lord Chatsfield, boarding an LCA at Reading Bridge with a mayoral party, and travelling to Caversham Bridge for the opening ceremony. There were trips from the Promenade on the boat during the week and a German midget submarine was on show.[9]

At the end of the war there was still a stock of traditional Thames boats to be hired but shortages of specialist materials for repairs had led to changes in design. The fixed wooden rowlocks of the traditional skiff, something easily and frequently damaged, were replaced by swivelling metal versions. The bergère work that had been used for the backs and sides of the passenger seats of the skiffs was replaced with wood. Frank Pearce, tired of repairing well-used oars which had been snapped near the leather collar, designed a light-weight curved metal plate to be let into the wood to prevent this happening. Edward and William Cawston had retired, and in 1945 Salters took from them the 60ft *River Queen* and the 88ft *Majestic*, and continued to run them as part of their own fleet until 1969 and 1974 respectively. Arthur Cawston continued the lido and boat-letting on the island.[10] Maynard's 95ft *Queen of the Thames* was sold to Shorts of Kingston after the war and acquired by Salters in 1948. They continued to run her until 1964. There were still customers for the punts and skiffs but they were a declining number.

In the period immediately after the war peo-

The families of Thames Side, Brigham Road, Thames Avenue and a section of Caversham Road held a street party to celebrate victory.[11]

ple, looking for somewhere to live in a period of housing shortage, bought the hulls of assault and personnel landing craft (LCAs and LCPs), now no longer needed, and converted them to houseboats or sometimes to pleasure boats. Moss had several of them on the moorings in 1946 or 47. The right hand boat in the photograph has had superstructure added to the basic 'bath tub' shape of the hull but its naval number, LCA 875, and its looped ropes are still visible and confirm that it is the same style of boat as LCA 1894 launched by Elliott's a few years earlier. In the left hand boat, where conversion is complete, there is a doorway at the stern, above what was the ramp, approached by a railed area. It is now a reasonable-sized houseboat.

Ex-naval pontoons were brought upstream after the war to be used as landing stages and for mooring. Frank Pearce used two of these large stable platforms to raise a boat which had sunk off the island after a flood. He fixed lifting tackle on each, anchored one on each side of the wreck and used them as leverage points from which to

LCAs converted into houseboats after the war.

bring the boat to the surface. Torpedo-shaped metal tanks or cases also appeared on the river after the war, converted into something between a single-seater canoe and a kayak but, as they were unstable and easily sunk, they were a short-lived fashion.

Floods were the major event of 1947 and they came after five years when the Conservancy had carried out only urgent repairs and another two years when they had done only a very little work. The bad weather began in November 1946 when heavy rain raised the river level so that Hill's Meadow, part of King's Meadow, the

Swimmers at Freebody's lido.[12]

towpath to Horseshoe Bridge and part of the Promenade were under water. The Kennet and the Loddon overflowed and there were floods at Sonning, Shiplake and Henley. The river was running at 10 knots, and its level was almost the same on either side of the Clappers. J Burns, the lock-keeper, pulled the last of Caversham sluices at the end of November and this was significant because Caversham was regarded as the key weir for controlling the upper Thames. By the beginning of December 1946 the homes on the Purley Estate were flooded and then at the end of the month temperatures dropped below freezing. In the spring floods came after heavy snowfall and a sudden thaw. It was not just the height to which the water rose: it was also the speed at which it moved, bringing with it boats torn from their moorings, trees, garden sheds, timber, bales of straw and drowned animals, which all finished up across the weir where they caused further build-up of water. The level was particularly high and the flow strong around Piper's Island and through the narrow channel of the Freebody backwater. The water levels came up to the fronts of the

houses in Thames Side but no further. Lower Caversham was badly affected although some of the flooding was caused by water backing up through drains, not just as a direct result of the rise in the river level. The water reached the bottom of Donkin Hill.

To cross the river during the flood Frank Pearce rowed upstream in a skiff, keeping near to the Berkshire bank until he was close to Caversham Bridge. He then moved into the centre of the river and came down with the current, crossing towards the Oxfordshire bank to land on the island to check mooring ropes and the trees and piles to which they were made fast. The houseboats and cruisers were a heavy responsibility in these conditions because they were bigger and more valuable than the boats on the moorings during any pre-war flood and there were more of them. They would do more damage if they broke loose and would cost more to repair if they were damaged. One of the LCAs or LCPs on the moorings sank during the flood and there were concerns that the force of the water would break the ropes and that the boat would be carried down to the weir. A vessel of this size below water level could have blocked the sluice gates and raised the flood levels even further so a diver had to go down, complete with helmet and suit, to secure the boat to prevent this happening. As the water level fell, Frank had to continue to check that boats did not settle on some obstruction and become holed.

In 1947 the lock-keepers again put in a claim for higher wages, increased leave and better housing and working conditions, particularly for extra clothing coupons to buy their footwear. This time they did get most of what they asked for, an acknowledgement of the increase in river traffic. A lay-by was built at the lock to hold launches and houseboats while they waited to go through. There were still some barges working on the Reading reach carrying timber, but they were few in number. George Lewis, timber merchant, was the only businessman on the Caversham reach who continued to use the traditional transport at this date.

Getting back to normal

When the war ended a series of photographs was taken in Reading for the Ministry of Information as propaganda material to show that everyday life was continuing normally, despite austerity and rationing. Freebody's was one of the sites selected. Throughout the war and afterwards river swimming at the lido was popular and the area was crowded in fine weather because there was plenty of room on the grass for sunbathing or picnics and a designated area for safe swimming. The photograph opposite shows it at its busiest.

Endnotes

1   Robert Gibbings *Sweet Thames Run Softly* (Dent 1940), introduction.

2   RLSL, *Air Raid Precautions* County Borough of Reading.

3   This photograph is from the private collection of Martin Andrews to whom thanks are given for its use.

4   RM, REDMG 1946/52/53, Elliott's launch an LCA.

5   TNA, HO 207/1051 Deep tunnels at Caversham 1940/41

6   I Currie, M Davison, B Ogley *Berkshire Weather Book* (Westerham, 1994), p 63–65

7   'The Thames at War' exhibition at the River & Rowing Museum, Henley-on-Thames in 2003.

8   'The Thames at War'. Elliotts produced Percival Proctor frames, and later Walruses and Albemarles. They mounted engines in Halifaxes and made Horsa glider parts, military vehicles, mobile nursing units, and dummy aircraft to fool enemy reconnaissance.

9   *Berkshire Chronicle* 12 October 1945.

10 A R Cawston, Freebody and Moss were the three local names listed as boatbuilders and repairers in the *Motor Boat and Yachting Manual* of 1943–44.

11 Miss Reed from the shop at the corner of Caversham Road and Thames Avenue is nearest the camera, Mrs Newport of Caversham Road next to her, Mrs Bates of Thames Avenue the first adult standing on the other side.

12 This photograph of Freebody's lido is copyright to Mrs Jenny Freebody. It is not one of the propaganda photographs.

17 Post-war changes along the river: 1947–1960

Post-war boating

The war accelerated both the design of marine engines and the construction of boats for all waters. Bigger engines could drive bigger boats. There were developments in materials for boat-building: the use of plywood and fibreglass and the introduction of pre-fabrication. These changes speeded up the pre-war trend away from the traditional unpowered wooden boats towards those driven by petrol engines and, by the end of wartime conditions and petrol rationing, they had affected every business on the river.

The table below of numbers of boats registered on the Thames shows how the scene changed during a period of just over ten years. By 1947 there were a thousand more petrol-driven boats on the river than there had been in 1939. When petrol rationing finished in 1950 there was a further increase in numbers and size of boats.[1] Although the term 'houseboat' was still in use at the end of the decade, the big pre-war luxury vessels like the *Satsuma* and the *Shopgirl*, furnished with a piano and servants' quarters, and used by the wealthy as a place to entertain, were gone. The term was

by 1946 applied to a boat used as living accommodation or to a 4 or 6-berth holiday boat with basic facilities. Over the decade the number of small boats declined. The skills needed for their maintenance were no longer available, and the pleasure of small boating was spoiled by the wash generated by the launches.

The demand in the hire business during the 1950s was increasingly from a customer who wanted to arrive by car and take a launch by the hour or a cabin cruiser for the day or for longer periods, depending on size. The Thames Hire Cruiser Association was formed in 1955. There was also an increase in private ownership of bigger motor boats. To survive, companies had to decide whether to raise capital to invest in fleets of boats for weekly summer lets (and still have seasonal trade, damaged boats and winter storage problems) or to serve the private owner in some other way. Companies or individuals that had taken part in wartime boatbuilding gained a post-war technical advantage from their experience. Moss's had the island which provided safe mooring and winter storage for privately-owned boats and it was in this direction that the business went.

Moss's also had a reasonable amount of parking space inside and outside the shed and enough ground to let customers and the Island Bohemian Club members park their cars. The club had remained open throughout the war but had held no social functions. By 1946 members and

Year	Petrol launches	Houseboats	Small boats
1936	1,240	80	10,202
1939	1,595	–	9,826
1946	2,193	92	8,670
1947	2,569	121	8,253

visiting teams were playing tennis and bowls throughout the summer season but they were still using the original buildings. Members and players were taken across the river by Len Hazell, ferryman and groundsman. Len kept the greens in perfect condition, rowed across all the deliveries from the brewery, kept the generator running and switched it off at 11 pm before he ferried the last group back to their cars.

Harry Isaacs had died in 1942, having continued to enjoy winter bathing to a good age. Moss Boat Company was then run as a private limited company with Frank Pearce and his wife Joan as directors. They were able under new legislation to buy the lease of the site. They also purchased the part of Fry's Island between George Lewis's garden and the Reading Rowing Club that held the large, open-ended, wooden building on the Caversham side that had been used by Lewis for barge building and repair. Here Frank installed a slipway big enough to lift out large cabin cruisers for repair work or for under-cover winter storage. He designed and built it himself, utilising the old barge ramp, securing the sides and embedding a

pair of old railway lines into the ground on which to run the trolley. He constructed a gantry over the top of the slipway for lifting engines. Motive power came from an ex-naval winch and electrical power was from a generator. Frank also designed and built a tall metal gantry outside the main shed for lifting boats from trailers or engines from boats. The advent of power tools made working life a little easier, in particular pumps which made short work of emptying flooded boats. Income at this time was principally from moorings, storage, installations and repairs. There were still a few customers with small boats stored in the shed and still a few canoes, skiffs and punts for hire but the changes allowed Frank to use his technical skills and to move away from boatbuilding. However he did any repairs needed to the racing eights stored in the main shed for Sandhurst Military Academy and used by the cadets in about 1950.

The photo below shows a hire cruiser belonging to the Maidline fleet that has come alongside Moss's frontage for service.[2] The company did not advertise that it provided fuel, water or disposal services but would have allowed the hirer

A Maidline cruiser on the Moss landing stage.

The owners of *Havelock* greeting friends.

to occupy the landing stage while a problem was sorted out and would not have refused a request for water or even for petrol if there was some to spare. In the photograph on the previous page Frank Pearce is holding a canoe for one of his own customers alongside two dinghies which were used to cross to the moorings on the island. Cruisers are double moored at the head of the island. This is a good illustration of the landing stage, looking very uneven and patchy after wartime shortages of materials and time for repairs. One small but significant change about this time was the introduction of sheets of peel-off adhesive letters to make boat names, a cheaper and quicker alternative to calling in a signwriter to paint them.

By the mid 1950s Frank had bought two 12 or 14ft ex-naval boats. They were jolly-boats, purely working boats, with powerful engines and fitted with a central metal pole for anchoring tow ropes. They were very manoeuvrable. The boats were primarily used for fetching and returning customers' boats to the moorings, this being part of the service offered, for ferrying customers to

moorings or slipway and for general river work. The only place to sit was on the gunwale. A portable motor pump was always on board.

Typical of the customers with day boats on the moorings at this time were Derek and Rita Baylis, from the shops of that name, with *Derita*, and Sydney and Nora Album of Frameco with *Synor*. Guthrie Allsebrook, whose agricultural machinery business was in Crown Street, was another customer. They used their boats, cabin cruisers with open cockpits, rather as they used their cars, to go for a trip for a few hours in the evening or at the weekend. George Dunnaway, scrap metal merchant, who came with his daughter Kathy, was more of a river enthusiast. Later in the 1950s two retired couples, Peter and Kitty Hobson, first with the cruiser *Havelock* and later with the launch *Cremyl* and Jack and Gladys Lakey, with the *Letty*, were regular river users all the season, enjoying their boats as second homes. Another regular customer was Mr Badnell of Thorneycrofts, Alderman and Mayor of Reading, who had an open launch, the *Margaret*. All these boats stayed on the moorings all the summer and some all the winter too.

Loading up *Letty* ready for a day out.

Others were pulled out on the slipway for repair and painting during the winter.

Across the other side of the river in the 1950s Mrs Rose Dorothy Freebody, yet another in the family's line of women who managed the company, was running, with her three sons, a thriving boatbuilding and boat-hire business, including hire cruisers. Her husband, Ernest William, had died in 1946. The lido closed in the mid 1950s but Mrs Freebody recognised the attraction that it had had for the public and was planning how best to utilise the site to bring people back to it. She visualised a new building with a restaurant and dance hall with balconies overlooking an outdoor river pool that would be an asset to the town. She offered the site to Reading Borough Council as a development opportunity but it was rejected and she tried without success to interest local businessmen in her plan.[3]

Dorothy's son Ernest designed and built a hydroplane, something which had been his ambition for many years. The concept of a hydroplane, a craft which skims the water, was not new. It had been put before the Admiralty in 1872 and the idea

Mrs Dorothy Freebody.[4]

was developed, patented and put into practice by Sir John Thornycroft. The first hydroplanes appeared around 1910 and were built with a step in the underside of the hull which allowed them to rise above the surface, leaving the rudder and propeller in the water. A development in the 1930s added two riding surfaces which, with the propeller, were the contacts with the water. The lack of drag let the boats achieve high speeds. The hull of the Freebody hydroplane, called the *Mark F Flyer*, was made of spruce and plywood and cost £95 without the outboard engine. It could travel at 60 mph. The craft reached an international market, selling in America, Canada, and the Belgian Congo. In 1956 the company received more than 60 building orders from the Boat Show and had five cruisers, sixteen motor boats and nearly 40 small craft for hire.

All in the working day

Being called to accidents and emergencies, particularly the rescue of adults and children who had fallen in the water, was part of the working day for all the professionals on the river because they had the skills and the equipment to respond. Frank Pearce helped the police in the recovery of a body in 1954 and in the rescue of a dog that had fallen through ice in 1958. Access to a motor boat made a quick response possible when a child fell off a cruiser as it went downstream, enabling him to reach it and pull it out of the water, to catch up with the boat at the lock, and return the child before its parents had missed it.

On another occasion Frank worked with the police to get officers across to Fry's Island after dark without being heard. De Montfort House, on the end of the island, was used for a café and a club during the 1950s and it was popular with American servicemen. Its isolated position made possible after-hours drinking and other illegal activities. When the police became aware of this they made a surprise raid on the club one night and, as a result, it was closed and the premises disqualified.

A regular sight in the Caversham Road area in the 1950s was the herds of cattle being driven from the cattle market in Great Knollys Street, or from the railway sidings, to fields where Rivermead now is. Sometimes the cattle were taken over

the bridge, up Priory Avenue, down Priest Hill and along Hemdean Road to fields near Bugs Bottom. A day or so later they would make the return journey. The herds were big enough to take up the entire width of the road. They were driven along at quite a fast pace by inexperienced lads who really did not have full control of them. The animals were frightened and sometimes one would break away to run down one of the side roads. Thames Avenue and Brigham Road were places where this could happen and where, within a short distance, the animal would find itself approaching the river, unable to distinguish its grey surface from the tarmac of the road, and unable to stop. Of course, as with any problem along the riverside it was the boat companies who were the first port of call for help in getting the terrified animal out of the water before and after the professional teams arrived.

Swans could also confuse tarmac and river and come into land on the road surface. The birds could be herded back towards the water, or picked up with one hand on the neck and other round the body, without much trouble. On land they are not usually dangerous but in the water or near their nests they can behave very aggressively to men or to other swans. They drive off their own cygnets once the young ones are old enough for the white feathers to show through the brown. The signs of aggression, the wings raised and the neck curved backwards so that the head is low, are very clear and they can swim fast. One swan will fight another to the death, pinning the head of its rival under water with the beak and controlling its body with wings and feet. Frank, having worked at Turk's, the Queen's Watermen and Swan Uppers, had no problem in handling swans and he was able to help to remove a particularly aggressive one from the river because it had been attacking oarsmen. The numbers of swans on the Caversham reach increased substantially from the 1950s and they seem now to exist in flocks there without too much in-fighting, an apparent change in behaviour. The beak marks to distinguish the birds belonging to the Queen, the Dyers' and the Vintners' livery companies are

Broadcaster Hywel Davies interviewing Frank Pearce aboard *Tolly*.

well documented (replaced in 1998 by ringing) and conservation ceremonies in July each year are widely reported.

A television broadcast

On 31 July 1954 the outside broadcasting team of the BBC transmitted a one-hour, live programme from the Promenade above Caversham Bridge called 'The River in Summer'. The presenter was Hywel Davies. The themes for the afternoon were the range of activities and uses of the river, the skills needed by individuals and teams to manoeuvre in safety on a busy Bank Holiday and the nuisance and dangers created to all users by badly-handled equipment or craft. A range of traditional boats were shown in use; a sailing canoe, fours and scullers from a rowing club, a cutter belonging to local Sea Rangers, kayaks, and a punt being paddled and poled. One of the team demonstrated 'gadgets and equipment' for fishing and camping and an angler from London was interviewed about his catch. Hywel Davis then began an interview with Frank Pearce, sitting in *Tolly*, his working boat, discussing with him the

safe handling of small craft and asking him to explain how to get in and out of a skiff safely and how to bring it alongside, while family and friends demonstrated how to do these things, and how not to do them. Finally Frank showed the presenter how to scull a dingy over the stern, a skill which he had been using all his working life.[5]

Angling

Angling was still very popular and well on the way to achieving the position it holds now of the sport with the highest rate of participation in the country. Ye Olde Thames Valley Angling Club, Reading Fishing Club, Reading and District Angling Association, Rabson's Sports Club and South Reading Community Centre Youth Club were among the groups active in the area. Huntley and Palmers recreation club had a fishing section and Berkshire Printing Company and Miles Aircraft had angling clubs.

The river should have been well stocked after five war-time years when there had been very little fishing, but the quality of the water was not improved by the presence of large petrol-driven

An angling club event on the Promenade.

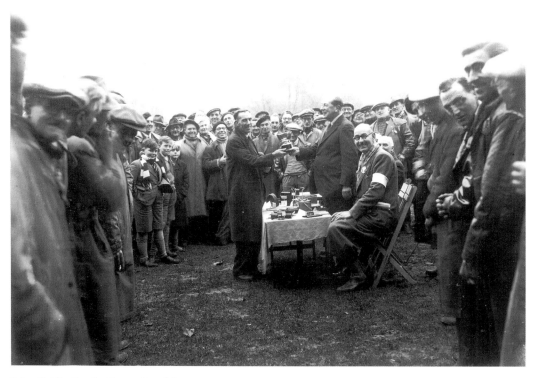

Prize distribution for the angling club group.

boats. They stirred up the mud and the fine silt was slow to settle, lowering the amount of light available for green weeds. When it did settle it coated the weeds, especially the broad-leaved varieties. The wash from the boats was strong and it damaged banks and stranded small animals and fish fry. In July 1954 there was an effort to restock with more than a thousand pike, perch, roach, dace and grayling, followed by another larger batch of fish later in the same week. The press report does not say who was doing the restocking but this was not a good time of year for introducing new fish. It would have been better to have done it when the water was colder.[6] There was an otter seen regularly along the Berkshire bank one summer in the mid 1950s but it did not stay.

Eels were a special case. Their levels had been much reduced since the days when elvers and adults could be taken on a commercial scale. Long-term pollution in the Thames tideway since the 1920s had prevented the migrant fish getting through it in either direction. The young could not get upstream to replenish the stock and adults, reaching maturity at about 10 years old, could not get down to the sea to breed.

However adult eels were being caught in the Thames at Tilehurst in the 1950s and 1960s and there are two independent sources to confirm this. A local fisherman, Michael Wheeler, can remember catching eels there and the former owners of the Fishery in the Warren recall that parties of eel fishers came to stay at their house at this period. There was no apparent explanation for the re-appearance of the eels above the pollution barrier but the author Tom Fort has recently provided an answer. He said that 'after the enforced departure of the Germans from the elver depot at Epney on the Severn just before the outbreak of war, the Ministry of Agriculture had transported several thousand Severn elvers and put them in the nearest part of the Thames.' Thus an eel population was able to mature in the Upper Thames. This resurgence was only temporary and lasted only the lifetime of the adult eels. There was a huge post-war effort at clearance of pollution and treatment of effluent along the river, and

eel stocks did increase, particularly in the River Loddon, a tributary that comes into the Thames near Wargrave, but not sufficiently to re-establish the species on a sound basis.[7]

Most anglers fished from the bank and came equipped with a seat and a large umbrella and during club competitions they would be at spaced intervals for very long distances. An undated book, probably written in the 1950s, said that the water from Whitchurch Bridge to Tilehurst was in the hands of fishing clubs or private owners. Below Tilehurst most of the waterside was owned by Reading Borough Council (the Promenade, Christchurch Meadows, Hill's Meadow and King's Meadow) and individuals could fish free of charge but clubs needed permission. From the Kennet Mouth down to Sonning the riparian owners did not exercise their rights and fishing was free. The Reading and District Angling Association controlled the Kennet as far as the Co-op Jam Factory (opposite the junction of Waterloo and Elgar Roads) and the public could fish there free except at the weekend when there was a charge of 1 shilling per head.[8]

The place of Bill Moss as the most knowledgeable and skilled fisherman of the Caversham reach had been taken by George Lamden of Thames Side. He had his own fishing boat from which he made some exceptional catches. Reg Witts and Willy Wyer were also keen fishermen in the 1950s and the latter turned a hobby into a business by opening a bait and tackle shop in Southampton Street.

The two photographs of an angling club and its prizegiving on the Promenade were taken by P O Collier of Thames Side. Although they are undated, the style of clothing being worn by members and supporters suggests that the event took place just after the war. The interest in these photographs is in the numbers and ages of the people taking part, showing the broad appeal of angling at this time. The prizes on the table were sensible and practical: primus stove, alarm clock, torch, zipped pouch, a round tin perhaps for live bait, and a box labelled 'Lurefly'.[9]

University of Reading Head of the River, 1950s.

Rowing

The rowing clubs had a better start after the war than they had in 1918. Reading Tradesmen's Rowing Club made a good start with a regatta in 1945. Reading Amateur Regatta and Reading Working Men's Regatta were both held in 1946. Reading Boys Clubs held a regatta on the Dreadnought reach in 1948.[10] Reading Rowing Club held an event over a shorter course than usual, rowing the half-mile from Reading Bridge to the top of Fry's island. Len Habbits was still an active member and two others on the list of officers in 1950, Norman Lipscombe and Stanley Latham, were longstanding and valued members. The entries for the club regatta grew over the next few years and ways of accommodating them had to be found.

A new endeavour by the Reading Working Men's Regatta Committee in the 1950s was the introduction of rowing into more local schools. Blue Coat School already rowed from the Working Men's boathouse and shared it with Woodley Hill Grammar School and with crews from the Reading Police and from Huntley

and Palmers. Their first eight was stored in the Reading Tradesmen's boathouse. Crews from Newtown, Sutton, Battle and Ashmead Schools competed with them in regattas organised by the Committee and umpired by Leo Waldron. The women of the Iris Rowing Club rowed on the Dreadnought reach in the 1950s.

Reading Town Regatta, the new title of the former Reading Working Men's Regatta, was adopted in 1966, differentiation between professional and clerical occupations and manual workers no longer having any relevance. Rowing was one of the last sports to eliminate such segregation, the two governing bodies, the ARA and NARA, finally amalgamating in 1956.

Between the wars the Regatta was a popular August Bank Holiday function, but following the transfer of the Bank Holiday to the end of the month for an initial trial period in 1965, the Regatta was moved to mid July, immediately prior to the end of term, with the aim of attracting school entries.

The presence of the University men's and women's rowing clubs was a positive influence. They had

'Happy' Haslam with a women's four leaving the boathouse to take to the water in the 1950s.

a landing stage in front of the war memorial with a fixed-tub training boat attached to it, in which a learner could sit and row with an oar whose blade had holes in it to let the water through. The oarsman made no progress and those who used it said that it was a very unpleasant experience and nothing like the real thing. The University's Head of the River had begun again in 1946 with 49 entries and grew to 136 entries in 1952. It was held in March when the river was often high and running fast and it continued to attract a very large entry. For some years Frank Pearce acted as safety steward, stationed in *Tolly* below the finishing post near the head of the island. The boats had slowed down by this time, ready to go down the main stream and up the backwater to the University landing stage. He had much experience of using a boat to rescue people from the water and was very confident of his skills but he knew the danger of shock to exhausted crewmen tipped into the water, having been present at an unsuccessful rescue attempt of an oarsman, and this particular job was not one he enjoyed.

At this time the University had a boatman, 'Happy' Haslam. He was a Caversham man who looked after the boats and the premises. He sometimes acted as coach and travelled on international trips with the Reading crews with whom he was very popular. As an employee (and thus a professional) it was only after the amalgamation of the ARA and NARA in 1956 that he was permitted to coach the amateur crews.

Young people on the water

A new element on the water was the involvement of young people in clubs and formal groups other than rowing: there were canoe clubs along the Warren; the 79th Reading Scouts had an island at Norcot; the Sea Rangers in *SRS Achilles* and *SRS Euryalus* and the 1st YMCA Reading Sea Scouts all had riverside bases in the rectory garden or along the Warren.

The Central Boys Club had kayaks at Cawstons. The Sea Cadet boat, *Jervis Bay*, a grey ex-naval vessel, was moored permanently by the Thames Water Authority's premises at Reading Bridge.

The Chief Constable, Mr Jesse Lawrence, presents the trophies to officers of Reading Borough Police. PC Milton is on the left, PC Stroust next to him, PC Barrett, winner on handicap, receives the cup, PC Emans is next but one and PC Bell is on the right.

Devizes to Westminster Canoe Race

A canoe race that began as a bet in the 1920s, and was repeated in 1947, then became an annual event. There were just two crews in 1948 but since then the number has increased greatly. The competitors start at Devizes on the Kennet and Avon Canal and pass through Pewsey, Hungerford and Newbury to Reading. They then enter the Thames at Horseshoe Bridge and continue downstream to the tidal zone at Teddington and finish at Westminster. The course is 125 miles in length with 77 locks and the original time of 77 hours has been reduced to less than a quarter of that figure. The race, which attracts large numbers of international entries from men and women in various age groups, is recognised as the 'Everest' of canoe events.

River swimming

River swimming was still popular in the 1950s from the river bank, and from the lidos at Cawston's and Freebody's boathouses, but sometimes there were accidents caused by inexperience or failure to recognise danger. A lido at Scours Lane, which was a very popular place for young swimmers, was on a sandy bay where the river was relatively narrow and it was outlined by floating markers.

When a passing cruiser was seen to be towing a tender (a small dinghy) behind it, a group of boys would sometimes swim towards it and hang on to the stern to be towed along with it. They could tip the tender over and sink it or the tailboard of the boat could be pulled out by their weight. The boys were back among the swimmers and

Aerial view of British Technical Cork on the site of Caversham Mill.

indistinguishable from them before the boat's crew could do much about it.

Long distance river swimming was a regular event in the 1950s, half- and quarter-mile downstream swims that finished at Caversham Bridge. Reading Swimming Club had a half-mile for men and a quarter-mile for women. The Reading Championship half-mile was won in 1954 by Johnny McGuirk, a well-known local swimmer. The police swim was the best reported and it was a mile-swim that took place in July. The undated photograph taken at Cawston's boathouse on Piper's Island shows the Chief Constable, Jesse Lawrence, presenting the prizes to the winners.[11] This was an event that continued into the 1970s, a long time after most people had deserted the river for the heated pools.

The move away from river swimming was hastened by the increasing number of swans which were believed to carry avian TB, by the risks imposed by the larger boats that were commonplace and by the sewage that some boats, belonging to major fleet owners, discharged from chemical toilets, quite against all regulations.

British Technical Cork Company

The site of Caversham Mill was redeveloped by the British Technical Cork Company and their trade card had on one side a street map of Lower Caversham showing how to reach them and on the other an aerial photograph of the site. The factory occupied the whole of Mill Island and extended to the mainland, incorporating some of the old mill buildings. The gardens on View Island appear in the photograph as well kept. King's Meadow is below them and Hill's Meadow on the top right of the picture.

New tenants in Moss's premises

In about 1957 The London Metal Company, trading as Brookside Metal, took over the former Browne and Lilly site in Thames Side and installed a public weighbridge. They wanted more space to extend their scrap metal business and Frank Pearce rented to them most of the main boat shed for this purpose. The photograph overleaf, taken on 17 May 1959, shows the old punt shed, Bill Moss's original

The site of Moss's boathouse in 1959, then occupied by Brookside Metal Company.

The former boathouse frontage now fenced off for storage of cars for Harry Markham with the completed Excel Bowl in the background.

Access to the island kept open during the freeze of 1962–63 by a channel and a fixed line to pull a boat across.

Large boats on the Freebody frontage have been kept clear of ice to protect them from damage.

premises, closed up but Lewis's timber yard behind it is still open. The cars in the foreground belong to members of the Island Bohemian Club. The ferry can just be seen in the bottom left hand corner of the photograph and some members have disembarked and are just going to their cars while others are in the boat ready to cross to the club.

When the London Metal Company no longer wanted the boat shed it was let to Harry Markham who had a car-repair business in Caversham Road and needed space for cars waiting to be worked on and for employee parking. For a while there was a small dry-ski run attached to the big shed where customers of Carters in Caversham Road could try out their purchases. The frontage was fenced off to protect the stored cars and later willow trees were planted along the edge.

The winter of 1962–63

Frank let the slipway to Len Leach but kept the upstream end of Fry's Island and the moorings and so was still in the boat business during the freezing winter of 1962–63. There had been low temperatures and snow since Christmas 1962 and by mid-January ice floes were forming on the river. It froze over completely along its entire length soon after this and remained frozen for two months. Access to the island and to the moorings was kept open by pulling a boat across on a fixed tow line through a channel kept free of ice. There were also large boats moored on Freebody's site but here too they had to be kept free of ice.

Fry's Island from the air.

Frank and Joan Pearce in *Tolly*.

Final closure for Moss and Freebody

The aerial photograph of the riverside and Fry's Island opposite was taken in the late 1960s. The Promenade and the Caversham Bridge Hotel are on the left, above the twin arches of Caversham Bridge. Below the bridge are commercial buildings, including those occupied by the London Metal Company, followed by the Victorian villas in Thames Side. The road in front of them can be seen to be closed to traffic by barriers, as it was on Good Friday each year, to maintain its status as a private road. Bill Moss's sheds are still standing. Piper's Island, immediately below the bridge, is surrounded by moored boats and the Freebody premises are opposite. Christchurch Meadows are on the Caversham bank. The Island Bohemian Club is open, the bowling rinks and tennis courts are ready for play and the ferry is on the mainland stage. At the bottom left of the photograph, redevelopment has begun of the site formerly occupied by George Lewis, timber merchant, to become the Excel Bowl. This marks the beginning of major changes on both banks.

The Freebody family sold their site in the late 1950s and retired from the boat business in Caversham 200 years after Thomas had established the wharf at the White Hart. Frank and Joan Pearce sold their part of Fry's Island and the mooring rights to the Island Bohemian Club in 1966, just short of 100 years since Bill Moss set up in business at Caversham Bridge, and they were then free to move away.

Endnotes

1   *The Thames Conservancy 1857–1957*, produced by the Conservators. The figures in the table also come from this source p 65–67 and the 1936 figures from a TC report to Berkshire County Council.

2   Maidline Cruisers of Thames Ditton.

3   *Berkshire Chronicle*, 20 January 1956.

4   Photograph copyright to Mrs Jenny Freebody.

5   Original script of the outside broadcast team.

6   *Berkshire Chronicle*, 30 July 1954.

7   Thanks are given to Michael Wheeler for the information from his own experience about eels at Tilehurst and for pointing out the explanation in Tom Fort *The Book of Eels* (HarperCollins, 2002), p 217. Also to Richard Wise, for information about The Fishery.

8   Bill Taylor *Famous Fishing Rivers: Upper Thames, an Angling Times book*, (undated) p 13.

9   MERL, P DX 323 M31/19–21 angling club meeting.

10 *Berkshire Chronicle* 7 October 1948.

11 Thanks are given to Michael Vince and to Ken Wells, Curator of the Police Museum, for making this photograph available.

18 Conclusion

Time to look back

One of the central themes of this account, the local boatbuilding and boat-hire companies of Moss and Freebody at Caversham, came to an end 40 years ago. This is a good length of time across which to look back and to review some of the other themes in this book and see how they have developed or concluded.

Boats and boatyards

Cawston's *Majestic*, the last steam-driven steamer in Salter's fleet, was withdrawn in 1966. The number of pleasure boats of all categories on the non-tidal Thames peaked in the 1970s and since then has fallen by about one-third. In 1980 there were 12,000 private and 800 hire boats and in 2002 only about 9000 and 150 respectively. There were also about 200 day boats for hire and 60 passenger boats. Since the Kennet and Avon Canal reopened in 1990 there has been an interchange of boats between it and the Thames, and narrowboats from other waterways are seen on both. The Thames locks downstream from Oxford were modified in a programme begun in 1956 to a hydraulic ram system, which speeded up their action, but left them without their manually-operated balance beam gates.

The Freebody connection with the Thames continues. Peter Freebody, grandson of Ernest William and Dorothy, carries on his family boat-building tradition downstream at Hurley. He is known world-wide for his superb restorations of Thames boats of all kinds, including in 1995 the 13ft motor dinghy *Cuthbert* built by the family business in the 1950s.

There are two boat companies on Fry's Island: Bridge Boats in the old barge sheds where Frank Pearce built his slipway, and Caversham Boat Services in the former Reading Rowing Club building. Thames Rivercruise operates a fleet of large, covered boats from Piper's Island which are popular for scheduled trips and evening group outings, thus continuing to supply the market which Bona developed. The Better Boating Co is a major presence at Mill Green. Salters Steamers still operate in their familiar black and white colours and offer round trips upstream from Reading and scheduled ones downstream to Henley.

Rowing

The University men's boathouse was destroyed by fire in 1989 and replaced by a new one. Reading Rowing Club moved the same year into a new boathouse above Caversham Bridge on a Reading Borough Council site, having occupied during the 1970s (after they left Fry's Island) a building that was once Bona's, and later East's and Cawston's. Rowing is still a major part of the river scene. Reading Amateur Regatta continued to thrive throughout the 1980s and 90s and achieved a record entry of 334 crews in 1996, but suffered a record rainfall in 1997 when the event had to be cancelled. Improvements to the layout and length of the course, and to the water, by the elimination of umpire boats, improved the racing, putting the adjudicators back on the bank (though not, as Mr Blandy in 1896, in the saddle !). The Head of the River continues to attract high-quality crews.

A national dimension has been given to rowing at the Caversham Lakes. These are extensive inland waters where there were once gravel pits on what was Deane's Farm. David Sherriff, chairman of the Thames & Kennet Marina at the lakes, was both a generous donor and instrumental in creating a training site for British rowing, called the Redgrave Pinsent Rowing Lake, managed by the Amateur Rowing Association. It is 2000m by 100m and can accommodate six lanes of racing boats, and there are all the necessary facilities for coaching and training on site. Reading Sailing Club and the Isis Ski Club each have a base there. The Lakes are also where The Thames Traditional Boat Society, the society for unpowered boating, is based. There is a Traditional Boats weekend rally after Henley Royal Regatta and new and restored boats of all kinds attend, including many from Peter Freebody's boatyard. In 2004 two old Caversham boats were there, a skiff called *Tara* built by Samuel Gyngell, and the *Eclipse*, a steam boat built by Edward Cawston.

Riverside development: the Thames

In the 1970s the riverside on the Reading bank, always a commercial area, began a period of change – following on from the building of the Excel Bowl – as great as the one that began in the 1870s. In 1978 Reading Borough Council published a plan for Reading's waterways, recognising that future pressure for development was likely to be intense and that it was important that it, as planning authority and principal landowner, should ensure that the use of the belts of open riverside land was to the advantage of

public and commercial interests.[1] In the same year the Fisheries and Recreation Committee of the Thames Water Authority recommended that £20,000 should be contributed towards repairing towpaths along the Thames. Of this, £10,000 was to go towards repairs between Caversham and Reading Bridges with an equal amount being contributed by Reading Borough Council.[2]

The Lorco sign is a reminder of the pressure from industrial development on the Berkshire bank at the time.

The coffee stall at Caversham Bridge, which was run by Reading Temperance Society, closed in the 1960s. Plans were put forward in 1984 to convert the Victorian cast-iron buildings at the bridge into a tea room but they were rejected by the council on the grounds that the site was earmarked as part of a wider development plan. The former toilets were removed and the site became Chronicles Restaurant. The Caversham Bridge Hotel was replaced by the Holiday Inn, renamed Crowne Plaza, and the former osier meadows beyond it have been used for the Reading Festival and Womad. Piper's Island and The Thames Valley Hotel site were redeveloped in 2005 and both are restaurants and entertainment centres. The drinking fountain put up in memory of Frank Attwells, manager of the Reading Theatre, mayor and river man, was moved from its original place in the road outside the hotel and is now in the public car park behind it.

Reading Borough Council is restoring the gardens of William Alexander's Striped House, now Caversham Court, and has uncovered the foundations of the Tudor building. The former stables have become small industrial units. There are flats on the Freebody site, houses and retail and residential development behind the University Rowing Club and Christchurch Meadows, and more flats on the opposite side on the Lorco site, once Browne and Lilly.

The Moss site was eventually sold in the early 1990s and since then has been redeveloped as flats. These changes have put land ownership into the hands of small numbers of commercial companies who retain the freeholds while leasing the properties to the occupiers. Fry's Island has changed very little. Templecombe is still there, the Island Bohemian Club continues as a bowling club, and De Montfort House is still a private residence. The mill site was cleared in 1983 and houses with their own moorings were built and the area given the name of Heron Island. Clearwater Court, an attractive circular building above Reading Bridge, is the business centre of Thames Water Utilities Ltd.

Riverside development: the Kennet

There has been substantial development along the banks of the Kennet. In Reading town centre the Oracle shopping centre has brought attention to the riverside once again, and the banks of the central section from Seven Bridges to High Bridge are busy with restaurants and clubs. On either side of this, the Fobney and Duke Street areas have been developed by companies to provide leasehold flats and apartments. In summer the waterway is busy with residential and pleasure boats and in winter there are still a few moored in the town centre. The weir near Blake's Lock was rebuilt in 2002, retaining the original paddle and rymer construction, and the lock gates replaced since then, but retaining the balance beam gates.[3] The pumping station and related buildings are retained as a small museum and as a restaurant. Reading Waterfest is an annual event on the Kennet at Chestnut Walk. The Kennet and Avon Canal Trust is a registered charity, formed to restore the waterway, which now works in partnership with British Waterways and the riparian local authorities to safeguard the navigation.

Open spaces

The huge numbers of swans and Canada geese make a mess of the grass on the Promenade and Christchurch Meadows, where there is still a children's playground and sports fields. Hill's Meadow has a car park and a skateboard and BMX site. A proposal to rebuild the Hexagon on the site produced a strong local reaction against it. View Island is a public park. King's Meadow is dominated by Tesco (where there are now public moorings and free fishing) and blocks of flats. It is the site of Reading Beer and Cider Festival and the Gay Pride Festival and there are still football pitches where Reading Football Club played its first game in 1872. Osiers are once again under cultivation and being cut for basket-making along the Napier Road edge of King's Meadow, where there are also full grown willow trees of a variety of species.

The Environment Agency and Reading Borough Council were in 2003 hoping to attract a developer to rejuvenate Caversham Lock Island and part of the King's Meadow recreation ground as 'mixed use' development. The site extended to almost three acres and incorporated the derelict King's Meadow Swimming Pool, formerly the Ladies' Bath. On 22 July 2004 Jane Griffiths MP, (Lab, Reading East), presented a petition of 2000 of her constituents to the House of Commons which opposed 'the plan to tear down the King's Meadow swimming baths, and to develop King's Meadow and Caversham lock on the green banks of the Thames into a hotel, apartments and other developments. The petitioners would like the area to be retained as a public amenity.' The petition was granted and the following month the swimming bath was given listed building status by English Heritage. In 2007 the King's Meadow Campaign was still asking the Council to consider the restoration of the baths to public use.

The building is one of a very small number remaining from the Edwardian and Victorian riverside scene in Reading, the others being the former Reading Rowing Club building, De Montfort House and Templecombe, all on Fry's Island, and the five Thames Side houses opposite

De Montfort House on the downstream end of Fry's Island.

the island. There is a strong feeling that a basic right to continue to use King's Meadow as a public facility is under threat.

River management

At the beginning of this account there was no management body on the river. The story has followed the work of Thames Navigation Commission and the Thames Conservancy as they resolved the conflicts of interest between millers and bargemasters for the right to the flow of water that William Pearce described to the House of Commons, and managed the introduction of steam, electric and petrol engines and the influx of new people the technology brought to the river. It has shown the contribution they have made in providing and maintaining towpaths, river banks, locks, weirs, managing the river flow and the traffic and enforcing the byelaws.

The management of the river passed in 1974 to the Thames Water Authority and in 1990 to the National Rivers Authority. In 1996 the management of the Thames, and of the Kennet up to and including Blake's Lock, was transferred to the Thames Region of the Environment Agency, which now looks after all navigational, recreational and environmental matters and attempts to maintain a balance between all their interests.

The Thames is now a clean river along its entire length and excellent for angling. A survey in 1982 found 100 species of fish.[4] Since 1992 there has been a single national rod licence issued by the National Rivers Authority replacing the earlier regional licences organised by the water authorities. This brought consistency of charge and transferability between waters. It was upgraded in 1994 by a two-level system that differentiated between salmon and sea trout and non-migratory trout and coarse fish.

The salmon is back with fish passes built in 1995 to help its migration, though lack of breeding grounds may prevent the establishment of the species, something which many anglers are not too unhappy about. They feel that it is fine as a symbol of clean water but rights to fish it would be valuable and riparian owners might want to restrict bank fishing.

The otter is now making a return to local waters. A survey in 2000–02 found that 10 of 32

Caversham weir pool: always a popular place for fishing.

sites in the Upper Thames were positive for otters where none of them had been so ten years before. In 2003 it was announced that they were also back in the River Loddon and their settlement was being supported by the placement of otter holts by the Countyside Services of Wokingham District Council.[5] Tom Fort hopes that the liking of the otter for eels as part of its diet will draw attention to the needs of that species too.[6]

The towpath is still there but its usage has increased way beyond the original purpose and it is now used by walkers as part of the Thames Path as well as by local pedestrians. It is also used by anglers and in parts by cyclists, the riparian rights of some landowners restricting its full use. Floods during the summer of 2007 were narrowly averted in Caversham through good communication and management as the bulge of torrential rain that had fallen throughout the Thames Valley drained into the tributaries and was then moved down the river. The town was reminded that the meadows on either side of the lock were part of the flood plain.

Safeguarding the river

There are substantial pressures on the Thames Region of the Environment Agency in managing the waterway. There is a rising population in the river valley with high expectations of clean water, recreational use of the river and its banks, drought management, protection from increasing risk of flooding as the climate changes and even of generation of electricity from turbines in the weir streams.

With such pressures on river management, there is a place for an impartial forum to act as a watch dog on issues that affect the well-being of the river from source to tideway. It was for this reason that the River Thames Society was founded as a registered charity in 1962.[7] Its aims are to preserve the amenity value of the Thames and to encourage its use in a sustainable manner. It supports the protection of the waterway and of land and buildings of historical and architectural interest alongside it. One of its present concerns is the loss of boatyards to exclusive residential developments, as has happened in Caversham and in Reading. It has active branches at local level and its river warden scheme uses volunteers to monitor the condition of the Thames Path, and the banks and water of the River Thames. The society works with Natural England, the Port of London Authority and the Environment Agency to monitor and improve the river environment. It is represented on River User Consultative Forums the length of the river. Its presence is a necessary safeguard to maintain the river and riverside as places of work and leisure.

This story has covered a period of nearly one thousand years and has followed the changes of land ownership along the riversides from the church, via the Knollys estate, to local authority and commercial interests. It has shown how goods traffic on the water has been replaced by pleasure boating and competitive rowing. Fisheries, ferries and mills have gone but angling remains popular. The river banks still retain their importance as places of business and recreation. This account has put people into the landscape and shown how they have responded to new opportunities, and adapted their businesses to changing technology. It has pointed out the pressures that all these activities put on the environment of the river itself, the living system that supports it all. While there are protective systems and safeguards

Still in place today – the metal bollard on the site of the first Freebody wharf, alongside the White Hart, where barges were moored and where Maynard tied up the *Queen of the Thames* after she was launched.

in place, it remains to be seen whether they will be strong enough. In the future, will it be the river banks and the surrounding areas which will experience the greatest changes or will it be the river itself ?

Endnotes

1   *Reading Waterways: a plan for the River Landscape* (Reading Borough Council, 1978). The Lorco sign image is taken from the plan with permission.

2   *Berkshire Chronicle* 4 August 1978.

3   Information from display board at Blake's Lock Museum.

4   Information from a display on the history of fishing at the River and Rowing Museum at Henley in January 2005.

5   Environment Agency Fourth Otter Survey of England 2000–02. www.environment-agency. gov.uk/commondata/105385/Thames_region. pdf. In the Upper Thames section of the survey, 10 of 32 sites were positive for otters in 2000–02 compared with zero in 1991–94. The Otter Trust introduced 17 otters in 1999.

6   Tom Fort *The Book of Eels* (HarperCollins, 2002) p 219.

7   Angela Perkins 25 *Thames years: a history of the River Thames Society* (The River Thames Society, 1987); http://www.riverthamessociety.org.uk/; The society's journal *Thames Guardian* is produced quarterly.

Reading waterways workers: 1423–1930

Trade	Name	Year	Boat or property	Information source	Location
Bargeman	Adkyns Johannes	1639		Guilding Vol 3 p452	RLSL
Boatbuilder	Allen John	1841	Katesgrove Lane	Census	RLSL
Bargemaster	Andrewes Charles	1675		Will	TNA
Fishmonger	Andrewes Peter	1587		Will of John Thorne	TNA
Fishmonger	Andrewes Peter	1607		Will	TNA
Bargeman	Atkyns John	1625		Guilding Vol 3 p165-7	RLSL
Fishmonger	Bagley John	1630		Will	TNA
Bargeman	Barr William	1844	High Bridge Wharf	Reading St Lau. Bap. Reg.	BRO
Bargeman	Beasely James	1835	Abbey Wall	Reading St Lau. Bap. Reg.	BRO
Barge Owner	Beasley Mr	1806		Rusher's Directory	RLSL
Bargeman	Bedford George	1841	Sims Court, Kennet Side	Census	RLSL
Bargeman	Benham John	1841	Katesgrove Lane	Census	RLSL
Bargeman	Benham William	1835	Abbey Wall	Reading St Lau. Bap. Reg.	BRO
Bargeman	Benham William	1841	Abbey Wall	Census	RLSL
Boatbuilder	Bennett George	1803		Will	TNA
Bargebuilder	Bennett Thomas	1901	Elm Villa, Mill Green	Census	RLSL
Bargeman	Benster Thomas	1841	Bridge Street	Census	RLSL
Bargemaster	Biggs John	1762		Will	TNA
Bargemaster	Biggs John	1804		Will	TNA
Barge Owner	Biggs Mr	1801		Rusher's Directory	RLSL
Bargemaster	Biggs Samuel	1776		Will	TNA
Wharfinger	Blake Robert	1713		Will of Edward Wilder Senior	BRO
Wharfinger	Blake Robert	1727	Kennet Wharf and Lock	Will	TNA
Barge Owner	Blandy William	1812	*Adventurer*	Barge Register	BRO
Bargeman	Bloxham Stephen	1832	Abbey	Reading St Lau. Bap. Reg.	BRO
Wharfinger	Bourman William	1632		Guilding Vol 3 p165-7	RLSL
Bargemaster	Bowsher Robert	1820		Will	TNA
Barge Owner	Bradford John	1639		Will of A Edwards, Partner	TNA
Barge Owner	Bristow John	1812	*Industry*	Barge Register	BRO
Barge Owner	Bristow Mr	1814		Rusher's Directory	RLSL
Bargeman	Brompton William	1841	Kings Road	Census	RLSL
Wharfinger	Brown John	1841	Friar Street	Census	RLSL
Wharfinger	Buncombe Richard	1842	Abbey Wharf	Snare's Directory	RLSL

Trade	Name	Year	Boat or property	Information source	Location
Wharfinger	Buy William	1717	Sivier Street, London Street	Will	TNA
Bargemaster	Camplin Wm	1739		Will	TNA
Bargeman	Cane John	1841	Ivy Court, Coley Lane	Census	RLSL
Bargeman	Chesterman Steven	1633		Guilding Vol 3, p187	RLSL
Barge Owner	Clement Mr	1801		Rusher's Directory	RLSL
Boatbuilder	Clement Richard	1796		Will	BRO
Barge Owner	Cobb Richard	1769		Malt Tax Claim	BRO
Bargeman	Collier Fred	1841	Palmers Wharf	Census (Overnight Stop)	RLSL
Bargemaster	Collier Frederick	1842	Birmingham Wharf	Snares' Directory	RLSL
Bargemaster	Collier Frederick	1843	High Bridge Wharf	Reading St Lau. Bap. Reg.	BRO
Bargemaster	Collier Samuel	1743		Will	BRO
Bargemaster	Collier Samuel	1843	High Bridge Wharf	Reading St Lau. Bap. Reg.	BRO
Bargemaster	Conwaye William	1632	*Doves*	Guilding Vol 3 p165-7	RLSL
Lock-keeper	Cooper	1865	Islands Duke Street	Macauley's Directory	RLSL
Bargeman	Cox James	1841	Whitley Street	Census	RLSL
Waterman	Creed Wiliam Strange	1840	Cross Street	Reading St Lau. Bap. Reg.	BRO
Lock-keeper	Cuper John	1841	Islands, Duke Street	Census	RLSL
Barge Owner	Deane Robert	1812	Mill Boat	Barge Register	BRO
Barge Owner	Deane Robert	1824		Will	TNA
Bargebuilder	Downing Daniel	1865	K&A Wharf Bridge Street	Macauley's Directory	RLSL
Boatbuilder	Downing Daniel	1874	Seven Bridges	Webster's Directory	RLSL
Bargemaster	Drewe John	1842	Victoria Wharf	Snares' Directory	RLSL
Bargemaster	Duglas John	1693		Will	TNA
Bargeman	Dunn Thomas	1830	Abbey	Reading St Lau. Bap. Reg.	BRO
Wharf Owner	Dye Simon	1638		Guilding Vol 3 p434	RLSL
Bargeman	Dyson Wm	1849	Abbey Wall	Reading St Lau. Bap. Reg.	BRO
Waterman	Edwards Abraham	1639		Will	TNA
Boatbuilder	Eels (?) Hy	1841	Muner Court	Census	RLSL
Bargebuilder	Elkins George	1841	Abbey Wall	Census	RLSL
Boatbuilder	Elkins Henry	1851	Caversham Bridge	Census	RLSL
Boatbuilder	Elkins John	1841	Abbey Court	Census	RLSL
Bargeman	Evans Daniel	1841	Lime Court, Coley Lane	Census	RLSL
Bargeman	Fowler Thomas	1632	Maidenhead	Guilding Vol 3 p165-7	RLSL
Waterman	Freebody Lester	1881		Census	RLSL
Waterman	Freebody Peter	1861	Castle Street	Census	RLSL
Barge Owner	Freebody William	1812	*Brittania*	Barge Register	BRO
Bargeman	Frewin James	1815		Bap. Reg.	BRO
Bargemen	Frost John	1806		Will	BRO
Bargebuilder	Fuller James	1871		Census	RLSL
Bargeman	Gibbons Samuel	1841	Kings Road	Census	RLSL
Bargebuilder	Goatley Thos	1841	Abbey Brook	Census	RLSL
Bargeman	Grase Frederick	1841	Salem Place	Census	RLSL
Bargemaster	Greenaway John Sen	1737		Will	BRO
Bargemaster	Greenaway Thomas Sen	1731		Will	BRO
Bargemaster	Greenaway William	1737		Beneficary of John Pudsey	BRO
Bargeman	Griffin John	1841	Starling Court, Silver Street	CensusB	RLSL
Bargeman	Hackett William	1632		Guilding Vol 3 p165-7	RLSL
Barge Owner	Hall John	1634		Guilding Vol 3 p248	RLSL
Bargeman	Hatt Wm	1830	Hookers Green	Reading St Lau. Bap. Reg.	BRO

Trade	Name	Year	Boat or property	Information source	Location
Boatbuilder	Hawkins James	1874	6 Thames Street	Webster's Directory	RLSL
Bargemaster	Hedges William	1842	Buncombe's Wharf	Snares' Directory	RLSL
Bargemaster	Hedges Wm	1828	Abbey St, Buncombe's Wharf	Reading St Lau. Bap. Reg.	BRO
Bargeman	Hill Richard	1632		Guilding Vol 3 p165–7	RLSL
Boatbuilder	Hope John	1841	Southampton Street West	Census	RLSL
Bargebuilder	Hope William	1841	Islands Duke Street	Census	RLSL
Boatbuilder	Hope William	1842	Islands Duke Street	Rusher's Directory	RLSL
Bargebuilder	Hope Wm	1826	Abbey	Reading St Lau. Bap. Reg.	BRO
Bargeman	Hulins Thomas	1712		Will & Inventory	BRO
Bargeman	Humphrey Wm	1835	Abbey	Reading St Lau. Bap. Reg.	BRO
Fisherman	Ide John	1423	Gutter Lane	Title Deeds	BRO
Wharfinger	Irvine Edward	1776		Will of Samuel Biggs	TNA
Bargemaster	Jackson Robert	1817	West Street	Reading St Lau. Bap. Reg.	BRO
Pondkeeper	Johnson William	1851	Kennet Side	Census	RLSL
Wharfinger	Kent Robert	1721		Will	TNA
Bargeman	Kenting John	1783		Will	BRO
Barge Owner	Kinner Mr	1806		Rusher's Directory	RLSL
Bargemaster	Kinner Robert	1812	Rosebud	Barge Register, based Henley	BRO
Bargemaster	Kinner Robert	1813		Will of Brother	BRO
Barge Owner	Kinner Samuel	1812	Jubilee	Barge Register	BRO
Bargemaster	Kinner Samuel Jun	1813		Will of Father Samuel Kinner	BRO
Bargemaster	Kinner Samuel Sen	1813	Abbey	Will	BRO
Bargeman	Laster Henry	1632	Wargrave	Guilding Vol 3 p165–7	RLSL
Barge Owner	Law Edward	1812	Friend	Barge Register	BRO
Barge Owner	Law Edward	1812	Old London	Barge Register	BRO
Barge Owner	Law Edward	1812	Stroud	Barge Register	BRO
Barge Owner	Law Mr	1801		Rusher's Directory	RLSL
Bargeman	Lewis Henry	1769		Malt Tax Claim	BRO
Waterman	Lighting Robert	1841	Friar Street	Census	RLSL
Ropemaker	Linain John	1841	Broad Street	Census	RLSL
Bargemaster	Lovegrove Matt Sn	1746		Will	BRO
Waterman	Lyford Charles	1845		Bap. Reg.	BRO
Waterman	Lyford Richard	1841	Near Caversham Rectory	Census	RLSL
Bargebuilder	Lyford Richard	1841	Bath Court	Census	RLSL
Bargebuilder	Mackie James	1901	Buck Side	Census	RLSL
Bargeman	Male John	1841	Kennet Side	Census	RLSL
Bargeman	Marsham Charles	1826	Broad Street	Reading St Lau. Bap. Reg.	BRO
Waterman	May Alfred	1871		Census	RLSL
Wharfinger	May John	1717		Will of Wm Buy, Partner	TNA
Bargeman	Maynard John	1825	Friar Street	Reading St Lau. Bap. Reg.	BRO
Bargeman	Mills John	1841	Starling Court, Silver Street	Census	RLSL
Barge Owner	Mills Richard	1812	Beanshell	Barge Register	BRO
Barge Owner	Mills Richard	1812	Mary Anne	Barge Register	BRO
Barge Owner	Mills Richard	1812	Venture	Barge Register	BRO
Bargemaster	Mills Richard	1827	Abbey Brook	Reading St Lau. Bap. Reg.	BRO
Bargemaster	Mills Robert	1814		Will	TNA
Bargeman	Moss John	1841	Blandy's Wharf	Census	RLSL
Boatbuilder	Mulford William	1874	28 Whitley Street	Webster's Directory	RLSL
Wharfinger	Osborne Edward	1804	Duke Street	Will	TNA

Trade	Name	Year	Boat or property	Information source	Location
Wharfinger	Osborne Edward	1804	Blakes Wharf	Will of John Biggs	TNA
Bargemaster	Paice Wm	1775		Will	TNA
Wharfinger	Parfett Arthur	1861	Church Walk	Census	RLSL
Bargeman	Parry Philip	1632	Twyford	Guilding Vol 3 p165-7	RLSL
Bargemaster	Patey James	1784		Beneficiary of John Plumridge	BRO
Bargemaster	Pearce William	1750		House of Commons Dep.	RLSL
Bargemaster	Perry Thomas	1827	West Street	Reading St Lau. Bap. Reg.	BRO
	Piggott William	1806		Will of Grandfather William Salter	BRO
Bargemaster	Piggott Wm	1698		Will	TNA
Bargebuilder	Piper James	1865	Caversham Bridge	Macauley's Directory	RLSL
Barge Builder	Piper Jas	1851	Caversham Bridge	Census	RLSL
Barge Builder	Piper Jas	1851	Caversham Bridge	Census	RLSL
Wharfinger	Plevier John	1841	Abbey Court	Census	RLSL
Bargemaster	Plumridge John	1784	*Dreadnought*	Will	BRO
Bargebuilder	Pope Charles	1871	Stephens Lodge	Census	RLSL
Lock-keeper	Provis Richard	1930	Caversham Lock	Kelly's Directory	RLSL
Bargemaster	Pudsey John	1737		Will	BRO
Bargeman	Reddings Nathaniel	1841	Kennet Side	Census	RLSL
Bargeman	Reddings Robert	1841	Kennet Side	Census	RLSL
Bargemaster	Reid Alexander	1841	Kings Road	Census	RLSL
Bargemaster	Reid Alexander	1844	Kings Road	Reading St Lau. Bap. Reg.	BRO
Bargeman	Rider Richard	1841	Islands Duke Street	Census	RLSL
Boatbuilder	Robins John	1826	West Street	Reading St Lau. Bap. Reg.	BRO
Bargeman	Salter Wm	1746		Will	BRO
Fisherman	Saunders Thomas	1841	Coley Street	Census	RLSL
Boat	Searle George	1841	Katesgrove Lane	Census	RLSL
Boatbuilder	Self Thomas	1840	Abbey Place	Reading St Lau. Bap. Reg.	BRO
Bargeman	Shopham Joseph	1841	Coley Terrace	Census	RLSL
Wharfinger	Simmond John	1725		Will	TNA
Boatbuilder	Simmonds Thomas	1826	Blakes Wharf	Reading St Lau. Bap. Reg.	BRO
Bargeman	Simmons Solomon	1842	Kings Road	Reading St Lau. Bap. Reg.	BRO
Bargeman	Slatter George	1743		Admin Bond	BRO
Bargemaster	Smith Samuel	1773		Will	TNA
Bargebuilder	Sparkes Thomas	1901	Buck Side	Census	RLSL
Boatbuilder	Springall John	1817	Friar Street	Reading St Lau. Bap. Reg.	BRO
Boatbuilder	Stocken Charles	1841	Laud Place	Census	RLSL
Bargebuilder	Swain James	1865	Blakes Wharf	Macauley's Directory	RLSL
Wharfinger	Swain James	1870		Probate	BRO
Boatbuilder	Swain SJ	1874	Kings and Queens Road	Webster's Directory	RLSL
Bargebuilder	Swan Charles	1871	North Place	Census	RLSL
Bargebuilder	Talbot Richard	1865	Caversham Road	Macauley's Directory	RLSL
Bargebuilder	Talbot Richard	1871	Bridge House	Census	RLSL
Bargebuilder	Talbot Richard	1874	Caversham Road	Webster's Directory	RLSL
Bargeman	Terrent Edward	1632		Guilding Vol 3 p165-7	RLSL
Wharfinger	Terrell William	1759		Will	TNA
Bargeman	Thatcher Richard	1844	High Bridge Wharf	Reading St Lau. Bap. Reg.	BRO
Fisher	Thorne John	1587	Lane to St Mary's Church	Will	TNA
Bargeman	Townsend Edward	1784		Beneficiary of John Plumridge	BRO
Bargemaster	Truss Charles	1713		Will of Edward Wilder Sen	BRO

Trade	Name	Year	Boat or property	Information source	Location
Bargemaster	Truss Charles	1751		Thacker	RLSL
Bargemaster	Truss Charles	1781		Will	TNA
Bargemaster	Truss Charles	1815		Will	TNA
Bargemaster	Truss Charles Sen	1731		Will	BRO
Bargemaster	Tubb Francis	1747		Will	TNA
Bargemaster	Tull Thomas	1738		Will	BRO
Bargeman	Ward John	1738		Will of Thomas Tull	BRO
Bargemaster	Ward William	1753	London Street	Deeds	BRO
Bargemaster	Ward William	1776	Mill Lane	Will	BRO
Bargeman	Warwick John	1841	Salem Place	Census	RLSL
Bargeman	Webb William	1905	Willow Street	*Berkshire Chronicle*	RLSL
Bargeman	Westall Frances	1861	Salem Place	Census	RLSL
Bargeman	Westall William	1841	Orts Road	Census	RLSL
Bargemaster	White James	1842	Katesgrove Lane	Will	BRO
Bargemaster	Whitehouse Jeremiah	1837	Kings Road, Blandy's Wharf	Reading St Lau. Bap. Reg.	BRO
Bargemaster	Whitehouse Jeremiah	1840		Will	BRO
Bargemaster	Whitehouse Jeremiah	1839	10 Acre and Hither Meadow	Tithe Plot 7	BRO
Bargebuilder	Wicks James	1826	Abbey, Yield Hall	Reading St Lau. Bap. Reg.	BRO
Bargeman	Wigg Wigmore	1640		Guilding Vol 3 p478	RLSL
Bargemaster	Wigginton John	1718	*Lamb of Reading*	Will	TNA
Bargemaster	Wilder Ed Sen	1713		Will	BRO
Bargemaster	Wilder Richard	1751		Will	TNA
Barge Owner	Williams Benj	1812	*Halford*	Barge Register	BRO
Bargeman	Williams Edward	1841	London Street	Census	RLSL
Bargemaster	Winter John	1587		Will	TNA
Bargeman	Wright George	1841	Saw Court, Friar Street	Census	RLSL

Sources

BERKSHIRE RECORD OFFICE (BRO)

R/AT1/106 Grant of a property in Gutter Lane, Reading 1423; D/P 96/6/42/1–19, Deeds of property in St Giles' parish 1753; R/JQ/1/7, Quarter sessions: bargeman's deposition in connection with malt lost in sinking of barge 1769; D/EX 1457/1/130, Register of barges on the Thames 1812: D/P 97/1/10 and 11 Register of baptisms, Reading St Laurence 1831–1859; D/P 98/27/A, Reading St Mary tithe awards; Archdeaconry Wills under the general reference D/A1, indexed by occupation.

READING LOCAL STUDIES LIBRARY (RLSL)

Microfilm of *Berkshire Chronicle* and of census of Caversham and the Reading parishes St Giles, St Mary and St Laurence; J M Guilding (ed) *The Records of Reading: Diary of the Corporation* vol III 1630–1640 (1896); F Thacker *The Thames Highway* (David and Charles, reprinted 1968).

THE NATIONAL ARCHIVES (TNA)

Wills are in the on-line series PROB/11.

Index

Accidents *33, 74, 91, 147, 169, 178*

Adams & Gyngell *94–96, 102, 104, 110, 112, 116, 118, 121,125*

Air raid shelters *168*

Alexander or Milward
  Richard *7–10*
  William *7–11*

Allen & Simmonds, Iron Founders *152, 163*

Amateur Rowing Association *154*

Andrews, Ned *56, 65*

Angling – see also Eels and Fishing
  catches *65, 84, 93*
  competitions *81, 145, 181*
  equipment *54, 66–67, 81,*
  fence or closed season *64–66*
  fly-fishing *66*
  live bait *67, 145*
  poaching *85*
  spinning *67*

Angling Associations and Societies
  Angling Preservation *145*
  Caversham and District *145*
  Piscatorial Society *64*
  Reading and District *83, 86, 144, 145*
  Reading Fishing Club *179*
  Reading Waltonian *74, 81, 111, 145*
  Royal Counties Angling and Preservation Society *145*
  Thames Angling and Preservation *64, 73*
  Ye Olde Thames Valley Club *179*

Attwells, Frank *92, 95, 114, 191*

Badcock, E B, timber and slate merchant *141*

Bargebuilding *36, 59, 71*

Bargemasters *15, 25, 29, 31, 32, 36, 39*

Bargemen *15, 25, 30, 36, 43*

Barges
  crews *36*
  depth *30*
  design *37*
  haulers *27*
  steam *41, 46*
  tackle *31, 32*
  weight and capacity *29, 30, 37, 38*

Barge trade
  cargoes *14, 15, 18, 32–34, 43, 48, 60, 71,*
  communities *31*
  maltsters *34*
  mealmen *20, 33*
  partnerships and trusts *23, 31, 32*
  towing *27*
  towpaths *30, 34*
  working practices *22, 27–29, 31, 33, 39, 46*

Basketmaking *49, 71, 126*

Berkshire Cricket Club *121*

Biggs
  John *32*
  Samuel *32*

Blagrave
  Anthony *20*
  John *21*

Blake, Robert *25, 38*

Blake's Bridge *21*

Blake's Lock *22, 35, 39, 48, 84*

Blount, Sir Charles *17*

Boatbuilding *70, 135, 160, 177, 190*

Boat-letting *69, 75, 89–96, 124, 128, 139, 157–160, 165, 190*

Bona, Antonio *75, 88, 89, 97, 119, 123, 124, 129*

Bourman, William *15*

Bowsher, Robert 32

Bradford, John 15

Brigham
    Anthony 4
    Thomas 7

Brigham's Mead 59, 112

Brookside Metal Company 185

Browne
    Sir George 11
    Sir John 18

Brunel's Bridge 45

Bull, A H 105

Cadogan, William, Baron of Reading 19

Canal network 35

Care and Comforts for the Wounded 151

Cart[w]right
    Edward 20
    Thomas 20

Caversham Bridge 3, 5, 17, 19, 61, 96, 156

Caversham Bridge Hotel 124, 191

Caversham Court – see Old Rectory, The

Caversham Lakes 191

Caversham Lock 41, 72, 192

Caversham Lock Island 41, 192

Caversham Manor 3, 14

Caversham Mill 2, 3, 4, 14, 19, 56, 124, 125, 190

Caversham Park 16, 17, 53, 61, 116, 162

Caversham Weir 2, 148, 156

Cawston
    Arthur Reuben 164
    Edward 69, 75, 90, 118, 124, 134
    Edward William 135, 164

William Edward 135, 164

Chalmers, Patrick 67, 71

Champion
    John 58
    Joshua 58, 125

Chapels
    Holy Ghost 6, 19
    Our Lady 3, 19
    St Anne 3

Charging stations 116

Christ Church, Oxford
    Dean and Chapter 4, 7, 18, 52, 130

Christchurch Meadows 131

Civil War 15

Clappers, The 80, 124, 148

Clark, William 84

Clarke, Edwin and Co, Stroud 90, 117, 134

Collier, P O 51, 122, 137, 141, 181

Conwaye, William 15

County Lock 35, 84

Craven, Lord 15, 17

Crawshay, William Thompson 53, 116, 123, 148

Cricket 110

Dalby, John 20

Darvill, Peter 25

Deane
    Henry 39
    Robert 19, 39, 44, 56
    Robert Micklam 39, 57

Dean(e)'s Farm 1, 123

de Montfort, Robert 1

De Montfort House 141, 178, 192, 193

De Montfort Island – see Fry's Island

Disease
    plague 15
    smallpox 25

typhus 16

Dreadnought reach 80, 104, 155, 170, 182

Dundas, Henry 96, 113, 123, 141

Dyer, Mrs Amelia 80

East, Arthur 94, 104, 112, 113, 120, 124, 128

Edwards, Abraham 15

Eels – see also Angling and Fishing
    bucks 20, 53, 82, 132
    fare 83
    fishing 66, 82, 181

Eighteen, John (Jack) 105, 107, 152

Electric launches 116

Elliott, Samuel and Son 152, 154, 170

Englefield, James 64, 68, 82

Environment Agency 192

Essex, Earl of 17

Ferries 2, 4, 5, 14, 61, 98, 110, 113, 175

Fishery, The 124, 181

Fishing – see also Angling and Eels
    bailiffs 84, 145
    equipment 23, 54
    fisheries and fishing rights 20, 53, 86
    fishery protection 83, 144
    professional fishermen 14, 22, 23, 56, 65, 70, 71, 75, 81
    restocking 84, 86, 181

Flash lock 2, 4, 5, 28, 29, 41, 57

Flash timetable 42

Floods 61, 97, 98, 129, 149, 151, 171

Fobney Lock 25

Football 110

Franciscan Friary 2, 4

Freebody
 Ann 54
 Ernest 124, 134, 177
 James 23
 Kate 69, 75, 90
 Lydia Elkin 54
 Mary 54, 134
 Peter 55–56
 Rose Dorothy 177
 Thomas 22, 53, 65, 91, 124
 William 22, 23, 39
Freebody, Peter & Co, Hurley 190
Freeze 93, 108, 169, 187
Fry, John 59
Fry's Island 6, 58, 101, 107, 112–114, 123, 141, 190, 192
Gibbings, Robert 167
Gifford, William 1
Great Western Railway 45, 47, 122
Griffin, The 55, 80, 85, 101, 133
Gyngell, Samuel 94–96, 110
Habbitts, Len 155, 182
Haslam
 Dryland 74, 133
 Happy 183
Haslams, Estate Agents 45, 119, 162
High Bridge 21
Hill's Meadow 156, 192
Hines, Frederick 121
Horse racing 109
Horseshoe Bridge 99
Houseboats 68, 174, 177
Huntley and Palmers 42, 46, 48, 104
Isaacs, Harry 135, 152, 157
Island Bohemian Club 128, 137, 141, 160, 174, 187, 188, 192
Jones, Richard 18

Katesgrove Iron Works 46
Keel, Joseph 89, 147
Kennet, River 14, 25, 35, 37, 85, 98, 192
Kennet and Avon Canal 25, 35, 37, 39, 46, 91, 190
Kildare, Earl of 19
King Alfred training ship 145
King's Meadow 18, 21, 44, 45, 109, 110, 111, 192
Knight
 Frederick 84
 George 71, 84
 Henry 71, 84, 125
 Ward 147
 William 71
Knollys
 John Weldale 41, 57, 58, 162
 Sir Francis 5, 21
Lamden, George 181
Lewis
 George 72, 101, 112, 113, 123, 163
 Henry 34
Lidos 164, 170, 172, 184
Life-saving 108, 132
Lock-keepers 73, 121, 146, 156, 173
Loveday
 John 19
 Thomas 18, 19
Lovegrove, Matthew 32
Lyford, Richard 54, 55
Manning, Edward 14
Mapledurham House 17
Marsack, Major Charles 19, 53
Maynard, E J 129
Millers 20, 56
Mill Green – see Caversham Mill
Mills, Robert 32
Milward or Mylward –

see Alexander
Moderation Inn 81
Moss, William (Bill) 69, 74, 79, 84, 112–114, 122, 124, 135, 137, 145, 151
Moss Boat Company 138–140, 157–160, 163, 174–176
Motor boats 130, 148, 150, 165–166, 174–175, 178
New Woman, The 102
Norcot Scours 80, 108, 119
Notley Abbey 1, 3
Nott, Manford 44, 54
Old Rectory, The 7–11, 18, 51–53, 133–134, 166
Orts Estate 44
Osier cultivation 48, 71, 126, 192
Otters 84, 86, 193
Paice, William 31, 32
Palmer, George MP 104, 111
Pearce
 Frank 132, 151, 157, 168, 179, 188
 Joan 168, 188
 William 27–29
Pembroke, Earl of 3
Piper (later Moss), Selina, 68
Piper's Island 61, 69, 124, 190
Plumridge, John 32
Poor's land 21, 44
Promenade, The 131, 192
Punting 56
Punts and skiffs - see Boatbuilding and Boat-letting
Reading Abbey 1, 3, 4
Reading Amateur Athletic Club 110
Reading Annual Industrial Exhibition 120

Reading Borough boundary 5

Reading Boys Home 74

Reading Bridge 156

Reading Cricket Club 110, 121

Reading Football Club 110

Reading Quoits Club 113

Reading Swimming Club 107, 132, 137

Reading United Quoits Club 113

Redgrave Pinsent Rowing Lake 191

Regattas
Head of the River 155, 183
Henley Royal 159
Reading Amateur 78, 103–105, 149, 154, 182, 190
Reading and Caversham 55, 101
Reading Rowing Club 182
Reading Tradesmen's 105
Reading Working Men's 79, 104, 111, 182

River management 34, 41, 46, 60, 72, 130, 144, 148, 150, 155

River Thames Society 194

Rob Roy canoe 70

Rowing, amateur and professional status 55, 104, 154, 182, 183

Rowing Clubs
Kennet Alliance 154
Reading 79, 101–103, 104, 111, 112, 113, 133, 149, 154, 155, 182, 190
Reading Tradesmen's 105, 154, 182
Reading University 104, 154, 155, 183
Royal Berkshire Yeomanry 111, 119

Salter, John 117

Salters' Steamers 117, 150, 164

Simonds
Blackall 52, 53
Henry C 133
Henry John 83, 103
James 104, 110, 131, 133
William Blackall 19, 51

Skating 108

Skiffs and punts - see Boatbuilding and Boat-letting

Smith, Peter 84, 145, 147

Southcote Lock 25

Steamers 117, 129

Steam launches 73, 124

St Peter's Church, Caversham 1, 4, 7, 19, 52

Suttons Seeds 42, 86

Swan ownership 4

Swimming 107, 132, 135–136

Talbot
Charles 60, 71, 96
Edward 59
Fred 102
George 60, 71, 152
Richard 59, 71
Robert 59

Temperance Hotel 120

Templecombe 113

Terrent, Edward 15

Thames Bank Iron Works 122

Thames Conservancy 60, 66, 72, 98, 107, 132, 144, 148, 150, 155, 163

Thames Hire Cruiser Association 174

Thames Navigation Commissioners 14, 30, 34, 41, 46, 72

Thames Punting Club 56

Thames Side (formerly Thames Bank) 118, 122, 124, 141, 163, 171

Thames Valley Hotel 133, 191

Thorne, John 14

Treacher
George 35, 47
John 34, 35

Truss, Charles 32, 38

Tubb, Edward 57

Upper Thames Patrol 169

Vasterns, The 15, 59

Vasterns Hotel 120

View Island 125, 148, 185, 192

Wallop, Sir Henry 15

War memorial 164

Wharfs
Bear 48
Blake's 39, 48
Blandy and Palmer's 37, 43
Boult's 36, 37
Freebody's 22, 33
Gasworks 43
High Bridge 48
Huntley and Palmer's 43
Kennet and Avon Canal Co 43
Kings Road weighbridge 48
Provis and Brown's 37
Seven Bridges 38
Talbots 60, 71
Williams' Commercial 43

White Hart, The 22, 53, 59, 123, 124

William, Earl Marshall 2

Willow Grotto 69

Wing, William 78, 123

Winter, John 14

Winter Bathers 107, 132, 135–136

World War I 149–153

World War II 168–171